Evolution

Evolution

Secular or Sacred?

BRADFORD McCALL

Foreword by Thomas Jay Oord

WIPF & STOCK · Eugene, Oregon

EVOLUTION
Secular or Sacred?

Copyright © 2020 Bradford McCall. All rights reserved. Except for brief quotations in critical publications or reviews, no part of this book may be reproduced in any manner without prior written permission from the publisher. Write: Permissions, Wipf and Stock Publishers, 199 W. 8th Ave., Suite 3, Eugene, OR 97401.

Wipf & Stock
An Imprint of Wipf and Stock Publishers
199 W. 8th Ave., Suite 3
Eugene, OR 97401

www.wipfandstock.com

PAPERBACK ISBN: 978-1-7252-6765-7
HARDCOVER ISBN: 978-1-7252-6764-0
EBOOK ISBN: 978-1-7252-6766-4

Manufactured in the U.S.A.   05/22/20

Contents

Dedication   vii

Foreword by Thomas Jay Oord   ix

Introduction   xi

Part 1: Programmatic Essay upon the Secular Evolutionary Worldview

1   The Secular Evolutionary Worldview
An Introduction and Critique   2

Part 2: Philosophical Perspectives on Evolution

2   Charles Sanders Peirce, Evolutionary Developmental Teleology, and Kenotic Causation   34

3   Alfred North Whitehead, Chance, and the Immanently Creative Spirit   49

4   Derrida and Nonhuman Animals
An Exploration of Shared Animality   64

Part 3: Theological Perspectives on Evolution and Divine Involvement (Activity)

5   The God of Chance and Purpose   82

6   Augustine's Theolog(ies) of Creation
Simultaneous Creation, "Seminal Seeds," and Genesis 1–3   94

7   Nondualistic (Macro-)Evolution
An Exercise in Mystical Immanence and Divine Involvement in an Evolutionary World   115

| 8 | Evolutionary Christology Adoptionism and Jesus of Nazareth | 129 |

Part 4: Theological Perspectives on Evolution and Responsive Divine Love

9	The Connection between Kenosis and Emergence	148
10	Nygren and Oord on Love: A Critique	169
11	Necessary, Kenotically Donated, and Self-Giving Love	185
Bibliography		195

Dedication

I dedicate this book to Prof. Arthur Tyson, the man who gave me the primordial inspiration and desire to pursue biology in higher education. When I met Prof. Tyson in 1996 as my academic advisor at Middle Georgia St. University, in Cochran, Georgia, I was but a mere brain-damaged peon, barely knowing how to read and write after my TBI in 1995. He placed me in his own General Biology course my first semester of college—it was an immense "culture shock"! I went on to take another two biology courses from him before transferring elsewhere. The way that Prof. Tyson taught us—by giving vivid and stimulating lectures, by questioning our presuppositions, etc.—has left an indelible mark upon me. I have yet—in my twenty-three years of subsequent higher education post-Tyson—ever taken an "exam" that met with his rigor of difficulty. He was the right man in my life at the right time: as a TBI-recovering individual, I necessitated both intellectual rigor and open compassion: Prof. Tyson was both of these things and infinitely more. In no small way, I can honestly say that he forever reoriented my trajectory in life, and that for the better. What more can be said for—or even expected of—an educator? While he would probably not agree with everything I have written in this book, the foundation for higher, critical thinking skills that he bestowed to me and in me made it possible. Thanks, as one of my more astute fellow students used to say, Mr./Dr. Tyson!

Foreword

Bradford McCall says we've got it wrong. That is, we've been thinking about God and evolution the wrong way. And this has not led to much progress. Wrong thinking rarely leads to much good.

Theists worried about evolution have been thinking about evolution in the wrong way. McCall encourages believers to read the evolutionary story through a different theological lens than many have been reading it. Instead of thinking God is a distant architect or a controlling micromanager, what if we read evolution in light of a God of love? What if this God's love is creative, relational, and uncontrolling?

McCall's project is not some cursory idea thrown up without support. This book isn't fluff unsubstantiated by indepth analysis. McCall dives headlong into the details. He explores and evaluates proposals from the leading philosophers, scientists, and theologians of our day. And he explores many from yesteryear. He faces challenges without flinching.

The loving God described here is present with us and all creation. This God is immanent in the working of the world, including evolution. But being present and active does not mean the world reflects exactly what God desires. This lens of love proposal overcomes the primary problems raised by anti-evolution voices. And yet the God McCall offers for our consideration is no wimp or creature.

While McCall draws from and is influenced by a myriad of relevant voices, this book offers novel proposals too. In many ways, it integrates the best of various disciplines and theories. Innovation emerges when drawing together the many into the one. This work is courageous and much needed. It is intellectually robust and interdisciplinary.

I'm convinced by these arguments. I'm especially drawn to McCall's vision of divine love at work in the world of evolution. I suspect some scholars in philosophy and science will be skeptical when first hearing the idea that a loving God creates without controlling. But McCall lays out a robust foundation for this claim. And theologians worried about his view will find McCall up to the task of defending its merits.

Near the end of the 20th century, Imre Lakatos famously explored the scientific method. He proposed what he called "research programs," which attempted to place up their philosophical assumptions at the fore. Scholars at the science-and-theology interface have used this approach to find frameworks for their profoundly important work. But it remains controversial, insofar as the disagreement about what philosophical (and theological assumptions) should be embraced.

This book might be understood as providing a "McCall research program." And I for one am impressed with the fruitful framework and winsome proposals Bradford McCall offers.

THOMAS JAY OORD
author of *The Uncontrolling Love of God* and many other books

Introduction

Is evolution secular or sacred? Are the processes of evolution endowed with meaning? Admittedly, I *cannot*, *do not*, and *will not* assert that the evolutionary process provides "proof" of a God—that is a natural theological enterprise. John Haught has noted that events in life can be "seen" or "read" from multiple perspectives. I agree with such a contention. Since I concede that notion, I will be attempting to "read" the processes of evolution. Indeed, I will herein and do elsewhere contend that the processes of evolution can be "read" in a manner that is consistent (key term!) with the notion of God, particularly with the notion of a God who (somehow; more on this later) interacts with the natural world in a creative, responsively loving, and uncontrolling manner. This argument will proceed over eleven chapters. In what directly follows, I will proffer an overview, of sorts, of the remainder of the title.

In the first chapter, which serves as a programmatic essay for the remainder of the volume, I explicate the Secular Evolutionary Worldview (SEW) in light of various strengths and weaknesses that I perceive in such a worldview. The chapter is centered around two individuals: Michael Ruse of Florida State University, and Elliot Sober of the University of Wisconsin-Madison. I have selected these two representatives of the SEW to focus upon, for though they be secular evolutionists, they are not belligerently anti-spiritual advocates of the worldview. Indeed, I have chosen them in part because they offer a very nuanced and sustained—though not vociferous—critique of the worldview that I—and many of my readers also—hold so dear: that is, theism, broadly defined. At the onset, I proffer a definition of the terminology regarding "worldview," and then elucidate various (almost a dozen) aspects and theses of this "worldview" that I distinctly define as "secular": the notion of progress; the roles and entailments of adaptation/ism, selection/ism, and adaptation/ism, with the subtheses of *natural and sexual selection* and the *units of selection* (with corresponding subtheses of the *individual vs. group selection* debate, which is explicated by the altruism subtopic).

Within chapter 2, which begins part 2 of the title, covering Philosophical Perspectives on Evolution, I argue that Charles Sanders Peirce's teleology is more than a mere purposive pursuit of a predetermined end; it is a developmental teleology. Peirce's "developmental teleology" is applicable to his idea of teleology in general. Thus, final causes evolve, and they are not static. Peirce's view pictures teleology as evolving and it is to be seen as a general goal versus having a definite end-state or goal predetermined, which is a corollary to the uncontrolling love of God. Teleology emerged out of the increasing complexification of life on Earth, and continues to be general, not specific, and is conceived of, herein, as at least partially self-determining. In Peirce's agapasm, God gives himself away in an act of uncontrolling love without any conditions regarding the potential responses to that love, as well as to what responses may fulfill that love; it is merely a display of completely reckless overflowing love. Seen as such, the many and varied manifestations of complexity that macroevolution has given rise to what can be seen as a fulfillment of the teleological goals of God. Further, the kenotic creating Spirit, who *donates* uncontrolling love to her creation, is present "in, with, and under" the processes of biological evolution and should be seen to act teleologically within the causal nexus of creation (i.e., natural law and later human action), a point that my Wesleyan-derived brothers and sisters should be able to promote without difficulty.

In chapter 3, it is argued that God through the Spirit is both the immanent and eminent principle of creativity, ever wooing and empowering the advancements in complexity within biological evolution. I argue herein also that God, particularly in and through the activity of the Spirit of creativity, was fully present *in* and *with* and *under* what is oft called "creation," from the very beginning of created time—and will be to the end of time, *proleptically present* as the expression of the principle of creativity. I maintain that the Spirit, by her kenosis *into* the natural world, imbibed nature with an evolving fertility that has continually manifested itself in and through the increases of complexity in the natural environ. This primal imbibing of herself into the world of nature caused the world to become marked by what principally amounts to an *activation* of the naturally occurring, inherent potentialities within nature, thereby producing a distinctive self-creativity within the world. Somewhat akin to Peirce, who said that we need a "thoroughgoing evolutionism or none," I contend that we need a thoroughly *immanent* God or none, all the while noting that both *immanent-* and *self-* creativity are marks of this overall poietic process known as biotic evolution.

The fourth chapter covers sections of Jacques Derrida's corpus that explored the human animal/nonhuman animal binary. Indeed, in his writings, Western thought regarding the binary is examined, as well as its inherently anthropocentric framework. Derrida successfully, however, deconstructs its systems and highlights why the binary—largely—remains in place. He wrote more than eight hundred pages explicitly devoted to the animal, most of which has appeared in print only after his death, which thereby makes animality one of his central philosophical themes. The HA/NHA binary has a long philosophical history, going all the way back to Aristotle—who, in his *The History of Animals*, established a hierarchical HA/NHA opposition. Aristotle rightly attributes intelligence to animals, and he thought that this differs only in quantity when compared to human animals. Derrida deconstructs the binary by dissolving the perceived superiority of HAs, in part through a critique of the attributes that HAs have historically been used to separate themselves from nonhuman animals.

Chapter 5 begins part 3, which explicates Theological Perspectives on Evolution and Divine Involvement (Activity). Particularly, this fifth chapter notes that in *The Structure of Evolutionary Theory*, Gould emphasizes the importance of recognizing both the reality of structural constraint and the idea that structures have an element of historical contingency. According to him, the history of life is not progressive and it is certainly not predictable. The Earth's living systems have evolved through a series of unexpected, unplanned, and accidental events, any one of which could have occurred differently and thereby led evolutionary history on a pathway that possibly could not have led to the derivation of consciousness. Perhaps the most sustained critique of Gould's contingency argument has come from Conway Morris. He notes that in the phenomena known as convergence similar patterns appear in widely divergent groups and he has employed examples of convergence to argue that despite apparent contingency, evolution is far more predictable than admitted by Gould.

The sixth chapter is comprised of an essay that dialogues with Augustine's Theolog(ies) of Creation. It asserts that Augustine's theology of creation is a muddled mess. In fact, one would be more apropos in referring to his "theologies of creation." This essay argues that his theologies of creation worked in a backward fashion: that is, he was more correct at the onset of his extensive writings than he was at the end of his magnificent corpus output. Indeed, the posit of an allegorical interpretive framework for the "days" of creation as set forth in his *Against the Manichees* text, written very early in his theological career, was closer to the reality of the situation, from our post-Darwinian perspective, than his textual acrobatics in his later writings. It is concluded, then, that with respect to Augustine's writings, one must go backwards to go forwards.

Chapter 7 explores Nondualistic (Macro-)Evolution, and asserts that it is an exercise in mystical immanence and divine involvement in an evolutionary world. Whether ultimate reality is to be conceived as a personal God or an impersonal principle somehow at work in the world is an issue which tends to divide major world religions into opposing camps. Furthermore, even within a given religion philosophers and theologians may differ on how God or ultimate reality is to be conceived. It is a commonplace that while Asian philosophy is nondualistic, the West, because of its uncritical reliance on Greek-derived intellectual standards, is dualistic. Dualism is a deep-seated habit of thinking and acting in all spheres of life through the prism of binary opposites which leads to paralyzing practical and theoretical difficulties. In general, Asian philosophy can provide assistance for the future a Christian nondualism, even though the West finds Asian philosophical nondualism, especially that of Mahayana Buddhism, nihilistic. However, (late-)/postmodern thought may deliver us from the dualisms embedded and embodied in modernity.

The eighth chapter is an admittedly provocative one, one that reimagines the incarnation of God through Jesus of Nazareth in terms of adoptionism. Indeed, I propose therein an evolutionary Christology. Adoptionism has a long history of being promoted—and suppressed!—throughout the Christian era. Succinctly, this essay argues that we may need to revisit this understanding of Jesus of Nazareth in order to make the doctrine of God understandable and (even?) palatable for the twenty-first-century faith context. In its most basic form, adoptionism argues that Jesus of Nazareth was born a man, like any other human. However, due to his pristine and perfect fulfillment of God the Father's will for his life, he was adopted into the godhead and deemed worthy of dying for the mass of men and women. I propose that such an understanding of Jesus's life retains the import of his unification with all of humanity, and honors the intentions of the church fathers to stress Jesus' uniqueness. Jesus' exceptionality was once and forever cemented at his baptism by John, and marked by the descent of the Spirit upon him, thereby constituting his anointing and empowering him to carry out the salvation of all who believe in him. He is, thereafter, pneumatologically constituted to be the Son of God.

Chapter 9 begins the fourth part of this text, which explicates Theological Perspectives on Evolution and Responsive Divine Love. In fact, this ninth chapter explores the connection(s), if any, between *kenosis* and emergence. I begin by noting that modern advances in scientific study reveal a vastly more complicated world than the reductionist program of the late nineteenth and twentieth centuries ever envisioned. In this essay, I seek to offer a new approach to creation, building upon the notions of emergence and kenosis. Pointedly, I proffer the notion that the existence and viability of emergence theory depends upon the primal kenotic act of God the Spirit *pouring* herself *into* creation. I review and interact with Clayton's seminal work, *Mind & Emergence*. I then present the biblical basis of kenosis of the Spirit *into* creation, and discuss former conceptions of the kenosis and science connection. Thereafter, I make my own contribution of the connections between kenosis of the Spirit into creation and emergence theory.

Chapter 10 is the first of two interrelated essays that dialogue with Thomas Jay Oord's conceptioning of the uncontrolling love of God. Both of these chapters appropriate Oord's position in differing manners and in different guises. The first of the two, chapter 10, asserts a *fully* kenotic concept of God's love that is *fully* consistent with Thomas Jay Oord's portrayal of an essentially kenotic God who has an eternal nature marked by others-centered and others-empowering uncontrolling love. This uncontrolling love, as the contingentist (a word that I have recently coined to refer to someone who highly emphasizes contingency in his or her philosophy of life) Oord likes to say, necessarily provides full freedom and agency to each species within the natural world—especially human animals—with God working to empower and inspire creation toward well-being and wholeness. Regardless of our attitude about religion, there is something very compelling about this radical image of self-giving as the epitome of love; one can hardly argue with it, for there is enormous power in it. In this essay, I seek to build on the insights regarding love by both Nygren and Oord, with an assist by Karol Wojtyla. I seek, further, to illustrate the notion that God's kenotically donated love is a synergistic symbiosis enacted through the Spirit of creativity that achieves greater evolutionary results combined than either aspect of the symbiosis alone.

The final constructive chapter is composed of an essay that responds to a prompt given by the Wesleyan Theological Society's 2020 call for papers. The prompt was related to whether or not God is necessarily loving, or if he is freely loving (?). I dialog with Thomas Jay Oord, who is a giant when it comes to the exposition of Christian love. Further, I reiterate a minority view on the meaning and extrapolation of the Greek term *kenosis*—that is, that the term refers to, variously, a "kenotic donation," a "self-offering," a "self-donation," or a "self-giving." Indeed, the love to which God calls us is multidimensional and multiexpressive. As such, it takes many forms. God calls his creatures to express "full-Oorded" love, because God's love is full-orbed. This kenotically donated, "full-Oorded" love onsets an evolving fertility within the natural world, which is a result of the panentheistic relationship of God and world. This panentheistic relationship was initially wrought by the kenotic donation of God's very self *into* chaotic matter eons ago, and is now continually sustained and upheld by the repetitive imbibification of the creating Spirit—i.e., the impartation of her very self—into the natural world. Thereafter, marked by the Spirit of contingency within evolution, the natural world progressed in a serpentine manner into the advancement of greater complexity, of which *Homo sapiens sapiens* are the pinnacle (at present, anyway).

Part 1

Programmatic Essay upon the Secular Evolutionary Worldview

1

The Secular Evolutionary Worldview

An Introduction and Critique

In this chapter, one will find an exposition of the overarching "Secular Evolutionary Worldview" (SEW) of the biological sciences. The core of the SEW is well summarized by George Gaylord Simpson: "Man is the result of a purposeless and natural process that did not have him in mind. He was not planned. He is a state of matter, a form of life, a sort of animal, and a species of the Order Primates, akin nearly or remotely to all of life and indeed to all that is material."[1]

Secular Science is grounded in Darwinian evolution. Carl Sagan states simply, "Evolution is a fact, not a theory."[2] Huxley exclaims, "The first point to make about Darwin's theory is that it is no longer a theory, but a fact . . . Darwinianism has come of age so to speak. We do no longer have to bother about establishing the fact of evolution."[3] Antony Flew is scandalized by the notion that there was a time, "unbelievably," when the Vatican questioned "the fact of the evolutionary origin of the species."[4] I will first define what a worldview itself contains and connotes, for it is only after defining "worldview" appropriately that I can then shift to the individual scholars individual

---

1. Simpson, *Meaning of Evolution*, 345.
2. Sagan, *Cosmos*, 27.
3. Huxley, "At Random." See also Tax, *Evolution of Life*, 1.
4. Kurtz, ed., *Humanist Alternative*, 110. An interesting development since Flew made these remarks is that Dr. Flew has left his atheistic position for some form of deism.

scholars about whom I wish to write (primarily the secularists Michael Ruse and Elliot Sober, though I will include five anthologies that contain works by various other authors). After defining the term "worldview," I will then highlight about a dozen topics and theses in a logical sequence, consisting of: the notion of Progress; the entailments of Adaptation/ism, with the subtheses of *natural and sexual selection*, the *units of selection*, and *functions*; the process of *speciation*, with the subtheses of the *causes of speciation* and of *species concepts*.

The meaning of the term "worldview" (also seen to be used as "world-view" or "world view" by various authors) seems self-evident: an intellectual perspective on the world or universe. But it has many characteristics. Indeed, the online edition of the *Collins English Dictionary* defines worldview as a "a comprehensive, esp. personal, philosophy or conception of the world and of human life."[5] The *CED* similarly defines the German noun *Weltanschauung*—from which we get our English term worldview—as "a comprehensive, esp. personal, philosophy or conception of the universe and of human life."[6] In "The Question of a *Weltanschauung*," from his *New Introductory Lectures in Psycho-Analysis*, Sigmund Freud describes *Weltanschauung* as "an intellectual construction which solves all the problems of our existence uniformly on the basis of one overriding hypothesis, which, accordingly, leaves no question unanswered and in which everything that interests us finds its fixed place."[7]

But this does not mean that the meaning of the term worldview as I use it herein does not have other connotations, some of which I will now unpack. Indeed, notably, in the *Discipleship of the Mind*, James W. Sire defines worldview as "a set of presuppositions" which we hold "about the makeup of our world."[8] Worldview, then, represents one's most fundamental beliefs and assumptions about the universe they inhabit. It reflects how he would answer fundamental questions about who and what we are, where we came from, *et cetera*. Worldviews operate at both the individual level and the societal level.

Rarely will two people have exactly the same worldview, but within any society certain worldview types will be represented more prominently than others, and will therefore exert greater influence on the culture of that society. The elements of one's worldview, the beliefs about certain aspects of Ultimate Reality, are one's: *epistemology*, which could be defined as beliefs

---

5. https://www.collinsdictionary.com/us/dictionary/english/worldview.
6. https://www.collinsdictionary.com/us/dictionary/english/weltanschauung.
7. Freud, *New Introductory Lectures in Psycho-Analysis*, 158.
8. Sire, *Discipleship of the Mind*, 136.

about the nature and sources of knowledge; *metaphysics*, which could be defined as beliefs about the ultimate nature of reality; *anthropology*, which could be defined as beliefs about the nature and purpose of humanity, in general, and oneself, in particular; *axiology*, which could be defined as beliefs about the nature of value, what is good and bad, what is right and wrong; *cosmology*, which could be defined as beliefs about the origins and nature of the universe, life, and especially humanity; and *theology*, which could be defined as beliefs about the existence and nature of God.[9]

The various definitions just given are essentially in accord with one another. However, it is in Freud's sense of the meaning of *Weltanschauung* that I will use the term worldview in this chapter. As such, a worldview is the set of beliefs about fundamental aspects of reality that ground and influence all one's perceiving, thinking, knowing, and doing. Since the Patristic Era, Western civilization, largely, has been dominated by a Christian worldview. But in the last couple of centuries, for technological and theological reasons—but most explicitly the scientific ones—the traditional Christian worldview has lost its dominance, and competing worldviews have become far more prominent, including at least the following: 1) *modernism*, in which all things in the physical world can be explained by "modern," scientific processes; 2) *postmodernism*, in which there are very few or no objective truths and moral standards, and "reality" is a human social construction; 3) *pantheism*, in which God is the sum total of all reality, as each thing or entity within it is itself also divine; 4) *pluralism*, in which different world religions represent equally valid perspectives on God, the Ultimate Reality—as such, there are many valid paths to salvation; 5) *panentheism*, in which God is the totality of reality—however, while God is in all things, God is more than all things at the same time; and 6) *ontological naturalism*, in which there is no God, humans are just highly evolved animals, and the universe is a closed physical system. It is this last worldview that is predominant within the biological sciences today, and which I have termed the Secular Evolutionary Worldview (SEW).

---

9. It is, therefore, no mistake that secular evolutionary biology has characteristics of a classical "religion." Some evolutionists claim, unabashedly, that a Darwinian worldview possesses no religious content. However, this notion is not well supported by Neo-Darwinian philosophers, who themselves admit to such religious overtones within Darwinian thought. For example, Michael Ruse, a leading Neo-Darwinian, states the following: "Evolution is promoted by its practitioners as more than mere science. Evolution is promulgated as an ideology, a secular religion. . . Evolution is a religion. This was true of evolution in the beginning, and it is true of evolution still today" (Ruse, "How Evolution Became a Religion," B1).

MAJOR TOPICS, THESES, AND SUBTHESES OF THE SECULAR EVOLUTIONARY WORLDVIEW

Progress Defined and Defended

> I do think that progress has happened, although I find it hard to define precisely what I mean.[10]

The Christian Louis Agassiz contributes much to the Secular Evolutionary Worldview. It may seem strange to start a chapter on the SEW of biological science with an open and deliberate (even "belligerent" or pugnacious) theist, one who in many ways was a progenitor of the not-so-modern Creationist movement, but I will do so regardless, for his notion of progress serves as the foundation of SEW's *formulation of* and *response to* the notion of progress. Indeed, the Swiss-American ichthyologist Jean Louis Rodolphe Agassiz (1807–1873) was a Christian paleontologist, who is often recognized as the proverbial father of glacial geology and the science of glaciology. More commonly known as Louis Agassiz, he proposed and argued for threefold parallelism with respect to progress insomuch as the order of living beings, the ontogenetic development of individual organisms, and the history of life as seen in the fossil record all gave evidence to the notion of progress being exhibited in the natural (or in his case, "created") world. Indeed, claimed Agassiz, the unifying thread of all of reality, but especially of the Earth, is that of progress: 1) from simple to complex, 2) from the uniform to the highly differentiated, and 3) from monad to man.[11] Therefore, there is a *scala naturae* all the way from invertebrates, to rodents, to primates, to mankind. For all of the problems with Agassiz's proposal, it had an influence far beyond what he envisioned.[12] Michael Ruse argues for a modern-day possible threefold parallelism, different in many respects to Agassiz but similar in making central the notion of progress; his is a parallelism between: 1) the development of society, 2) the development of science, and 3) the evolutionary development of organisms.[13]

---

10. Smith, "Taking a Chance on Evolution."

11. Interestingly, this last phrase serves as the basis of the title for one of Michael Ruse's most popular titles, *Monad to Man*.

12. Cf. Bowler, *Fossils and Progress*.

13. Ruse, *Evolutionary Naturalism*, 109–35. Notably, Ruse was not always—seemingly—a progressionist; indeed, in his earlier texts, prior to the turn of the millennium, he was ever careful to distinguish between forms of progress, apparently attempting to employ a sort of verbal gymnastics. He would openly speak of what he termed "comparative" progress and "absolute" progress, or even "improvement," but only reluctantly

Ruse argues that the history of the Darwinism movement can be understood only as an expression of the idea of social and anthropic progress. Indeed, he links the rise of evolutionism to the prevailing faith in the idea of progress. He believes that the scientific credentials of the theory were never strong enough to convince anyone not predisposed to accept it on ideological grounds.[14] Ruse also stresses the extent to which the founders of the synthesis (~1930–1940) still clung to the concept that *progression is philosophy*, so popular in the previous century. Indeed, Ruse is keen to point out that the idea of progress in biological advancement was not quick to disappear, persisting at least until the modern synthesis in the middle of the twentieth century (some, myself included, would contend that the notion still persists unto this day). It is normally assumed that liberal theology saw individual effort (teams led by competition) as the driving force of progress. But as Desmond and Moore argue, there was a period in the early nineteenth century when a less optimistic form of liberalism reigned, and Malthus's principal was part of his nonprogressive viewpoint.[15] Darwin became part of the ideology of progress of only the later, more confident era of liberalism.

Many modern SEW scientists are reluctant to concede that Darwin was a progressionist, because they themselves reject the concept of progress

---

affirm what I term "objective" progress in evolutionary biology (cf. Ruse, "Evolution and Progress," 55–59). He notes, particularly, that comparative progress is a Darwinian notion, centering on selection, and "at the microlevel, all would agree that it occurs" (Ruse, "Evolution and Progress," 55). Ruse states, in fact, in one of his earlier texts, "Progress that people desire, especially when (by and large) everyone has an interest in the end result, centers on value. Progress against some standard, which may or may not be valued, centers on evaluation. We can think of them as *absolute* progress (or 'progress' without qualification) and *comparative* progress. If one arrives at the Heavenly City, one has made absolute progress. If one makes a bigger and better atom bomb, one has made comparative progress. Although value judgments are required in both cases, it is the former which really interests us. Whether and how the latter will arise in our discussion is a question for the future" (Ruse, *Monad to Man*, 20). Controversy arises, he says in this "Evolution and Progress" article, when one tries to take the hypotheses and findings of microevolution and apply them to the geological timescale, which is the concern of the (macro-)evolutionist (Ruse, "Evolution and Progress," 55). He goes on, asserting that two particular points of dispute exist: namely, over significant new adaptations—"innovations," as he terms them—and that over protracted shifts—what he terms "trends" (Ruse, "Evolution and Progress," 56). Innovations open new ecological niches or to the seizing of niches already occupied (Nitecki, *Evolutionary Innovations*). In this process, an entity has an "adaptive breakthrough" (Ruse, "Evolution and Progress," 56). Defining an innovation as something that has crossed a functional threshold, it has been claimed that they are the mainsprings of macroevolution (Jablonski and Bottjer, "Ecology of Evolutionary Innovation," 253–88).

14. Cf. the entirety of Ruse, *Monad to Man*.
15. Desmond and Moore, *Darwin*, xii.

as being too value laden, and there is a temptation to assume that the founder of the movement shared our own perception of the theory. Robert J. Richards accuses many historians of falling into this trap and thereby ignoring much evidence for Darwin's commitment to the idea of progress.[16] Richards' interpretation fits in with Ruse's thesis on the more general link between biological evolutionism and progressionism. Most historians now accept that Darwin cannot be seen as a nonprogressionist in this (late-) postmodern sense. Ruse argues that the evidence for evolution was never strong enough to persuade anyone by itself: people converted to Darwinism because it underpinned their faith in progress, and those who oppose the theory to do so because they rejected that faith, perhaps on religious grounds.[17]

Following the Dominican priest biologist Francisco J. Ayala—again, oddly!—one person who has made much effort with the notion of what I term "objective" progress in biology,[18] Ruse contends that the concept of progress requires change, and that this in some sense involves change in a linear direction. As such, mere cyclical change could not qualify as progress, even though there is constant change in cyclical movements.[19] But, "progress is more than just change . . . Progress implies that there is change in a certain *direction*. You must be going somewhere to have progress."[20] However, according to Ruse, what is important is the recognition that directionality alone is not enough. Progress is a value notion; progress implies that things are in some sense getting better—at least, progress in any absolute sense has this implication. But, going beyond Ayala, Ruse stipulates that it is useful to distinguish between evaluation and valuing.[21] Only the latter is absolute, whereas the former occurs against any arbitrarily specified standard.

According to Ruse, SEW science (biology) is Heraclitean, that is, always moving. No one would deny this, although, conversely, no one would deny that biology moves irregularly—now leaping forward, then equilibrating, and so forth.[22] But is there any meaning to the movement? Does the back-and-forth of biology make sense? Is there any pattern to it? Is biology progressive, and if it is, what is the nature of this progress and what is its

  16. Cf. Richards, *Meaning of Evolution*.
  17. Ruse, *Monad to Man*, 179.
  18. See, e.g., Ayala, "Concept of Biological Progress," 339–54; Ayala, "Evolutionary Concept of Progress," 106–24; and Ayala, "Can 'Progress' Be Defined as a Biological Concept?," 75–96.
  19. Cf. Ruse, *Evolutionary Naturalism*, 110.
  20. Ruse, *Monad to Man*, 19.
  21. Cf. Nagel, *Structure of Science*.
  22. Ruse, *Evolutionary Naturalism*, 114.

cause? Speaking of scientists qua scientists—that is, excluding the things that scientists say when being self-reflective—they are strongly committed to the belief that their subject matter both has a pattern and makes sense. In particular, scientists believe in progress (of science/biology), and by "progress" they mean "getting closer to the truth."[23] Moreover, scientists qua scientists are philosophical realists,[24] and by "getting closer to the truth" they mean making their theories better correspond to the empirical facts. For example, modern molecular genetics is, in a sense, "better" than Mendelian genetics because the unit of inheritance is the near-particulate DNA molecule.

For Ruse, it also is true that the general progressivist view of science (biology) is one which has been widely accepted by commentators upon science.[25] At least, this is true of those closest to the philosophical end of the spectrum, although belief in scientific progress has come under attack from radical thinkers within historical, sociological, and literary disciplines.[26] The two most recent commentators on the nature of science (biology) are, undeniably, Karl Popper[27] and Thomas Kuhn.[28] As is well known, Popper believes that the mark of science—the "criterion of demarcation," in fact—is *falsifiability*, which means that science moves forward as scientists face problems, propose tentative solutions, and then others attempt to proverbially knock them down. Even in the process of refutation, however, progress is made, and the body of knowledge grows.[29] Kuhn is at times read to be a nonrealist, but Ruse contends that it is better perhaps to read him in a Kantian way: that is, as seeing reality in an important sense defined and created by the inquiring mind.[30] He certainly does not see the aim and end of science as some kind of finished absolute knowledge, for there is always the possibility for another paradigm switch. Yet, in a passage which is often ignored—or, better yet: misunderstood—Kuhn, not much different than Popper, shows a virtual commitment to the notion of progress in science:

> The analogy that relates the evolution of organisms to the evolution of scientific ideas can easily be pushed too far. But with respect to the issues of [this book] it is very nearly perfect. The

---

23. Ruse, *Evolutionary Naturalism*, 115. Cf. Davies, *Storm Over Biology*.
24. Ruse, *Evolutionary Naturalism*, 115.
25. Cf. Losee, *Historical Introduction*.
26. Ruse, *Evolutionary Naturalism*, 115.
27. Cf. Popper, *Logic of Scientific Discovery*; Popper, *Conjectures and Refutations*.
28. Cf. Kuhn, *Structure*.
29. Cf. Popper, *Objective Knowledge*. Popper denies, however, that one can ever get to the truth per se.
30. Ruse, *Evolutionary Naturalism*, 117.

process described [by me] as the resolution of revolutions is the selection by conflict within the scientific community of the fittest way to practice future science. The net result of a sequence of such revolutionary selections, separated by periods of normal research, is the wonderfully adapted set of instruments we call modern scientific knowledge. Successive stages in that developmental process are marked by an increase in articulation and specialization. And the entire process may have occurred, as we now suppose biological evolution did, without benefit of a set goal, a permanent fixed scientific truth, of which each stage in the development of scientific knowledge is a better exemplar.[31]

Purportedly, Charles Darwin had no penchant for biological progress and rigorously excised it from his published writings (I am reminded of a cautionary statement from his notebooks on evolution: "never say higher or lower . . ."). For all intents and purposes, this was probably due to his mechanism of selection. In the arms race, what wins is what wins, insomuch as it could be the prize specimen which has all of the offspring, or it could equally be the foolish simpleton. As one who used to interpret Darwin this way, Ruse currently believes that this story is admittedly alluring, but flat wrong.[32] While it is true that Darwin recognized branching to be a crucial part of the evolutionary process, it is true also that Darwin denied any simple upwardly progressive force in evolution. He saw that selection would lead to a kind of *relativistic* progress, where one improves *particular* adaptations, which could also be referred to as "comparative highness."[33] But, it remains true that Darwin thought *relativistic* progress would morph into *absolute* progress, marked by the ever-pervasive rise of complexity.[34] Curiously, Darwin saw humans—specifically, white males—at the proverbial top of the macroevolutionary heap.[35]

---

31. Kuhn, *Structure*, 172–73.

32. Ruse, *Evolutionary Naturalism*, 120. Cf. Ospovat, *Development of Darwin's Theory*.

33. Ruse, *Evolutionary Naturalism*, 120.

34. Cf. Darwin, *Origin*.

35. Cf. Darwin, *Descent*; see also, Greene, "Darwin as a Social Evolutionist," 1–27. In *The Vestiges of the Natural History of Creation* (1846), Robert Chambers, who was a prominent influence upon Darwin, regarded progress and evolution as part of the same proverbial family, with the former being the parent of the latter (Ruse, *Evolutionary Naturalism*, 142). Darwin was also a progressionist about society. But how could he not be? After all, he came from a rich, liberal family, with roots deep in the industrial British Midlands. And this progressionism was taken explicitly into his biology. For progressionists like Darwin, there was an easy movement from belief in change in the world of culture and society and science to a belief in change in the world of organisms—a movement, that is, from "monad to man." And, especially given that the progressionists

Interestingly, an endorsement of an *absolute* kind of progress—monad to man—can readily be found in rather recent SEW biological literature. For instance, entomologist and sociobiologist Edward O. Wilson:

> We should first note that social systems have originated repeatedly in one major group of organisms after another, achieving widely different degrees of specialization and complexity. Four groups occupy pinnacles high above the others: the colonial invertebrates, the social insects, the nonhuman mammals, and man.[36]

And then he goes even further, noting:

> The typical vertebrate society . . . favors individual and ingroup survival at the expense of societal integrity. Man has intensified these vertebrate traits while adding unique qualities of his own. In so doing he has achieved an extraordinary degree of cooperation with little or no sacrifice of personal survival and reproduction. Exactly how he alone has been able to cross to this fourth

---

were keen to judge our own species as the epitome of creation, it was natural to read the improvement of culture right into the processes and products of organic change. Macroevolution was thus seen to be progressive, with Homo *sapiens* as the end point, at which stage people turned around and read the progressiveness of the (macro-)biological record back into society. Ruse stresses that whereas after the *Origin* it was no longer necessary to appeal to progress to support one's belief in evolution, people nevertheless did (and still do! Cf. Ruse, *Evolutionary Naturalism*, 143). Indeed, Darwin provided what the earlier philosopher of science William Whewell (1840) called a "consilience of inductions," thus making the support of progress unnecessary (Ruse, "Darwin's Debt to Philosophy," 159–81). In this sense, Ruse argues, evolution had grown up. Just like a human adult, it no longer needed its parent—societal progress—to exist, and yet evolution did not leave home, alike unto how many young adults do not leave home today when they "should" do so. (Macro-)Evolutionists continued to be progressionists just as ardently after the *Origin* as they had before—even more so, in fact. Indeed, although Darwin attempted to caution himself to "never to speak of higher and lower," even in the first edition of the *Origin* there were strong allusions of Darwin's own progressionism. This came through most clearly in the flowery paragraph, closing the volume: "Thus, from the war of nature, from famine and death, the most exalted object which we are capable of conceiving, namely, the production of the higher animals, directly follows. There is grandeur in this view of life, with its several powers, having been originally breathed into a few forms or into one; and that, whilst this planet has gone cycling on according to the fixed law of gravity, from so simple a beginning endless forms most beautiful and most wonderful have been, and are being, evolved" (Darwin, *Origin*, 490). By the time of the third edition of the *Origin* (1861), Darwin's evolutionary ideas were a basic success, and thus he wrote candidly about his belief that evolution is essentially an "upward drive" towards humanity (Peckham, ed., *Origin of Species*, 222).

36. Wilson, *Sociobiology*, 379.

pinnacle, reversing the downward trend of social evolution in general, is the culminating mystery of all biology.[37]

The most articulate expression of this general thrust has come rather recently from the pen of John T. Bonner,[38] who argues that there has been and always will be a kind of biological pressure towards increase in bodily size, for bigness—as it were—has its virtues. For instance, when the early mammals retreated to the sea, the niches for small animals were overly crowded—but there was a plethora of room for *really* big animals. Hence the whales.[39] Continuing this theme, Bonner points out that the increases in bodily size requires a concurrent increase in size of internal support systems, which led to increased complexity, where this can be defined simply in terms of the different number of types of component parts. Complexity, in turn, led to improved selected-for adaptations, most importantly sophisticated social skills. So then, in Bonner's system, as in traditional accounts, primates—humans in particular—come out at the top of the heap again. As Ruse exclamates, progress reigns (again)![40]

Succinctly, one may confidently say that macroevolutionary evolutionary theory is a child of progress. Indeed, the belief that all organic beings have natural origins and are produced by the "normal" laws of nature was an idea that started to be accepted from the middle to the end of the eighteenth century. Ruse claims that it was not chance that evolution appeared at this time, nor was it chance that the virtually same idea appeared in France, England, and Germany along the same time frame. After all, the eighteenth century was one that invented, developed, and promoted the idea of progress: that is, the belief that it is possible to improve aspects of existence, and that this improvement can come about through human effort. Ruse avers that the birth of the one idea (progress) brought about the birth of the other (macroevolution).[41] Why progress, Ruse queries? In simple terms, it was because the more that was learned of the world of organisms, the more people realized that it is a world of change. There was, for example, an ever-growing data set of biological phenomena that seemed to point to perpetual *becoming* rather than dormant *being*. Additionally, there was the

---

37. Wilson, *Sociobiology*, 382.

38. Bonner, *Evolution of Complexity*; cf. Benton, "Progress and Competition," 305–38.

39. In what may argue against my notion of objective progress, in the retreat to the sea, mammalian backbones underwent a significant simplification (see McShea, "Complexity and Evolution," 303–24).

40. Ruse, *Evolutionary Naturalism*, 122.

41. Ruse, *Evolutionary Naturalism*, 140.

fossil record with its revelation of yesterday's organisms, of which there were no living counterparts.[42]

However, Ruse stipulates that between the years of 1930 and 1960, evolution separated from its proverbial parent, that is, progress. The "professionalizers of evolution" (also known as known as the "synthetic theorists") severed the bonds between the two; while (macro-)evolution had been capable of standing on its own two feet for nearly a hundred years, there was no reason for it to do so, so it failed to make the break.[43] Concluding my selective survey of biological progress, I pronounce that it is apparent that the notion of progress continues to be of concern to evolutionists—especially those interested in macroevolution. Indeed, progress is alive and well in today's macroevolutionary biology, calling it "arms race," "escalation," the "Red Queen hypothesis," or what have you. At the same time, many (macro-)evolutionists feel distinctly uncomfortable in discussing the very notion, and there is a tendency to push such discussions into the semi-popular realm.[44] Notable in his detestation and proverbial protest against this notion of progress in biology is George C. Williams, who points out that all standard measures of progress fail, and they even yield counter-intuitive results. For example, if one judges complexity over the whole of a life span, a good case can be made for saying that the liver fluke is a higher life form than humans.[45] In flat opposition to just about every progressionist mentioned above, one prominent evolutionist (G. C. Williams) has recently argued that progress entails the dipolar opposite of that which is adaptively advantageous, because he feels (with T. H. Huxley) that that which is morally good is rarely if ever that which is biologically good.[46] Additionally, some more recent work, for instance on measures of complexity, simply shows what people like Simpson (himself a progressionist) said all along—namely, that there is simply no good reason to think that complexity is a *necessarily* ever-increasing product of the evolutionary process, and hence there is no reason to affirm progress in a Rusean "absolute" or what I term "objective" sense.[47]

---

42. Cf. Bowler, *Evolution: The History of an Idea*; and also see Rudwick, *Meaning of Fossils*. Combined with this, there was the traditional viewing of the organic world as a chain of being, going from the most simple to the most complex. Of course, as we know, this belief goes back at least to Aristotle's *De Anima*, and it was reinforced by theological and philosophical arguments throughout the Enlightenment (cf. Lovejoy, *Great Chain of Being*).

43. Ruse, *Evolutionary Naturalism*, 147.

44. Cf. Smith, "J. B. S. Haldane," 37–51.

45. Cf. Williams, *Adaptation and Natural Selection*.

46. Cf. Williams, "A Sociobiological Expansion," 179–214.

47. Cf. McShea, "Complexity and Evolution," 303–324.

So then, an accounting of SEW's view upon progress is a mixed bag, even today, in the early twenty-first century.

The Roles of and for Common Ancestry, Selection/ism, and Adaptation/ism

Moving on from progress being a main topic of the SEW, I now advance to the notion(s) of *common ancestry, selection/ism*, and *adaptation/ism*, which will include both *natural* and *sexual selection* as main subtheses, as well as the *units of selection* (with corresponding subtheses of the *individual vs. group selection* debate, which is explicated by *altruism, evolutionary ethics*, and *fitness* subtopics).

Why did Darwin start with an explication of natural selection, and not an exposition of what (perhaps?) should be seen to be logically prior to the mechanism of diversity generation (i.e., common ancestry)? I propose that Darwin did not want to immediately offend his readers; indeed, had he started with common ancestry, his readers would have instantaneously made the mental connection between apes and humans, which he desperately wanted to avoid (at least in *The Origin*, though he later broaches that topic in his *The Descent of Man*). So then, Darwin begins *The Origin* by noting artificial selection, then extrapolates that principle to his own mechanism—natural selection—and then ends with overtures to common ancestry.

However, around 150 years post hence, SEW biologists can safely begin with common ancestry, for it is now more generally accepted—that is, after the "grunt work" of the mechanism of (macro-)evolution had been laid by Darwin in *The Origin*. So then, in orienting this section, I will invert Darwin's presentation of his ideas, so as to reflect the better logical sequence, insomuch as I begin with common ancestry, and only then move to expositing both natural and sexual selection. However, it should be noted that Darwin himself says that *The Origin* is "one long argument," so perhaps it is possible that I am reading too much into his chosen arrangement of the text. But I think, truly, that I am on to something.[48] Not only me, of course, but

---

48. Another explanation as to why Darwin put selection first in the *Origin* is provided by the thought that selection explains branching, which is given through his *Principle of Divergence* (cf. Darwin, *On the Origin of Species: A Variorum Edition*, 26). It is notable that Sober prefers this alternative explanation, whereas I prefer the former (Cf. Sober, *Did Darwin Write the Origin Backwards?*, 10053). In fact, Sober stipulates that there is a special feature of the relationship between common ancestry and natural selection in Darwin's theory. Natural selection and common ancestry fit well together, but only if selection has *not* been proverbially omnipotent, for if all traits evolve because there is (natural) selection for them, "Darwin's Principle" would conclude that we

SEW biologists seem to think so too. However, given how central the thesis of common ancestry is to SEW evolutionary reasoning, one might expect there to be a vast literature in which the evidence for that claim is collected and collated. But in fact, though the question is discussed, the literature upon it is hardly vast. For most SEW evolutionists, the similarities that different species share make it obvious that they have common ancestors, and there is no reason to puzzle further over the question.

That being said, Darwin tells us in *The Origin* that when it comes to finding evidence for common ancestry, the adaptive features that provide evidence for natural selection are precisely where one ought not to look:

> [A]daptive characters, although of the utmost importance to the welfare of the being, are almost valueless to the systematist. For animals belonging to two most distinct lines of descent, may readily become adapted to similar conditions, and thus assume a close external resemblance; but such resemblances will not reveal—will rather tend to conceal their blood-relationship to their proper lines of descent.[49]

That humans and monkeys have tailbones, and that human fetuses and fish have gill slits, are both evidence for common ancestry precisely because tailbones and gill slits are useless in modern-day humans. In contrast, the torpedo shape that sharks and dolphins share is (still) useful to both groups; understanding the concept of natural selection, one might expect this trait to evolve in large aquatic predators whether or not they have a common ancestor. This is why the adaptive similarity is insignificant to the systematist. Elliot Sober calls this "Darwin's Principle," which asserts that "adaptive similarities provide almost no evidence for common ancestry

---

have little or no evidence for common ancestry. Thus, what is needed is that selection causes branching *and* extinction but that some traits persist in lineages for *non*adaptive reasons. Darwin's claim that selection is not the exclusive cause of evolution plays an essential role in allowing him to develop his evidence for common ancestry. Indeed, Darwin's conjunction of common ancestry and natural selection would be unknowable, according to "Darwin's Principle," if the second conjunct described the only cause of phenotypic evolution. In broad outline, Sober notes, the evidential structure of Darwin's argument for his theory of common ancestry plus natural selection proceeds in this manner: 1) the argument for common ancestry, where neutral and deleterious phenotypes (i.e. vestigial organs, embryology, biogeography) do the main work; 2) it follows from 1) that populations have evolved across species boundaries; and 3) the argument that natural selection is an important part of the explanation of many adaptive traits, and artificial selection and the Malthusian argument for the power of selection are important, as are Darwin's many examples of adaptive phenotypes in nature. The order in the *Origin* has 3) first, and then 1), with 2) more or less implied (Cf. Sober, *Did Darwin Write the Origin Backwards?*, 10054).

49. Darwin, *Origin*, 427.

while similarities that are useless or deleterious provide strong evidence for common ancestry."[50] This principle, I aver, is important to grasp and apply in our talk of common descent, adaptions, and the concept of evolutionary convergence, a topic that my dissertation shall expound upon.

The Darwinian reconstruction of the history of phenotypic evolution uses the fact of common ancestry to infer the states of lineal ancestors from the states of collateral descendants. Parsimony considerations, applied to an independently attested phylogeny, of course also play an important role in testing hypotheses about natural selection. Take the example of the hypothesis that land vertebrates evolved four limbs to help them walk on dry land: biologists reject this hypothesis because the morphological phenotype was present in the lineage before vertebrates emerged out of the water. Why is such a contention palatable? I suspect it is because the phenotypes of collateral descendants allow one to infer the traits of lineal ancestors. So then, we infer from modern-day organisms (and from fossils) that the ancestors of land vertebrates had four limbs before vertebrates emerged upon dry land; thus, tetrapody evolved before walking in the vertebrate line—that is, in the sea. Darwin himself hints at this idea in *The Origin*, speaking of skull sutures:

> The sutures in the skulls of young mammals have been advanced as a beautiful adaptation for aiding parturition, and no doubt they facilitate, or may be indispensable for this act; but as sutures occur in the skulls of young birds and reptiles, which have only to escape from a broken egg, we may infer that this structure has arisen from the laws of growth, and has been taken advantage of in the parturition of the higher animals.[51]

Moreover, if we think of an ancestor as a species, we need to say what a species is; that is, we need to solve the notorious "species problem." One warning sign that this is not a path down which we should choose to tread is that the much-admired biological species concept[52] says that a species is a group of organisms that interbreed among themselves but which are reproductively isolated from other such groups. Understood in this way, a species must be made of sexual organisms. However, evolutionists agree that sexuality is a derived character; first there were asexual organisms. This means that the biological species concept is not the right choice if we wish to say that all life on Earth derives from a single species.[53] But the common ancestry hypothesis says that all current life forms derive from a single

---

50. Sober, *Did Darwin Write the Origin Backwards?*, 10051.
51. Darwin, *Origin*, 197.
52. Mayr, "Biology," 895–97.
53. Cf. Sober, *Evidence & Evolution*, 268.

organism, not a single species. An organism must be alive, of course. Darwin and present-day Darwinians would not be satisfied if all life on Earth derived from the same large slab of rock whose nonliving materials produced numerous separate start-ups of life that never melded together but instead led separately to the several groups of organisms we now observe.[54] After all, your grandparents produced your parents, and your parents produced this generation; ergo, your grandparents are among your ancestors.

But what is this begetting relation? It is natural to think of reproduction in terms of genetic transmission. You received half your nuclear genes from your mother and half from your father, and they, in turn, received half of their genes from each of their parents. However, it does *not* follow that you received one-quarter of your genes from each of your four grandparents. Instead, meiosis is a proverbial lottery, as one of your grandparents may have lost, meaning that you received exactly zero genes from him or her. As we consider ancestors of ours who are more and more remote, it becomes increasingly certain that some of them passed no genes at all to us. Ancestors have a shot at contributing genes to their descendants, but there is no guarantee that they succeed in doing so.[55]

Selection itself causes branching and extinction, which means that selection does explain why the life around us traces back to "one or a few original progenitors." SEW historians who study Darwin's work often say that he thought that natural selection is analogous to an agent (see, for example, Ospovat[56] and Young[57]). Of course, it isn't literally true that natural selection is "trying" to do anything or that it "chooses" who shall live and who shall die. Selection, after all, is a mindless process. But Darwin found the idea of natural selection as an agent useful, and so have evolutionary biologists down to the present, in thinking about what natural selection would achieve by thinking about what agents would achieve if they had certain aims and if their choices were limited to a given set of feasible options.[58] In view of such, the reason antelopes don't have machine guns with which to repel the attacks of lions is not that guns would not be useful; rather, this option was not available to them ancestrally.[59] Selection selects only among those options that are actually represented in a population. It is important

---

54. Sober, *Evidence & Evolution*, 269.
55. Cf. Sober, *Evidence & Evolution*, 269.
56. Cf. Ospovat, *Development of Darwin's Theory*.
57. Cf. R. Young, *Darwin's Metaphor*.
58. On discussion of how this "heuristic of personification" can lead one astray, however, see Sober, "Three Differences," 408–22.
59. Cf. Krebs and Davies, *Introduction to Behavioral Ecology*.

to remember that what is conceivable to an intelligent agent can differ from what is biologically possible for a species given its history.[60]

Another explanation may be phylogenetic inertia. Regarding phylogenetic inertia, consider the following remark by Roger Lewin:

> Why do most land vertebrates have four legs? The seemingly obvious answer is that this arrangement is the optimal design. This response would ignore, however, the fact that the fish that were ancestral to terrestrial animals also have four limbs, or fins. Four limbs may be very suitable for locomotion on dry land, but the real reason that terrestrial animals have this arrangement is because their evolutionary predecessors possessed the same pattern.[61]

There are two points that this passage suggests. The first is a simple chronological point: since the aquatic ancestors of land vertebrates already had four limbs, it is false that the trait initially became common in the lineage because of its utility for walking on dry land.[62] While this is no more controversial than the thought that cause must precede effect, once this point is granted, there is a second and more contentious thesis to reckon with, which is the claim that the correct explanation for why land vertebrates are tetrapods consists in the fact that their ancestors had four limbs—summarily, it is incorrect to maintain that the trait remained in place because there was selection for the trait due to the fact that it facilitated walking on dry land. Selection for the ability to walk on dry land of course does not explain the initial evolution of the tetrapod morphology; the question is whether, rather, the thesis that selection for walking was responsible for the trait's subsequent maintenance also should be rejected. The term "phylogenetic inertia" is sometimes used to refer to the explanation that Lewin favors, which might better be called "ancestral influence."[63]

60. Cf. Sober, *Evidence & Evolution*, 191.

61. Lewin, "Evolutionary Theory Under Fire," 886.

62. Cf. Eaton, "Aquatic Origin of Tetrapods," 115–20; and Edwards, "Two Perspectives," 235–54.

63. Cf. Sober, *Evidence & Evolution*, 244. See also, Wilson, *Sociobiology*; see further Harvey and Pagel, *Comparative Method*. Note that the word "inertia," seemingly, could misleadingly suggest that lineages have a tendency to continue evolving in a certain direction even after the initial "push" that got them started is no longer present. For example, if selection initially favors the evolution of longer fur in polar bears and evolution is "inertial," then fur length will continue to increase even if there ceases to be selection for longer fur. At the start of the twentieth century, the orthogenetic theory of evolution held that inertia in this sense explains why the Irish elk had such enormous horns; this view of evolution, however, is dubious, and inertia in this sense is not what "phylogenetic inertia" is now taken to mean.

The hypothesis of phylogenetic inertia and the hypothesis of stabilizing selection propose to explain the character state of a descendant in different ways; the former appeals to the lineage's ancestral state while the latter cites processes that the lineage subsequently in the future. Why are these two possible explanations in conflict? Cannot phylogenetic inertia and stabilizing selection both help explain why land vertebrates now have four limbs? This is not the position that Lewin takes in the quoted passage: phylogenetic inertia is said to be "the real reason"; not only is selection not the *whole* story, it isn't even *part* of the story. Lewin seems to posit that the hypothesis of phylogenetic inertia should be regarded as innocent until proven guilty, whereas the default assumption should be that ancestral influence is the right explanation unless the data force us to abandon that hypothesis.[64]

If what we observe is consistent with the hypothesis of phylogenetic inertia and also with the hypothesis of stabilizing selection, we should prefer the former, and even more if considerations of parsimony also suggest that we should prefer the one-factor inertia explanation over a pluralistic explanation that cites both inertia and selection.[65] Other evolutionary biologists have espoused other principles of default reasoning. Whereas George C. Williams (1966) asserts that adaptation is an "onerous concept" that should be embraced only if the data force one to do so, Ernst Mayr takes the opposite stance—that is, only after all possible selection explanations of a given trait have been explored and rejected can one tentatively conclude that the trait is a product of drift.[66] Default principles also have been defended that give precedence to some types of natural selection over others. Williams maintains that the hypothesis of group selection is more onerous (by which he means less parsimonious) than the hypothesis of individual selection; our default assumption should be that when a trait evolves by natural selection, it evolves because it is advantageous to the individuals who possess it, not because it helps the groups in which it occurs.

Adaptationism, as a claim about nature, is a thesis about the "power" of natural selection.[67] Those who debate its truth do not doubt the tree of life hypothesis; rather, the dispute concerns the mechanism, *not* the fact, of evolution. Adaptationists are inclined to answer this question in the negative; their approach to the evolution of a trait avers that natural selection is so powerful regarding of a population's evolution that such complications may safely be ignored. Indeed, adaptationists tend to expect nature to conform

64. Notably, Ridley recommends this policy in *Explanation of Organic Diversity*.
65. Sober, *Evidence & Evolution*, 245.
66. Mayr, *Towards a New Philosophy of Biology*, 150–51.
67. Sober, *Philosophy of Biology*, 120.

to the predictions of well-motivated models in which natural selection is the only factor described. They expect antelopes to be *fast* rather than *slow* (if fast is, indeed, the fitter phenotype). Adaptationists well realize that which phenotype is fittest depends on the biological details. Another qualification is needed in conjunction with the word "fittest": adaptationists might expect antelopes to evolve from *slow* to *fast* but will not expect them to evolve machine guns with which to counter lion attacks.[68] When adaptationists say that the fittest trait will evolve and survive, they mean the fittest traits *already present in the population*, not the fittest of all the traits we can imagine. Although adaptationists recognize that the outcome of selection is limited by the variation available, they expect that range to be quite rich. Natural selection will optimize with respect to *existing* variation, and it is reasonable to expect the existing variation to be rich. Still, no adaptationist holds that variation is *limitlessly* rich.

Adaptationism is a "tendency" of thought for SEWs. In practice, its proponents often hold that variation is less constraining than critics of adaptationism are inclined to maintain. An extreme adaptationist, for example, will conject that *every* trait evolves independently of every other, whereas an extreme anti-adaptationist will hold that *every* trait is enmeshed in a web of correlations that makes it impossible to change a part without systematically changing the whole. Practicing biologists rarely occupy either extreme, according to Sober.[69] Sober distinguishes three theses about the relevance that natural selection has to explaining why the individuals in some population X possess some trait T:

- (U) Natural selection played some role in the evolution of T in the lineage leading to X.
- (I) Natural selection was an important cause of the evolution of T in the lineage leading to X.
- (O) Natural selection was the only important cause of the evolution of T in the lineage leading to X.[70]

These theses are presented in ascending order of logical strength; (I) entails (U) but not conversely, and (O) entails (I) but not conversely. If (I) is true, then an explanation of the trait's evolution *cannot* omit natural selection; if (O) is true, then an explanation of the trait *can* safely ignore the

---

68. For this analogy, I admit my dependence upon Krebs and Davies, *Introduction to Behavioral Ecology*, 26.

69. Sober, *Philosophy of Biology*, 121.

70. This paragraph's statements are originally from Orzack and Sober, "Optimality Models," 361–80, as cited in Sober, *Philosophy of Biology*, 123.

nonselective factors that were in play. Adaptationism, as Sober understands the term, is committed to something like (O).[71] For adaptationists, models that focus on selection and ignore the role of nonselective factors provide *sufficient explanations*. Having described what it is to endorse adaptationism with respect to a single trait in a single lineage, Sober addresses the question of what adaptationism means *in general*. Adaptationists usually restrict their thesis to phenotypic characters; they often are prepared to concede that (O) and even (I) may be false with respect to molecular characters,[72] which makes it reasonable to formulate adaptationism as follows:

> Adaptationism: *Most* phenotypic traits, at least in *most* populations, can be effectively explained by a model in which selection is explicated and nonselective processes are effectually ignored.[73]

Notably, the above quasi-definition of adaptationism is a generalization of (O); similar generalizations of (U) and (I) also are possible (e.g., the more general form of (U) says that natural selection is *ubiquitous*). Adaptationism, as Sober construes it, does not demand that the process of natural selection maximize the fitness of the organisms (or the genes) in a population.[74] As is demonstrable in the problem of altruism, natural selection can reduce fitness. Adaptationism emphasizes the importance of natural selection; it is not committed to the thesis that natural selection always improves the level of adaptedness. Stronger versions of the adaptationism enunciated above can be obtained by replacing one or both occurrences of "most" with "all." The result of these substitutions would be to make adaptationism more falsifiable. If adaptationism were the claim that natural selection suffices to explain *all* phenotypic traits in *all* populations, a single counterexample would be enough to refute it. However, few biologists would be prepared to endorse this strong form of the thesis. The formulation that Sober suggests, though more difficult to test, is closer to the real issue that currently distresses biologists.[75]

It is commonly asserted, in genetics circles, that phenotypic variation must reflect genetic variation. SEW adaptationists, by and large, are inclined to maintain that if a phenotype were to become advantageous, then some gene combination coding for that alternative trait would probably—somehow!—arise (via mutation or recombination); although this assumption is not always correct, it is more true than not. Indeed, adaptationists expect

71. Sober, *Philosophy of Biology*, 123.
72. Cf. Smith, "Optimization Theory," 31–56.
73. This is adapted, highly, from Sober, *Philosophy of Biology*, 124. I admit my dependence upon him freely.
74. Sober, *Philosophy of Biology*, 124.
75. Sober, *Philosophy of Biology*, 124.

traits that have a significant influence on an organism's viability and fertility to be optimal. If *fast antelopes* are fitter than *slow antelopes*, then present-day antelopes should be *fast*. This expectation may be mistaken if the population has recently experienced a major change in its environment; indeed, if this has occurred, then the population may not have had sufficient time for the optimal phenotype to evolve (in this case, the traits one presently observes are *sub*optimal). Natural selection may be powerful, but even the most committed adaptationist will admit that it can lag behind extremely rapid ecological change;[76] after all, it takes time for novel variant traits to arise and time for those traits to be fixed in the population as well.

However, adaptationism has been criticized for being "too easy."[77] Suppose an adaptationist explanation is invented for trait T in population X and that we then find evidence against this explanation. The committed adaptationist can modify the discredited model or replace it with a different adaptationist account. Indeed, adaptationism seems to be so flexible a doctrine that it can be maintained no matter how many specific models are invented and refuted. The criticism lodged here is that adaptationism is, itself, *unfalsifiable*: the complaint is not that adaptationism is a false scientific doctrine, but that it is not a scientific claim at all—that is, not meeting the Popperian definition of science. But, according to Sober, *existence* claims cannot be falsified, in the Popperian sense, by their very definition.[78]

Curiously, it is not just the critics of adaptationism who have asserted that empirical investigations do not test the hypothesis of adaptationism. Indeed, even some advocates of it have stipulated such. For example, Parker and Maynard Smith say that when the optimality approach is used to address questions like, "Why do dung flies copulate for 36 minutes?," "the question is assumed to have an adaptive answer."[79] Likewise, Krebs and Davies make it quite clear that one of their "main *assumptions* is that animals are well adapted to their environments . . . We are not testing whether animals are adapted," but "rather the question we shall ask . . . is how does a particular behavior contribute to the animal's inclusive fitness."[80] According to critics and defenders alike, then, adaptationism seems to be an assumption rather than a hypothesis, per se.

76. Cf. Smith, *Evolution and the Theory of Games*.
77. Sober, *Philosophy of Biology*, 130.
78. Sober, *Philosophy of Biology*, 130.
79. Parker and Smith, "Optimality Theory in Evolutionary Biology," 27–33; italics added.
80. Krebs and Davies, *Introduction to Behavioural Ecology*, 26–27; italics added.

But ... what should we make of the claim that adaptationism *unfalsifiable*? Sober remarks that we must, first, be careful to distinguish *propositions* from *persons*.[81] Assuredly, some adaptation*ists* have been dogmatic; perhaps some have even been unwilling to consider the possibility that there might be nonadaptive explanations; but this says nothing about the falsifiability of the propositions they hold. Whether adaptation*ism* is falsifiable is a quite separate question from how adaptation*ists* behave. The next thing Sober notes about the thesis of adaptationism is that it does not have either a series of experiments or a singular "crucial experiment."[82] As such, there is no single observation that could refute the thesis, even if it is false. The word "most" that appears in the thesis above is enough to ensure that there can be no "crucial experiment" at all. In addition, the thesis says that for most traits in most species, *there exists* a selective explanation. As noted above, existence claims are not falsifiable in Popper's sense.

The fact that adaptationism is not falsifiable in the Popperian sense does not mean that it is not a scientific statement; instead, it means that there is more to science than is countenanced by Popperian philosophy. Adaptationism is like other *isms* in science: for example, behaviorism in psychology and functionalism in cultural anthropology. Adaptationism is testable only in the *long run*.[83] Its plausibility—or lack thereof—cannot be decided in advance of detailed investigations of different *traits* in different *populations*. Contrariwise, biologists investigating a specific trait in a particular population are engaged in a process in which models are developed and tested against an ever-expanding body of data. It is not impermissible that in the *long run* biologists will arrive at biologically well-motivated explanations of various traits. If biologists can do this, we then will be able to survey the body of results and decide how often adaptationist explanations turned out to be true; however, as Sober notes, the idea that we must decide whether adaptationism is true *before* we begin the project of constructing and testing specific adaptationist explanations puts the cart before the horse.[84]

Although no singular observation will determine whether adaptationism is true, this does not mean that the thesis has no scientific importance. Generalizations about how evolution proceeds are of considerable scientific interest. Adaptationism is, so to speak, a "monistic" approach to the evolutionary process; the alternative to it is "pluralism," which holds that evolution

---

81. Sober, *Philosophy of Biology*, 130.

82. Sober, *Philosophy of Biology*, 130.

83. This little allusion to the phrase "long run," which is frequently used by C. S. Peirce, is intentional.

84. Sober, *Philosophy of Biology*, 130.

is caused by a number of mechanisms of roughly coequal importance.[85] If adaptationism were unfalsifiable by scientific inquiry, however, pluralism would be unfalsifiable as well. Sober strongly contends that adaptationism is first and foremost a *research program*; after all, its core claims receive support if specific adaptationist hypotheses turn out to be well confirmed.[86] Only time will tell whether adaptationism deserves the fate of phrenology, for example.[87]

Natural Selection Explicated

All populations of organisms evolve through a law-bound process, which was described by Charles Darwin in his *The Origin of Species*. The modern explanation of this process, known as natural selection, can be briefly summarized as follows: the members of each population vary in heredity in traits of anatomy, physiology, and behavior.[88] Individuals possessing more beneficial combinations of traits survive and reproduce better than those with lesser beneficial combinations. As a consequence, the units that specify better physical traits—genes and chromosomes—increase in relative frequency within such populations, from one generation to the next. This change in better traits, which occurs at the level of the entire population, is the essential process of both (macro-) and (micro-)evolution. Although the agents of natural selection act directly on phenotypic traits and scarcely on the underlying genes (or chromosomes), the shifts they cause in the genes have lasting effects. New variation across each population arises through changes in genetic makeups, as well as their relative positions on the chromosomes.[89] Nevertheless, these changes (broadly referred to as mutations) provide only the raw material of evolution. Indeed, natural selection— differential survival and reproduction—determines the rate and direction of evolution.[90]

---

85. For this point, Cf. Gould and Lewontin, "Spandrels of San Marco," 581–98, who perhaps successfully decried the hegemony of adaptationism in biology. But for a hearty defense of adaptationism, see Cain, "Perfection of Animals," 3–29, who endorses a strong form of the adaptationist thesis. The anthologies edited by Rose and Lauder (*Adaptation*) and by Orzack and Sober (*Adaptation and Optimality*) collect a number of essays on the testing of adaptationist models.

86. Cf. Sober, *Philosophy of Biology*, 131.

87. Cf. Mitchell and Valone, "Optimization Research Program," 43–52.

88. Cf. Sober and Wilson, *Unto Others*, 104–5.

89. Cf. Ruse and Wilson, "Moral Philosophy as Applied Science," 555.

90. For nice coverage of these different components of natural selection, see the following texts: Roughgarden, *Theory of Population Genetics and Evolutionary Ecology*;

Although natural selection implies competition in an abstract sense between different forms of genes occupying the same chromosome positions or between different gene arrangements, pure competition, sometimes caricatured as "nature red in tooth and claw," is but one of several means by which natural selection can operate on the outer traits.[91] For SEWs, survival and reproduction can be promoted equally well—depending upon circumstances—through the avoidance of predators, efficient breeding, and improved cooperation with others.[92] In recent years there have been several much-publicized controversies over the pace of evolution and the universal occurrence of adaptation, of which my dissertation shall explore more fully.

But according to Ruse and Wilson, both in the SEW camp, these uncertainties should not obscure the key facts about organic evolution: that it occurs as a universal process among all kinds of organisms, that the dominant driving force is natural selection, and that the observed major patterns of change are consistent with the known principles of molecular biology and genetics;[93] according to them, such is the view held by the vast majority of the biologists who work on heredity and evolution. Ruse and Wilson simply state that there are no such crises. They cite Motoo Kimura, the principal architect of the "neutralist" theory of genetic diversity—which proposes that most evolution at the molecular level happens through random factors—because *even* he allows that classical evolution theory has demonstrated that the basic mechanism for adaptive evolution is natural selection acting on variations produced by changes in chromosomes and genes. Such considerations as population size and structure, availability of ecological opportunities, change of environment, life-cycle strategies, interaction with other species, and—to some degree—kin and group selection play a large role in our understanding of the process.[94]

Hartl, *Principles of Population Genetics*; May, ed., *Theoretical Ecology*; and Krebs and Davies, eds., *Behavioral Ecology*.

91. Ruse and Wilson, "Moral Philosophy as Applied Science," 556.

92. Salient reviews of the various modes of selection, including forms that direct individuals away from competitive behavior, can be found in Wilson, *Sociobiology*; Oster and Wilson, *Caste and Ecology in the Social Insects*; Boorman and Levitt, *Genetics of Altruism*; and Wilson, *Natural Selection of Populations and Communities*.

93. Ruse and Wilson, "Moral Philosophy as Applied Science," 556.

94. Cf. Kimura, *Neutral Theory of Molecular Evolution*.

Natural and Sexual Selection in Speciation

Although it was always his *major* mechanism, natural selection was *never* Darwin's *sole* mechanism of evolutionary change.[95] Further, Darwin was always a Lamarckian, in the sense of believing in the inheritance of acquired characteristics. Darwin's most prominent secondary mechanism was sexual selection: even in the earliest drafts of his theory, Darwin mentioned this kind of selection (Darwin and Wallace 1958);[96] indeed, within *The Origin* (1859) he spelled it out, albeit without developing it; and then in his seminal work on humanoids, *The Descent of Man* (1871), Darwin broached sexual selection in great detail, both as it applies through the animal world and as it applies to *Homo sapiens*. Ruse argues that not only was artificial selection crucial in Darwin's getting to this kind of selection, but it was essential for the place that Darwin gave it in his theorizing; in other words, without understanding Darwin's route to discovery via artificial selection, one cannot understand the structure of Darwin's argument.[97]

Moreover, Ruse claims that while sexual selection is not itself subjective, Darwin's treating it as an independent kind of selection is. First, there is the historical question of how Darwin got to sexual selection. There are hints of sexual selection in the evolutionary meanderings of Darwin's grandfather, Erasmus Darwin, as well as in the writings of others that Darwin read.[98] However, study of what Darwin produced makes it certain that the key to discovery for Darwin rested in the analogy from the domestic world and the individual breeder's power of selection.[99] Breeders, after all, select for two things: 1) attributes of animals and plants that are useful to humans, and 2) attributes that are pleasurable to us humans. It was this division that gave rise to the natural and sexual selection dichotomy.[100] In nature, these translated for Darwin into sexual selection through male combat and sexual selection through female choice.[101] One can see, therefore, that the analogy from artificial selection played a powerful role for Darwin when he came to introduce and justify sexual selection in *The Origin* and in later works.

---

95. Ruse, *Evolutionary Naturalism*, 25.
96. Darwin and Wallace, "On the Tendency of Species to Form Varieties," 46–62.
97. Ruse, *Evolutionary Naturalism*, 25.
98. See, e.g., Sebright, *Art of Improving the Breeds of Domestic Animals*; and Darwin, *Temple of Nature*.
99. Cf. Michael Ghiselin, *Triumph of the Darwinian Method*.
100. Ruse, *Evolutionary Naturalism*, 26.
101. Ruse, *Evolutionary Naturalism*, 29.

Units of Selection Explained

In biology, the debate over units of selection has centered on the evolution of seemingly altruistic behaviors that benefit others at the expense of the self; this is the paradox that makes altruism such an enthralling subject for biologists. As humans, we would like to think that altruism can evolve, whereas as biologists we see animal behaviors that appear altruistic in nature, yet almost by definition it appears that natural selection will act against them.[102] What has happened to produce this interesting—and counterintuitive—result? First, there must be more than one group; in fact, there must be a population of groups. Second, the groups cannot all have the same proportion of altruistic types, for then the results would not differ from a singular group; indeed, the groups must vary in the proportion of altruistic types.

Third, there must be a direct relationship between the proportion of altruists and the total amount of offspring produced by the group: altruistic groups need to be fitter than groups without altruists. Indeed, in order to be sufficient, the differential fitness of altruist groups must be great enough to counter the differential fitness of individuals within groups, that is, that which "naturally" selects and/or favors the selfish types.[103] Cheap individualism is meaningless; and no one explicitly endorses it. Even the most ardent individualists, such as George C. Williams,[104] Richard Dawkins,[105] and John Maynard Smith,[106] believe that there is something outside individual selection called group selection that in principle can evolve altruistic traits. Nevertheless, the history of individual selection from 1960 to the present has been a "slow slide" from valid individualism to cheap individualism.[107]

However, what is good for the individual can—and does!—conflict with what is good for the group; one's adaptation concept should reflect this fact. Rather than use "individual adaptation" as an all-encompassing label that is defined so that it applies to all adaptations regardless of whether they evolve by group or individual selection, Sober thinks it to be more useful to use "group adaptation" to name traits that evolve when group selection dominates the selection process and "individual adaptation" to name traits

---

102. Wilson, "Levels of Selection," 65.
103. Cf. Wilson, "Levels of Selection," 65.
104. Williams, "A Defense of Reductionism in Evolutionary Biology," 1–27.
105. Cf. Dawkins, *Selfish Gene*.
106. Smith, "How to Model Evolution," 117–31.
107. Wilson, "Levels of Selection," 66.

that evolve when individual selection dominates the selection process.[108] After all, why have two labels if one of them applies no matter what?

One of the main questions that has exercised philosophers writing about the units of selection problem in the twentieth century was *realism* versus *conventionalism*.[109] The realist view of the evolution of a trait notes that it is a factual question whether the evolution of a trait is influenced by selection at each of several levels—group and individual. Conventionalists—like Cassidy (1978),[110] Sterelny and Kitcher (1988),[111] Kitcher, Sterelny, and Waters (1990),[112] Waters (1991),[113] Sterelny and Griffiths (1999),[114] and Waters (2005)[115]—argue that the biological facts alone do not settle the matter. For them, the question concerns which type of explanation has the most utility. Conventionalists acknowledge that it is sometimes true that a trait evolves because of group or individual selection. But, for conventionalists, there is a pragmatic point in favor of a *genic* selection account (not herein expanded upon by me, note)—its generality. Conventionalism is *not* the position promoted by early foes of group selection such as Williams (1966), Maynard Smith (1964),[116], and Dawkins (1976), who argued that group selection hypotheses are factually false claims about nature.[117]

Sober describes the alternative to realism as *conventionalism*, not pluralism, because realism about units of selection and pluralism about explanation are compatible. Or, at least, he hopes they are, because he embraces them both; indeed, the explanatory pluralism that he endorses holds that, for any event, there are different true stories that explain why the event occurred.[118] Some describe more proximate causes while others describe causes that are more distal; some describe macro causes while others describe causes that are more micro (cf. Jackson and Pettit, 1992;[119] Sober,

---

108. Sober, *Did Darwin Write the Origin Backwards?*, 176.
109. Sober, *Did Darwin Write the Origin Backwards?*, 164.
110. Cassidy, "Philosophical Aspects of the Group Selection Controversy," 575–94.
111. Sterelny and Kitcher, "Return of the Gene," 339–60.
112. Kitcher, Sterelny, and Waters, "Illusory Riches of Sober's Monism," 158–61.
113. Waters, "Tempered Realism about Units of Selection," 553–73.
114. Cf. Sterelny and Griffiths, *Sex and Death*.
115. Waters, "Why Genic and Multilevel Selection Theories Are Here to Stay," 311–33.
116. Smith, "Group Selection and Kin Selection," 1145–46.
117. Sober, *Did Darwin Write the Origin Backwards?*, 164.
118. Sober, *Did Darwin Write the Origin Backwards?*, 165.
119. Jackson and Pettit, "In Defense of Explanatory Ecumenism," 1–22.

1984[120] and 1999[121]). Notably, Philip Kitcher claims that "one can tell all the facts about how genotype and phenotype frequencies change across the generations—including the causal explanations of the changes—without any commitment to a definite level at which selection acts."[122] Notice that Kitcher does not reject the factuality of causal talk in general; he is specific in that he thinks that causal explanations can be given without invoking a uniquely correct "level."[123]

Unlike the conventionalist philosophers just discussed, the biologists West, Griffin, and Gardner 2006; Gardner and Grafen 2009; and Wild, Gardner, and West[124]) do not deny that it is a factual question whether groups are ever units of selection. They agree with the viewpoint described by Sober that group selection means fitness variation among groups and individual selection means fitness variation within groups, and that it is a factual question what the pattern of fitness variation is in a given case.[125] However, these authors argue that units of selection must be distinguished from units of adaptation and that multilevel selection theorists fail to recognize this distinction, which leads them to fall into a "logical error."[126] These authors point out that multilevel selection models of the evolution of selfishness and altruism that separately represent the contributions of individual and group selection are predictively equivalent with models of kin selection that describe the inclusive fitnesses of the two traits; these kin selection models do not separate individual from group selection.[127]

Individual vs. Group Selection

The units of selection problem, since it concerns the kinds of adaptations found in nature, has to do with the kinds of selection processes that produced the traits that are observed.[128] Almost all of Darwin's selectionist explanations deploy the concept of individual, not group, selection. A trait that evolved because it benefited the organisms that possessed it is

120. Cf. Sober, *Nature of Selection*.
121. Sober, "Multiple Realizability Argument against Reductionism," 542–64.
122. Gasper, "An Interview with Philip Kitcher," 89.
123. Sober, *Did Darwin Write the Origin Backwards?*, 168.
124. Wild, Gardner, and West, "Adaptation and the Evolution of Parasite Virulence in a Connected World," 983–86.
125. Sober, *Did Darwin Write the Origin Backwards?*, 169.
126. Gardner and Grafen, "Capturing the Superorganism," 660.
127. Gardner and Grafen, "Capturing the Superorganism," 660.
128. Sober, *Philosophy of Biology*, 89.

an *individualist* adaptation; if it evolved because it benefited the groups in which it was found, then it is a *group* adaptation. Two features of these definitions are worth noting: first, the units of selection issue concerns evolutionary history, *not* current utility or usage. Groups may now possess various traits that help them avoid extinction, but it is a separate issue whether those traits evolved *because* they had that effect. If they evolved for another reason, then those traits provide incidental *group benefit* and are not *group adaptations*. The second point is that the definition allows that different traits may have evolved for different reasons and that a single trait may have evolved for several reasons. Perhaps one trait is an individualistic adaptation, while another is a group adaptation, and that even in the same organism. In addition, it is possible for a given trait to evolve because it simultaneously benefits objects at several levels of organization.[129]

There is an interesting passage in *The Origin* where Darwin provides a general description of the traits that selection will cause to evolve. He says the following in the first edition:

> in social animals it [natural selection] will adapt the structure of each individual for the benefit of the community; if each in consequence profits by the selected change.[130]

But what does the second occurrence of "each" refer to in the above passage? For Sober, evidently, it refers back to each individual.[131] If so, Darwin is merely saying that traits will evolve in benefit of the group if they also—by chance—benefit the individuals who possess those traits; however, the passage does not say that traits that benefit the group will evolve because they benefit the group—as such, there is no explicit endorsement of group selection in this sentence. Notably, Darwin kept this sentence as it was for the first four editions of *The Origin*, but he apparently grew to think that it needed to be rephrased. While working on *The Descent of Man*, he prepared the changes that would appear in the fifth edition of *The Origin*, published in 1869. His adjustment to the sentence above is modest but significant:

> in social animals it [natural selection] will adapt the structure of each individual for the benefit of the whole community; if this in consequence profits by the selected change.[132]

---

129. Sober, *Philosophy of Biology*, 90
130. Darwin, *Origin of Species* (1859), 87.
131. Sober, *Did Darwin Write the Origin Backwards?*, 82.
132. Darwin, *On the Origin of Species: A Variorum Edition*, 172.

After *The Descent* appeared in 1871, Darwin toys with the sentence again. Indeed, in the sixth edition of *The Origin* (1872), he changed it to read:

> in social animals it [natural selection] will adapt the structure of each individual for the benefit of the community; if the community profits by the selected change.[133]

At this time (1872, i.e.), seemingly, Darwin was openly endorsing the role of group selection, insomuch as traits that benefit the group are favored by natural selection because they benefit the group.[134] To explain the traits of individuals that promote sociality, Darwin was eager to endorse group selection, at least post-*The Descent* (1871). However, there are many traits in nature that are not like sociality. So then, Darwin's mature theory of natural selection begins with the idea of individual selection, but it does not end where it begins.

Altruism: Instances of Group Selection Exemplified

While the concept of altruistic behavior in everyday language seemingly necessitates an element of both motive and action, evolutionary biologists define altruism solely in terms of differential survival and reproduction.[135] The question of whether and how altruism can evolve has received an enormous amount of attention from evolutionary biologists. Edward O. Wilson even called it "the central theoretical problem of sociobiology."[136] In fact, Wilson popularized the term "sociobiology," (which I will not pontificate upon more in this chapter) as an attempt to explain the evolutionary mechanisms behind biological sociality such as altruism, aggression, and offspring nurturing. The fundamental principle guiding Wilson's sociobiology is that an organism's evolutionary success is measured by the extent to which its genes are represented in the next generation.

Elliot Sober asks, why isn't it a matter of convention whether one describes a trait as evolving for the good of the organism or for the good of the species? He gives the answer to this question in one word: *altruism*.[137] An altruistic trait is one that is deleterious to the individual possessing it but advantageous for the group in which it is found; as such, if the organism is

---

133. Darwin, *On the Origin of Species: A Variorum Edition*, 172.
134. Cf. Richards, *Darwin and the Emergence of Evolutionary Theories of Mind and Behavior*, 217.
135. Sober and Wilson, *Unto Others*, 17.
136. Wilson, *Sociobiology*, 3.
137. Sober, *Philosophy of Biology*, 91.

the exclusive unit of selection, then natural selection works *against* the evolution of altruism. However, if the *group* is a unit of selection, then natural selection—at times, anyway—*favors* altruistic traits. The important point about the units of selection problem is that there can be conflicts of interest between objects at different levels of organization: what is good for the group may not be good for the organism.[138]

Seemingly altruistic bees disembowel themselves when they sting intruders to the nest; thereby they sacrifice their own lives and help the group to which they belong. Similarly, some species of crows often issue warning cries when a predator approaches, which in the case of the individual crow is negative, whereas the other members of the group receive a benefit.[139] The evolutionary concept of altruism concerns the fitness effects, to self and other, of the behavior involved; thus—again seemingly—even plants and viruses can be altruistic, though they do not have minds. If organisms compete against other organisms within the confines of a single population, then natural selection will favor selfish organisms over altruistic ones, as the selfish individuals are the beneficiaries do not incur the cost of making donations themselves; on the other hand, if groups of altruists do better than groups of selfish individuals—and individual *groups* compete against other groups—then altruism may evolve, be maintained, and perhaps even become overly advantageous and therefore prominent within the populations (ref. "higher" primate societies).

I earlier said that almost all of Darwin's many selectionist explanations deploy the concept of *individual*, not *group*, selection. And while that is true in my opinion, there are a few contexts in which Darwin forsakes an individualistic interpretation of adaptation. One of them occurs in *The Descent of Man* in his discussion of human morality. Here is Darwin's statement of the case:

> It is extremely doubtful whether the offspring of the more sympathetic and benevolent parents, or of those which were the most faithful to their comrades, would be reared in greater numbers than the children of selfish and treacherous parents of the same tribe. He who was ready to sacrifice his life, as many a savage has been, rather than betray his comrades, would often leave no offspring to inherit his noble nature. The bravest men, who were always willing to come to the front in war, and who

---

138. Sober, *Philosophy of Biology*, 91.
139. Cf. Sober, *Philosophy of Biology*, 91.

> freely risked their lives for others would on average perish in larger numbers than other men.[140]

So then, we are left with a quandary: if altruistic self-sacrifice is deleterious for the individual, though good for the group, how can it evolve? Darwin responds to this question quasi-directly:

> It must not be forgotten that although a high standard of morality gives but a slight or no advantage to each individual man and his children over the other men of the same tribe, yet that an advancement in the standard of morality and an increase in the number of well-endowed men will certainly give an immense advantage to one tribe over another.[141]

A third example from *The Descent* is one in which Darwin discusses technological innovations that allow some human groups to outcompete others:

> Now, if some one man in a tribe, more sagacious than the others, invented a new snare or weapon, or other means of attack or defence, the plainest self-interest, without the assistance of much reasoning power, would prompt the other members to imitate him; and all would thus profit . . . If the new invention were an important one, the tribe would increase in number, spread, and supplant other tribes.[142]

As Sober notes, Darwin's discussion of human morality requires, in the lineage leading to modern human beings, that some individuals embraced an altruistic morality while others did not. This variation in phenotype may have been due to genetic differences between individuals, but Darwin's hypothesis is also consistent with a moral inclination to altruistic behavior evolving by cultural group selection.[143] Perhaps the traits are transmitted from one generation to the next by teaching and learning, not by genes.[144] Indeed, for Darwin and the Darwinian lineage, relatedness is the condition under which altruism evolves under the influence of group selection; it is not a condition that cancels the operation of group selection.

---

140. Darwin, *Descent of Man*, 163.
141. Darwin, *Descent of Man*, 163.
142. Darwin, *Descent of Man*, 161.
143. Cf. Boyd and Richerson, *Culture and the Evolutionary Process*.
144. Sober, *Did Darwin Write the Origin Backwards?*, 62.

Part 2

Philosophical Perspectives on Evolution

2

Charles Sanders Peirce, Evolutionary Developmental Teleology, and Kenotic Causation

INTRODUCTION

Charles Sanders Peirce was a novel thinker, in terms of both originality and in application. One area of his originality was his evolutionary developmental teleology. Another area of originality is his novel conceptioning of evolutionary causation, which is founded upon his foundational and fundamental three categories of Firstness, Secondness, and Thirdness. In what follows, I will argue the notion of a "developmental teleology" is applicable to Peirce's idea of teleology in general. Seen as such, final causes evolve, and they are not static. This contention means that teleology emerged out of the increasing complexification of life on Earth, and continues to be general, not specific, in its derivation. Moreover, in Peirce's agapasm, as explicated in the second part of this chapter, God gives himself away in acts of uncontrolling love without any conditions as to the potential response(s) to that love, as well as to what response(s) may fulfill that uncontrolling love. Rather, it is merely a completely reckless and overflowing display. Seen as such, the many and varied manifestations of complexity that macroevolution has given rise to are to be seen as a fulfillment of the teleological goals of God.

Wesleyan-related individuals of all stripes should find Peirce's thinking on teleology and causation to be amenable to their worldview, influenced as it is by a strong conception of the love of God, particularly that which is uncontrolling (cf. Tom Oord). Indeed, Oord's posit of God's uncontrolling love is potent in application to the presence of randomness and chance in the natural environment. I find that notion to be consonant with my view of a God who lures creation to higher levels of complexity through the processes of biological evolution, a contention which also should be welcomed by Wesleyan-derived theologians.

PEIRCE ON EVOLUTIONARY DEVELOPMENTAL TELEOLOGY

Charles Sanders Peirce's evolutionary philosophy was not bounded by classical determinism, as he stressed its illogicality. He notes, "We must therefore suppose an element of absolute chance, sporting, spontaneity, originality, freedom, in nature."[1] In what follows, I will explicate three models of evolution as presented by Peirce. His threefold description of evolution, comprised of tychism, anancasm and agapism, provides a plausible account of evolution that is in some sense explainable by reference to teleology, which would be a major development for theology and science in the twenty-first century. Moreover, I will explain how Peirce, by virtue of his developmental teleology, brought a unique understanding of reality to philosophy. Furthermore, I will dialogue with Peirce, drawing from him a developmental teleological view, which will then be applied to a modern rendition of teleology that may be palatable for the evolutionary sciences. An "evolutionary developmental teleology," based upon the implicit arguments found within Peirce's seminal writings, will be proposed, whereby the *telos* of evolution is seen to be, broadly, increased complexity, a *telos* which is ever growing and incessantly indeterminate.

According to Clatterbaugh, three major transitions occur during the years 1671–1739 in the modern causation debate regarding the nature of causation. First, the notion of causation is simplified. Second, the notion of causation is secularized. Third, the concern of the causation debate is changed from the metaphysical problem of causation to the attempt to identify true causal connections.[2] At the beginning of the debate regarding cau-

1. Peirce, "One, Two, Three: Kantian Categories," in *Essential Peirce*, 1:243.
2. Clatterbaugh, *Causation Debate in Modern Philosophy*, 12.

sation in the seventeenth century, there were four types of causes: material, efficient, formal, and final.[3] The discussion regarding causation culminates, according to Wang, with David Hume, who reduces the Aristotelian four causes to efficient causation only; causation and determinism thereafter became virtually equivalent.[4] Final causation, though being constantly neglected and forgotten since the beginning of modernity, I contend, remains the hidden foundation of all causal explanations and thus of mechanism itself. In order for this hidden foundation to come to light, we need first have a closer look at the inherent unity of four kinds of causes and the constant conjunction of efficient causation and final causation.[5] Peirce interprets the interdependence of efficient and final causation in this way:

> Final causation without efficient causation is helpless: mere calling for parts is what a Hotspur, or any man, may do; but they will not come without efficient causation. Efficient causation without final causation, however, is worse than helpless, by far; it is mere chaos; and chaos is not even so much as chaos, without final causation: it is blank nothing.[6]

At the same time, Peirce compares the relationship between efficient and final causation to that between the sheriff and the court. Final causation cannot be imagined without efficient causation just as "the court cannot be imagined without a sheriff." On the other hand, "an efficient cause, detached from a final cause in the form of law, would not even possess efficiency."[7]

Peirce's Three Cosmological Principles

For Peirce, there are three cosmological principles: tychism (or chance),[8] agapism (or love),[9] and synechism (or continuity).[10] Peirce's objective idealism involves a developmental teleology (a position between nominalism and realism), a view wherein final causes are not future certainties, but

3. Clatterbaugh, *Causation Debate in Modern Philosophy*, 15.
4. Wang, "Rethinking the Validity and Significance of Final Causation," 615.
5. More detailed and insightful discussion of the complementary relation between efficient and final cause can be found in Short, "Peirce's Concept of Final Causation," 376–79; and in Hulswit, "Teleology: A Peircean Critique of Ernst Mayr's Theory," 188–91.
6. Peirce, *Essential Peirce*, 2:124.
7. Peirce, *Essential Peirce*, 2:121.
8. Peirce, *Collected Papers*, 6:102.
9. Peirce, *Collected Papers*, 6:287.
10. Peirce, *Collected Papers*, 6:173.

present possibilities that may be attained in the future. Hence there is no fixed end of the world; rather, all things are marked by continual growth and change. Regarding his conception of evolution, Peirce writes, "Three modes of evolution have thus been brought before us: evolution by fortuitous variation, evolution by mechanical necessity, and evolution by creative love. We may term them tychastic evolution, or tychasm, anancastic evolution, or anancasm, and agapastic evolution, or agapasm."[11] The first kind of evolutionary theory discussed is represented by the Darwinian view, which views evolution proceeding "heedlessly" by discontinuities (or chance variations) appearing with no reason whatsoever.[12] Chance, for the tychistic type of evolution, is not associated with any particular "direction."

The second type of evolution discussed within Peirce's essay entitled "Evolutionary Love," is anacasticism, which Peirce characterizes as deterministic. He writes, "diametrically opposed to evolution by chance are those theories which attribute all progress to an inward necessary principle, or other form of necessity."[13] The necessity herein referred to is mechanical in nature. This anacasticism is deterministic; indeed, whether internal or external, the necessity works so that evolution proceeds through a succession of events from which they cannot deviate. Nothing is due to chance.[14]

The third type of evolution written of in "Evolutionary Love" affirms the presence of a form of love that plays a role in development.[15] *Agape*—which Peirce calls the operative principle of "evolutionary love"—is inherently open to variations and deviations to the laws and agencies of laws. This third type of evolution—also known as agapism—incorporates the other two types of evolution described within "Evolutionary Love." Agapasm is a form of evolution, then, that incorporates chance and necessity, but is not reducible to either, or merely the sum of the two together; it is a synthesis of these aspects with "something else," which I take as being a reference to, presumably, *telos*.[16] For Peirce, developmental teleology prevails at all levels and all stages of evolution.[17]

11. Peirce, *Collected Papers*, 6:302.
12. Peirce, *Collected Papers*, 6:287–97.
13. Peirce, *Collected Papers*, 6:298.
14. Hausman, *Charles S. Peirce's Evolutionary Philosophy*, 174.
15. Hausman, *Charles S. Peirce's Evolutionary Philosophy*, 174.
16. Hausman, *Charles S. Peirce's Evolutionary Philosophy*, 174.
17. Hausman, *Charles S. Peirce's Evolutionary Philosophy*, 16.

Peirce's Perspective upon Chance and Final Causality

Peirce contends that spontaneity will not be overcome by some final end or *telos*.[18] As such, Peirce notes that the universe will always contain some irregularity in it—in essence, there will always be an expression of both freshness and brute fact in the universe. Indeed, for Peirce, there must be some "absolute chance" in the universe and "at any time . . . an element of pure chance survives and will remain until the world becomes an absolutely perfect, rational and symmetrical system, in which mind is at last crystallized in the infinitely distant future."[19] It is important to the point of this chapter that Peirce notes that this will occur in the infinitely remote future, not in the near future. For Peirce, "no final cause is actual; every final cause is a general type."[20] Like Aristotle, Peirce avers that final causes work with efficient causes;[21] he argues for more than that, however, as "final causes tend to create or find the efficient causes that are necessary for their realization."[22] Entities, whether animate or not, attempt to "actualize in their own way the same general type or possibility actualized in the fullest possible way in God . . . a general type is a final cause because of the goodness that would characterize any actualization of it."[23] In fact, in Darwinian evolution, "random variation & tautology cooperate to produce order . . . [and] if a final cause is a general type, then it might be actualized in any number of different ways."[24] In this view, then, no matter what chance variation produces, God can work it into his overall *telos*.

In agreement, working from a Peircean view, Hulswit defines final causes as "general types that tend to realize themselves by determining processes of mechanical causation. Final causes are not future events, but general (physical) possibilities which may be realized in the future."[25] Employing Peirce's category of tychism, Hulswit notes that chance is central to teleology, and thus teleology is creative, exhibiting an irreducible novelty;[26] this unpredictability and irreducibility "is the reason why final causes cannot specify

---

18. Hausman, *Charles S. Peirce's Evolutionary Philosophy*, 17.
19. Peirce, *Collected Papers*, 6:33.
20. Short, "Peirce's Concept of Final Causation," 369.
21. Peirce, *Collected Papers*, 1:220.
22. Peirce, *Collected Papers*, 2:249.
23. Short, "Peirce's Concept of Final Causation," 371.
24. Short, "Peirce's Concept of Final Causation," 372.
25. Hulswit, "Teleology: A Peircean Critique of Ernst Mayr's Theory," 188.
26. Hulswit, "Peirce's Teleological Approach to Natural Classes," 746.

exact results."²⁷ It is for the same reasons that end states can be reached in different ways. By denying that final causes are static, unchangeable events, Peirce avoided the problems attached to classical essentialism, which beset the Aristotelian perspective on teleology in the Enlightenment—wrongly or rightly—and thereby provides a way to reintroduce final causation in a scientifically respectable manner in today's environ.²⁸

PEIRCE'S VIEW OF EVOLUTIONARY CAUSATION

This second part of this chapter now transitions to focusing upon Peirce's view upon evolutionary causation, and how it complements his view upon evolutionary developmental teleology, and could, in fact, be seen as an application of his thoughts upon the former issue. Peirce contends that bodies indeed obey the laws of mechanics, but it may be that if our means of measurement were better, or if we were able to wait inconceivable ages for an exception, exceptions to any law may be found. In fact, it may be that chance, in the Aristotelian sense of there being the absence of cause, has to be admitted as being relevant in our universe. The terms "causation" and "causality" are often used as synonyms. In *From Cause to Causation: A Peircean Perspective*, however, Hulswit makes a distinction between *causation*, or the *production* of an effect by its cause(s), and *causality*, which is defined as the *relationship* between cause and effect. Although Peirce never explicitly made this distinction, he implicitly did so by criticizing the principle of *causality*, and by elaborating a constructive theory of *causation*. In Peirce's conception, there is a triple *interdependence* of final causation, efficient causation, and chance.²⁹ It was to Peirce's merit to have stated the problem succinctly: "The great principle of causation which, we are told, it is absolutely impossible not to believe, has been one proposition at one period in history and an entirely disparate one [at] another and is still a third one for the modern physicist. The only thing about it which has stood . . . is the *name* of it."³⁰

This confusion is at least partly due to the complex evolution of the concept of cause. The modern concept of cause is the result of the interplay between the Aristotelian-Scholastic conception, according to which causes are *active initiators of a change*, and the modern scientific conception, according to which causes are the *inactive nodes in a law-like implication chain*. Although the Aristotelian-Scholastic conception of cause has remained an

27. Hulswit, "Teleology: A Peircean Critique of Ernst Mayr's Theory," 195.
28. Hulswit, "Peirce's Teleological Approach to Natural Classes," 766.
29. Hulswit, *From Cause to Causation: A Peircean Perspective*, 44–45.
30. Peirce, *Reasoning and the Logic of Things*, 197.

aspect of our commonsense idea of "cause," the modern scientific view is without question the most predominant in philosophical discourse. According to the latter view, causation means some sort of *law-like relation* between cause and effect, rather than the *production* of an effect by its cause. Peirce's conception of causation, however, is different, according to which each act of causation involves a *teleological*, an *efficient*, and a *chance* component. Peirce's conception of efficient cause in fact holds a middle way between the Aristotelian-Scholastic conception of cause and the modern scientific conception of cause.

Peirce's Highly Original View of Causation

In his 1902 paper "On Science and Natural Classes," Peirce developed an original view of causation that each act of it involves an efficient component, a final component, and a chance component.[31] The efficient aspect of causation is that each event is produced by a previous event (the efficient cause), whereas the teleological aspect is that each event is part of a chain of events with a definite tendency. The chance component is that each event has some aspect that is determined neither by the efficient nor by the final cause.

According to Peirce, *final causes* are general types that tend to realize themselves by determining processes of efficient causation. Final causes are basically habits: they direct processes toward an end state. The habits of nature (which we refer to as the laws of nature) are final causes because they display tendencies toward an end state. Moreover, these habits are not static entities because they may evolve in the course of time. Peirce called the possible evolution of final causes "developmental teleology."[32] Thus, final causes are not future events, but general possibilities, for the end state of the process to which the act of causation belongs can be reached in different ways. It is therefore a mistake to contend that a *telos* is referent to a future state of affairs influencing the present state of affairs. In fact, Peirce says this much in writing:

> we must understand by final causation that mode of bringing facts about according to which a general description of result is made to come about, quite irrespective of any compulsion for it to come about in this or that particular way; although the means may be adapted to the end. The general result may be brought about at one time in one way, and at another time in another way. Final causation does not determine in what particular way

---

31. Peirce, *Essential Peirce*, 2.115.
32. Peirce, "Law of Mind," 331.

it is to be brought about, but only that the result shall have a certain general character.[33]

The idea that efficient causation can only be understood within the context of final causation is central to Peirce's conception of causation. According to him, "efficient causation . . . is a compulsion determined by the particular condition of things, and is a compulsion acting to make that situation *begin* to change in a perfectly determinate way; and what the general character of the result may be in no way concerns the efficient causation."[34] The efficient cause functions as a *means* for the attainment of the end. Thus, "final causality cannot be imagined without efficient causality."[35]

Moreover, according to Peirce, every event is characterized not only by an aspect of final causation and an aspect of efficient causation, but also by an aspect of *objective chance*. Each natural process involves an aspect of objective chance at every stage of the process, which *cannot* be reduced to efficient or final causation. Above, I explained that Peirce's conception of causation is characterized by a triple *interdependence* of final causation, efficient causation, and chance. Keeping in mind that we earlier distinguished two mutually incompatible conceptions of cause—the Aristotelian-Scholastic conception and the modern scientific conception—I conclude that Peirce's conception of causation forms an ingenious middle way between these two conceptions. On the one hand, Peircean causes are the active initiators of a change (rather than the inactive nodes in a law-like implication chain). On the other hand, however, the action of a *cause* is essentially a case of the operation of a law, and in fact directly implies a law.

An Explication of Peirce's Three Categories

This section begins by highlighting the three original yet fundamental categories as outlined by Peirce. Peirce's entire system of thought, it could be said, rests upon his notion of three fundamental categories, which he called Firstness, Secondness, and Thirdness.[36] He derived these categories by two independent methods, one deductive and the other phenomenological. He summarized the categories as follows: "The First is that whose being is simply in itself, not referring to anything nor lying behind anything. The Second is that which is what it is by force of something to which it is second.

33. Peirce, *Collected Papers*, 1:211.
34. Peirce, *Collected Papers*, 2:120.
35. Peirce, *Collected Papers*, 1:213.
36. Peirce, *Essential Peirce*, 2:272–73.

The Third is that which is what it is owing to things between which it mediates and which it brings into relation to each other."[37]

Expanding on his category of Firstness, Peirce emphasized that because its nature is to be independent in origin from anything else, it can never be adequately grasped or described:

> The idea of the absolutely First must be entirely separated from all conception of or reference to anything else; for what involves a second is itself a second to that second. The First must therefore be present and immediate, so as not to be second to a representation. It must be fresh and new, for if old it is second to its former state. It must be initiative, original, spontaneous, and free; otherwise it is second to a determining cause. It is also something vivid and conscious; so only it avoids being the object of some sensation. It precedes all synthesis and all differentiation: it has no unity and no parts. It cannot be articulately thought: assert it, and it has already lost its characteristic of innocence; for assertion always implies a denial of something else. Stop to think of it, and it has flown![38]

So then, once we conceive of any phenomenon that manifests something of the nature of otherness, we meet the category of Secondness:

> The Second is precisely that which cannot be without the first. It meets us in such facts as Another, Relation, Compulsion, Effect, Dependence, Independence, Negation, Occurrence, Reality, Result. A thing cannot be other, negative, or independent, without a first to or of which it shall be other, negative, or independent . . . We find secondness in occurrence, because an occurrence is something whose existence consists in our knocking up against it . . . The idea of second must be reckoned an easy one to comprehend. That of first is so tender that you cannot touch it without spoiling it; but that of second is eminently hard and tangible. It is very familiar too; it is forced upon us daily: it is the main lesson of life.[39]

Finally, Thirdness is the category that introduces the possibility of mediation, which cannot arise from either Firstness or Secondness alone:

> First and Second, Agent and Patient, Yes and No, are categories which enable us roughly to describe the facts of experience, and

---

37. Peirce, *Essential Peirce*, 1:246.
38. Peirce, *Essential Peirce*, 2:248.
39. Peirce, *Essential Peirce*, 1:248–49.

they satisfy the mind for a very long time. But at last they are found inadequate, and the Third is the conception which is then called for. The Third is that which bridges over the chasm between absolute first and last, and brings them into relationship.[40]

Whereas the category of Firstness is characterized by an "airy-nothingness" and Secondness is characterized by the "Brute Actuality of things and facts," Thirdness "comprises everything whose being consists in active power to establish connections between different objects."[41] In this view, Thirdness is the source of meaning and intelligibility in the universe.[42] Peirce speculated that the order (Secondness) and intelligibility (Thirdness) of the universe evolved from a primordial condition of indeterminate chaos (Firstness):

> In the beginning,—infinitely remote,—there was a chaos of unpersonalised feeling, which being without connection or regularity would properly be without existence. This feeling, sporting here and there in pure arbitrariness, would have started the germ of a generalising tendency . . . Thus, the tendency to habit would be started; and from this with the other principles of evolution all the regularities of the universe would be evolved.[43]

Peirce developed his system of three categories into a highly original evolutionary cosmology. In fact, he proposed that there are three possible modes of evolutionary change, which parallels his three categories. The first mode of evolutionary change is "tychastic" evolution, which he regarded as the basic form of Darwin's theory. He wrote, "Natural selection, as conceived by Darwin, is a mode of evolution in which the only positive agent of change in the whole passage from moner to man is fortuitous variation."[44] Evolution by strict chance is a manifestation of Peirce's category of Firstness, because Firstness is the category in which a lack of determination by other events or entities is the chief characteristic. Peirce, ultimately, found Darwin's scheme—considered alone—unsatisfactory.[45]

The second possible mode of evolution, "anancastic" evolution, is that which is constrained completely by necessity, constraint, and determination by something other than itself. In contradistinction to this view, and in

---

40. Peirce, *Essential Peirce*, 1:249.
41. Peirce, *Essential Peirce*, 2:435.
42. Corrington, *Introduction to C. S. Peirce*, 135.
43. Peirce, *Essential Peirce*, 1:297.
44. Peirce, *Essential Peirce*, 1:358.
45. Peirce, *Essential Peirce*, 1:357.

support of Peirce's own position, many current positions regarding macro-evolutionary theory argue that the process of evolution reflects a balance of chance and necessity.[46] In Peircean terms, they argue for a balance between Firstness and Secondness. However, Peirce rejected the idea that such a balance—by itself—offers an adequate explanation of the world as we know it, proffering instead that a complete explanation of evolution requires the category of Thirdness beyond the categories of chance (Firstness) and necessity (Secondness).[47]

Peirce also regarded Thirdness as the category that gives to the universe "a vital freedom which is the breath of the spirit of love."[48] Therefore, he referred to this third mode of evolution as "agapastic" evolution, building upon the Greek term *agape*, which translates into English as "love." He commented regarding this mode of evolution that "Everybody can see that the statement of St. John [i.e., "God is love," 1 John 4:8] is the formula of an evolutionary philosophy, which teaches that growth only comes from love ... The philosophy we draw from John s gospel is that this is the way mind develops; and as for the cosmos, only so far as it yet is mind, and so has life, is it capable of further evolution."[49]

Peirce's Categories Interpreted Pneumatologically

I would like to suggest that pneumatology could add an important element to this depiction of Peirce's category of Thirdness. Indeed, the Spirit may be understood as manifesting the characteristics of Peircean Thirdness. According to a Christian rereading of Genesis 1:2, the Spirit (*ruach*), while sweeping over the formless void, brings order (Secondness) to the primordial chaos (Firstness). Furthermore, in the Old Testament the Spirit, again alike unto Thirdness, is described as the source of all life (e.g., Psalm 104:29–30), with regard to both human (e.g., Genesis 2:7) and nonhuman entities (e.g., Genesis 6:17; Psalm 104:25). In the New Testament, a shift occurs to the emphasis on the role of the Spirit as the source of *new* creation (e.g., Romans 8:11). Nevertheless, I contend that the Spirit, like Thirdness, brings the life-giving power of God to other entities.

In addition to the similarities between the Spirit and Thirdness as the source of life, there is a parallel in that the Spirit may be regarded as the

---

46. See, e.g., Bartholomew, *God of Chance*; see also Ward, *God, Chance, and Necessity*.

47. Peirce, *Essential Peirce*, 1:331.

48. Peirce, *Essential Peirce*, 1"363.

49. Peirce, *Essential Peirce*, 1.354.

source of openness to the future, which coheres with Peirce's notion that it is the category of Thirdness upon which freedom depends.[50] Yet another aspect of this parallel is that in Peirce's concept of *agapasticism* the openness to the future is closely connected with the nature of love. In historic Trinitarian theology, there is an understanding of the Spirit in terms of love, notably in Augustine's infamous identification of the Spirit as the bond of love between the Father and Son.[51]

These minimal considerations demonstrate that there are significant parallels between the characteristics of the Spirit and those of Peirce's category of Thirdness. A further question is whether it is justifiable to claim that, like Thirdness, the identifying characteristic of the Spirit is the function of mediation. Whereas neither scripture nor tradition has consistently made such an identification, I contend that such a connection is at least plausible. Some support can be found for an identification of the Spirit with the phenomenon of mediation, for example, in John's Gospel, wherein Jesus promises that the Father will give the disciples the Spirit as an "advocate" (cf. John 14:16) who will act as a mediator between Christ and the world. Moreover, in pre-Christian Greek literature, the word *paraclete*, usually translated as "advocate," can also mean "mediator."[52]

The apostle Paul uses the language of mediation when he declares that God's love has been poured into our hearts through the Holy Spirit (cf. Romans 5:5) and that the Spirit 'intercedes' for the saints (cf. Romans 8:26). Saint Augustine suggested that "the Holy Spirit is a kind of inexpressible communion or fellowship of Father and Son."[53] The idea that the primary characteristic of the Spirit is that of mediation is summed up well by Taylor and Wood when they call the Spirit "the Go-Between God."[54] As I indicated above, the scriptural and traditional understanding of the Spirit has significant parallels with Peirce's category of Thirdness. I suggest further that the role of the Spirit in creation may therefore be regarded as that of mediating between God and the world, bringing into relationship that which would otherwise be separated. This coheres well with the scriptural witness, according to which God enters the world in the incarnation through the mediation of the Spirit (see e.g., Matthew 1:20) and the reconciliation of the world to God is regarded as a function of the Spirit (e.g., Romans 8:1–27). According to Rahner, a symptom of the isolation of the doctrine of the

50. Pannenberg, *Systematic Theology*, 2:97–98.
51. Augustine, *Trinity*, 43.
52. Bauer and Danker, *Greek-English Lexicon of the New Testament*, 623.
53. Augustine, *Trinity*, 12.
54. Taylor and Wood, *Go-Between God*, 22.

Trinity from the rest of Christian theology, including the doctrine of creation, has been a recalcitrance to consider the possibility that the world may exhibit actual vestiges of the triune creator.[55] A model of the Trinitarian creation informed by Peirce's categories and evolutionary philosophy offers a new way of developing this neglected theological concept.

CONCLUSION

So what does this proceeding analysis of Peirce's thoughts upon evolutionary developmental teleology, in conjunction with a presentation of his views upon evolutionary causation, mean for modern Wesleyans? I suggest to my patient reader several things in what follows:

First, Peirce's teleology is "more than a mere purposive pursuit of a predetermined end; it is a developmental teleology."[56] Although Peirce used the term "developmental teleology" only in the discussion of the development of human personality, Hulswit points out that it is also "applicable to [his] idea of teleology in general: learning from the developmental aspect of our own human purposes, we can inductively infer that all final causes in nature are, at least in principle, subject to evolution."[57] This means that final causes are indeterminate, which may help explain the randomness that is everywhere present in our (uni-?)multiverse. Thus—as a second summary point—final causes evolve, and they are not static. The developmental teleology of Peirce is characterized by the continuity of the evolutionary process, and this principle of continuity is essential for his developmental teleology and his understanding of reality.[58]

Third, I maintain that a significantly revised conception of teleology must be developed, if it is to see a resurgence of widespread plausibility in today's somewhat scientifically literate populace, and fortunately modern Wesleyan theology has the resources in its disposal to revive such a concept. Indeed, as Wesleyan theology uniquely emphasizes God's love, such a picture is conducive to a proper theology of evolution and a pertinent theodicy. Moreover, I contend—fourthly—that the conception of teleology may need serious revision for it to even be maintained as a viable *theological* category. One contribution of Peirce's view is that it pictures teleology as evolving and as being a general goal versus a definite end state or predetermined goal. This helps explain a lot of the "evolutionary dead ends" to which our

---

55. Rahner, *Trinity*, 13–14.
56. Peirce, *Essential Peirce*, 1:331.
57. Hulswit, "Teleology: A Peircean Critique of Ernst Mayr's Theory," 197.
58. Cf. Peirce, *Collected Papers*, 5:436.

fossil record attests. In dialogue with Peirce, I argue—fifthly—that teleology emerged out of the increasing complexification of life on Earth, and continues to be general, not specific.[59] Such a contention as this bodes well in producing a thoroughly evolutionary paradigm. All of these points c/should be reviewed—and possibly appropriated—by the contemporary Wesleyan-relational movement.

Furthermore, as a sixth point, in dialogue with Peirce's insistence on the absence of teleology in anancasm, and the inclusion of it in agapasm, I conceive of teleology as at least partially self-determining. Self-determination is, in fact, fundamental to evolutionary developmental teleology, and Wesleyans would want to therefore preserve it. They find a pattern for doing so with respect to how Whitehead says that everything is self-creative. In his *agapasm*, Peirce has a condition that is permissible of future growth, and this condition does not negate any tendency that may seem at odds with it. As such, the "directedness" of the condition, then, may be characterizable in terms of the God that gives of himself in act of love without any conditions of potential responses to that love, and what responses may fulfill that love; it is merely a display of completely reckless overflowing, *uncontrolling* love. Seen as such, the many and varied manifestations of complexity to which macroevolution has given rise can be seen as a fulfillment of the teleological goals of God. Such a view places import on even the most minuscule species produced by evolution—everything has worth. God's nature, as it is pictured within the Wesleyan-relational tradition, is nothing short of "creative-responsive love," which is based upon, fundamentally, an infinitely *relational* God, who is *redemptively* present in everything that happens, from beginning to end. Those points comport well with the position of Peirce, as laid out in this chapter.

What's more, causation is a multifaceted event, comprised of previous actions which are determined, future developments which are at least projaculately anticipated by a final (teleological) component, and current effects which are affected and perhaps even effected by chance events, which are comprised by Peirce in his view that each act of causation involves an upon efficient component, a final component, and a chance component. This mode of causality—a theological synthesis between *kenosis* and the evolutionary complexification of matter, mediated by the *uncontrolling* love

---

59. Teleology is grounded in the physical realm via the kenosis of the Spirit into the natural world, but cannot be reduced to it, as the Spirit operates within the natural world as its empowerment. This is a point that is argued for in McCall, "Kenosis of the Spirit into Creation"; see also McCall, "Emergence and Kenosis: A Theological Synthesis," 149–64; also, reference the following essay for a further delineation of this position: McCall, "Emergence and Kenosis: A Wesleyan Perspective," 155–70.

of God through the creative Spirit—is potent in application to Wesleyan-relational theology and the contemporary theology and science discussion, and it should be incorporated into both. It is based fundamentally upon the conceptioning of "uncontrolling love" by Thomas Jay Oord in several books in the preceding years.[60] Oord's posit of God's uncontrolling love is potent in application also to the presence of randomness and chance in the natural environment. I find that notion to be consonant with my view of a God who lures creation to higher levels of complexity through the processes of biological evolution. As I see it, God does not determine the outcome of random events, but God instead constrains randomness by setting broad boundaries, after which the empowered particles, systems, and organisms interact according to natural laws within the aforementioned boundaries, which produces a wide range of beautiful results. Instead of opposing God and chance, I further contend that chance was God the Spirit's idea and that *she* uses it to ensure the variety, resilience, and freedom necessary—not to mention maximal population—to achieve her purposes within "creation."

---

60. Cf. Oord, *Nature of Love: A Theology*; and Oord, *Uncontrolling Love of God*, 1–29.

3

Alfred North Whitehead, Chance, and the Immanently Creative Spirit[1]

CONCEIVING THE SPIRIT AS CREATIVITY

In the present chapter, one will find several parts, followed by a suggestive conclusion. Each part of this chapter suggests an overall thesis that God through the Spirit is both the immanent and eminent principle of creativity, ever wooing, ever beckoning, and ever empowering the advancements in complexity over 15 billion years of cosmic history, and 3.6 billion years of earthly history, seen principally in the accompanying (or, rather, resultant) biological evolution. I will argue that via the primal *kenosis* of the Spirit's being-ness *into* the world, the fullness[2] of the deity is immanently present *upon* and *within* the Earth, which has been expanding with increasing complexity in virtual perpetuity,[3] insomuch as over a period of 3.6 billion years there has arisen entities that display and promote both the goodness

1. This article originally appeared as McCall, "Whitehead, Creativity, and the Immanently Creative Spirit," 337–50. Reprinted with permission.

2. Note here that Michael Weber stipulates that within the triune category of the ultimate, Creativity *cannot* work without the One and/or without the Many, and the Many cannot work without Creativity and/or the One.

3. Weber, *Whitehead's Pancreativism*, 149.

(defined as what God *does* for the "other") and the greatness (referent to the *intrinsic* character) of God.[4] I agree with I. C. Jarvie, who holds that creativity is interesting precisely because it is uniquely mysterious.[5] It is all the more mysterious since I posit that it is the Spirit who is the principle of creativity within the world, for the Spirit is often seen to be the hidden member of the Trinity, and not an active force prior to the ascension of Jesus. It should be noted that creative achievements are unique events, and as such they are not repeatable. However, we can nevertheless reconstruct this creativity post hoc, which of course is our perspective in the twenty-first century. As an attempt to explain why process is at the base of actuality, Whitehead introduces the concept of creativity. I follow Whitehead's lead in this chapter.

In this sense, then, this chapter argues that God, particularly in and through the activity of the Spirit of creativity, was not merely resting aloof on his proverbial throne for nearly twelve billion years before biotic entities arose upon the cooled Earth, but, rather, was fully present in and with what is oft called "creation," from the very beginning—and will be to the end, *proleptically present* as the expression of the principle of creativity. More often than not, God is understood (by Christians) to act particularly in the life of Christ, but cannot be said to do too much more beyond that. I maintain, however, that the Spirit, by her kenosis *into* the natural world, imbibed the natural world with an evolving fertility that has continually manifested itself in and through what we commonly term "creativity." This primal imbibing of herself into the world of nature created a situation in which the natural world became marked, virtually in and of itself, by the *gift* of creativity,[6] or what principally amounts to an *activation* of the naturally occurring, inherent potentialities within nature, thereby producing (in essence) a distinctive self-creativity within the natural environ.

What, then, is creativity? Generically, it is the defining trait of our species—but to answer what it is specifically, one must explore the various aspects of creativity. Carl R. Hausman offers the following conditions of it: creative outcomes have lucid constructions that are irreducible; creative

---

4. I herein take for granted that the readers of this chapter are familiar with my reimagining of the term *kenosis* as an *in*filling—a proverbial "pouring out" of the Spirit *into* creation, versus it being a mere "self-emptying." For a full exposition of this reappropriation, the fullness of which would take us too far afield, I point readers to several of my peer-reviewed essays, including: "God of Chance and Purpose"; "Thomistic Personalism in Dialogue with Kenosis"; "Evolution, Emergence, and Final Causality"; "Emergence and Kenosis: A Theological Synthesis"; "Emergence Theory and Theology: A Wesleyan-Relational Perspective"; and "Kenosis of the Spirit into Creation."

5. Jarvie, "Rationality of Creativity," 44

6. Weber, *Whitehead's Pancreativism*, 142.

outcomes are capricious; structures of creative outcomes are fundamentally instrumentally valuable; and the acts that lead to creative outcomes include an morsel of spontaneity.[7] In emphasizing the idea that the intelligibility of a creative outcome is discernible in a structure that is unpredictable, Hausman resists determinism because it excludes novelty and newness. After laying out his rationale for understanding the research undertaken by investigators of creativity, Hausman then adopts a descriptive premise that under constraints there is a select range of phenomena that is most clearly, undeniably, and unquestionably an example of creative acts and outcomes.

Again, then, what is creativity? For Edward O. Wilson, the two great branches of learning—science and the humanities—are complementary in the pursuit of creativity in that they share the same roots of innovative endeavor, as the realm of science is everything possible in the (*uni-/multi-*) *verse*, whereas the realm of the humanities is everything conceivable to the *human mind*.[8] Wilson admits that it "might seem—*feel* is perhaps the better word—that the human suite of intellect and emotion" is the only one that could have attained creativity. Somewhat a diagnostic trait of our species, some four billion years in the making, creativity might seem to require some "unique feature of evolution or else the hand of God extended special to our lineage."[9] But this is not the case at all. Other species of animal, particularly the gorillas, apes, monkeys, orangutans, chimpanzees, and bonobos (especially!), can display behavior that is akin to creativity in the human animal.

Because I am willingly constrained by science inasmuch as feasibly possible, I do not want to offer much more in this chapter than what could be considered prolegomena to my argument that will be successively developed over the ensuing years of doctoral study (especially regarding the causal joint), one that stays neutral with reference to most of the frameworks of contemporary science. Theologians would be wise to no longer attempt to make their hypotheses palatable to the scientists who are often so hostile toward them, and that often without reason (e.g., witness the vitriol by the likes of Richard Dawkins and Daniel Dennett to all things religious, especially to that which is "Christian"). This does *not* mean that theologians should be dismissive or ignorant of the developments in science. On the contrary, they should be well versed in science, but not attempt to force their ideas into an established scientific position; doing that is more of a capitulation than a strategy to influence the public and academy (and such

---

7. Hausman, "Eros and Agape in Creative Evolution: A Peircean Insight," 3–16, esp. 4.
8. Wilson, *Origins of Creativity*, 14–15.
9. Wilson, *Origins of Creativity*, 20.

has often led to a god-of-the-gaps argument, which subsequently gets filled, thereby leaving the Christians who advocate such in a worse position than the one with which they started). This chapter suggests a unique perspective on divine action that is exclusively pneumatological (related to the Spirit) and distinctly eschatological (anticipating the future), while being aware of varied proposals originating from the Divine Action Project (DAP), which was cosponsored by the Vatican Observatory and the Center for Theology and the Natural Sciences in Berkeley, California, from 1988 to 2003.[10]

In view of the conclusions of the DAP, which are far too varied and detailed to be explicated here, I postulate that the Spirit is ever *before* the advancement of complexity on the face of Earth. This *poietic* (creative) process was initiated long ago, but continues even unto this day. The infilling of the Spirit's nature *into* nature creates a panentheistic relationship between herself and the world, which has been continually employed by her in the perpetual and almost inexorable advancement of biota in general, the most magnificent display of which is *Homo sapiens sapiens* (our particular subspecies). The creative increase in complexity that is everywhere present is not a straight progression, however, for the Spirit is not the manipulator of the natural world, but its *empowerment* instead. In this conception, the deity is not the principle of order, but instead the very creativity—that is, the pure multiplicity—of the divine game itself, which is an affirmation that the complexification of the world is always "already all" of chance[11] and eminently influenced by the *uncontrolling love of God*.[12] This *uncontrolling love of God* is thoroughly empowering of the other, and not in any manner determinative of the outcome, much alike unto how God woos, lures, and beckons—but does not force or coerce—biologically complex organisms in the present era to do his bidding upon the Earth. In Whitehead, as with Thomas Jay Oord, the divine game is *not* about power, but *love* instead.[13] Further, for Oord, this uncontrolling love is self-giving. We will encounter Oord and Whitehead again later in this chapter, but it is worth pointing out that their critique (more so the latter than the first) of power had the net effect of philosophers largely exchanging "coercion" with respect to God's influence on the Earth, with "persuasion" regarding the same.[14]

---

10. For a stellar accounting of divine action as distinctly pneumatological and exclusively eschatological, along with a tidy review of the DAP, I point the reader to Yong, *Spirit of Creation*, ch. 3 (73–101) and ch. 4 (102–32).

11. Faber, *Divine Manifold*, 261.

12. Cf. Oord, *Nature of Love: A Theology*; Oord, *Defining Love*; and Oord, *Uncontrolling Love of God*, 1–29.

13. Faber, *Divine Manifold*, 260.

14. Whitehead, *Adventures of Ideas*, 166.

WHITEHEADIAN VIEWS OF CREATIVITY

It is interesting to notice that Whitehead does not mention the concept of creativity until *Religion in the Making*,[15] wherein creativity is the first formative element.[16] With regard to this Whiteheadian text, creativity is seen to be the process which underlies all creatures. In fact, "the universe exhibits a creativity with infinite freedom."[17] We see therein that creativity is a temporal, formative element, one that is nonactual; this is because the formative elements ground actuality and consequently are either nontemporal or nonactual. On its own, creativity is indeterminate and unable to bring about novel entities. However, in relation to the other formative elements—namely, God—creativity is the perpetual force that spurs the creative advance of the universe forward.

In *Process and Reality*, creativity is the universal of universals, that which characterizes ultimate matter of fact.[18] Moreover, creativity is an ultimate principle by which the *many*, which are disjunctively the universe, become the *one* actual occasion, which is the universe conjunctively. As such, it is the nature of things that the "many enter into complex unity."[19] In looking at this text, we can see that Whitehead is referring to the process whereby the objects of the world, which are subjects that have reached satisfaction and passed over into objective immortality, enter into the inner constitution of actual entities experiencing subjective immediacy. This creative principle is the base of actuality as the principal matter of fact; it is the base of both time and novelty.[20] Further, it is the event of in/finite becoming.[21] The word "creativity" is indeed appropriate to describe this process, as expressed in the notion of each occurrence issuing in novelty.[22] The ultimate reason why novel entities emerge is due to the "'creative advance'. . . the application of this ultimate principle of creativity to each novel situation which it originates."[23] A new entity is born in and through this process. Indeed, "[t]he many become one, and are increased by one."[24]

15. Cf. Whitehead, *Religion in the Making*.
16. Weber, *Whitehead's Pancreativism*, 184.
17. Whitehead, *Religion in the Making*, 115.
18. Faber, *God as Poet of the World*, 22–23.
19. Whitehead, *Process and Reality*, 21.
20. Whitehead, *Process and Reality*, 259.
21. Whitehead, *Process and Reality*, 104.
22. Faber, *Divine Manifold*, 210.
23. Whitehead, *Process and Reality*, 21.
24. Whitehead, *Process and Reality*, 21.

Providing the most accurate portrayal, Whitehead contends, the best of Ultimate Reality is through the cosmic principle of creativity. Creativity, in fact, is *the* universal of universals—and it is comprised of that which is only actual in relation to its accidents.[25] *Even God* is in a sense a "creature" of creativity. Inasmuch as full autonomy is granted to the natural world post its imbibing by the Spirit of God, *natural* creativity becomes self-creativity, which, in fact, is the process by which the world has become what it is.[26] Whitehead stipulates, "The world is self-creative; and the actual entity as self-creating creature passes into its immortal function of part-creator of the transcendent world"; "[t]he freedom inherent in the universe is constituted by this element of self-causation."[27] In fact, creativity is understood to be the self-actualization of events of the process.[28] Classic, essentialist science utterly failed to consider this "self-productivity" of nature.[29] Thinkers today such as Gordon Kaufman, however, are striving hard to make the status of incipient creativity as the deity palatable to a large(r) audience.[30] In the contemporary environ, we are better able to determine what distinguishes self-organization from self-creation than previous generations.[31] In Whitehead's own work, as for proponents of the new thinking regarding self-creation, the ideal of progress is totally insufficient to account for the virtual self-creativity of organisms. Similarly, for Whitehead, the concept of creativity is always creative in everything because it is only creativity to itself, and as such solely self-creativity of everything singularly bodied.[32] Hence:

> [T]he word creativity . . . if guarded by the phrases Immanent Creativity, or Self-creativity . . . avoids the implication of a transcendent Creator.[33]

---

25. Faber, *Divine Manifold*, 156–57.

26. Faber, *God as Poet of the World*, 154.

27. Whitehead, *Process and Reality*, 84, 88.

28. Cf. Bradley, "Transcendentalism and Speculative Reason in Whitehead," 155–91, as quoted in Faber, *Divine Manifold*, 156.

29. Whitehead, *Process and Reality*, 95.

30. Kaufman, *In the Beginning . . . Creativity*, 1–32.

31. Seemingly, Whitehead flirts with radical immanence, but he does not come close to the position of Gordon D. Kaufman, a position with which I largely agree. Indeed, whereas Whitehead defends a semblance of immanence by giving nature an autonomous capacity for generation, Kauffman offers a more radical conception of immanence in considering the everywhere-present possibility of chaos in the universe, which acts to promote a strictly evolutionary becoming.

32. Faber, *Divine Manifold*, 282.

33. Whitehead, *Adventures of Ideas*, 236.

MULTIPLICITY AND THEOPLICITY
WITH RESPECT TO CREATIVITY

For Whitehead, creativity is yet another multiplicity of multiplicities.[34] In fact, God the Spirit is the creativity of the future.[35] Further, both *immanent-* and *self-*creativity are marks of this overall poietic process. One could in fact say, moreover, that creativity is the becoming of multiplicity.[36] Further, in the dissolution of sameness into difference and immanence, multiplicity becomes the expression of in/finite creativeness.[37] For Whitehead, creativity functions as the ground or principle against the insinuation of unity, and instead presents us with that which is novel. Similar to how the concept of creativity is unrepeatable in its exactness, so too is novelty, which is the mainspring of much creativity. What I mean by that is this: novelty is in a sense the foundation of creativity insomuch as all that is novel will be, correlatively, creative. However, just because something is creative does not mean that it is necessarily novel. Nevertheless, it is the case, usually, that where you find one, you will also find the other. The divine game of ultimate and immanent multiplicity "becomes a poetics of theoplicity in which divine [auto-]*poiesis* affirms multiplicity by subtracting itself from any power-discourse of the Logic of the One, the Two, and the Many."[38] This "chance," in a paradoxical manner, is the production of beauty through the ever-expanding multiplicity of individual forms of biological complexity.[39] In fact, rather than accepting the view that chance is contrary to order and purpose, it is the position of this paper that it is actually *conducive* to the kind of world that one would expect a Christian-like God to create.[40]

In his book *The Uncontrolling Love of God*, Tom Oord claims that randomness and chance are real occurrences in the natural environment. I agree, for that notion is consonant with my view of a God who lures creation to higher levels of complexity through the processes of biological evolution. God does not determine the outcome of random events, but God instead constrains randomness by setting broad boundaries. After this constraint,

---

34. Whitehead, *Process and Reality*, 21.
35. Faber, *Divine Manifold*, 292.
36. Faber, *Divine Manifold*, 444.
37. Faber, *Divine Manifold*, 210.
38. Faber, *Divine Manifold*, 279.
39. Faber, *Divine Manifold*, 260.
40. According to Michael Weber, God's purpose in the advance of creativity is the introduction of new things, whether that be entities or energy. In fact, God's primordial nature is the spur of the world's advance in creativity and novelty (Cf. Weber, *Whitehead's Pancreativism*, 146).

in which the empowered entities and individuals interact according to natural laws, a wide range of beautiful results materialize.[41] Instead of opposing God and chance, I further contend that chance was God the Spirit's unit of instrumentation whereby the variety and freedom necessary to achieve her purposes within the created world are ensured. This, of course, raises theological problems, some discussion of which will directly follow.

In Arthur Peacocke's 1978 Bampton Lectures, later published as *Creation and the World of Science*, a positive function to chance in the purposes of providence is given, much alike to what I deem its role to be. In fact, implicit in the initial conditions of the world were many potential universes. Chance allowed all the inherent possibilities to be explored by continually mixing up the combinations of sorting, with this random sorting being the means by which potentialities become realized. According to Peacocke, "it would be more consistent with the observations to assert that the full gamut of the potentialities of living matter could be explored only through the agency of the rapid and frequent randomization which is possible at the molecular level of the DNA."[42] Indeed, chance mechanisms are an efficient means of exploring all the potentialities of matter, not just DNA, and thus are part of the initial structuring of the multi-/uni-verse.

This above consideration, I contend, is a clue to both a reasonable and acceptable interpretation of chance processes in nature. Notably, Arthur Peacocke cannot discern any reason why randomness should be seen as evidence of irrationality in the universe, a position with which I heartily agree.[43] Indeed, since many—if not most—of the laws of nature are *statistical*, it is entirely feasible to postulate that a creator could introduce quasi-random processes whose statistical behavior would have the result, in the long run (to use a Peircean phrase), to be achieved in due time. This process constitutes the "teleology" of the universal drive toward the multiplicity of biological entities displaying complexity.[44] The biological complexity just mentioned could be seen to be that which is marked by being "alive"; that is, it exhibits both *metabolism* and *growth*, and is additionally—according to Whitehead—accompanied by the influx of *beauty*.[45]

I also affirm that the "divine game" is bound to the affirmation of chance.[46] This affirmation of chance is reminiscent of—even comparable

---

41. McCall, "God of Chance," 221–24.
42. Peacocke, *Creation and the World of Science*, 34.
43. Peacocke, *Creation and the World of Science*, 34.
44. Whitehead, *Adventures of Ideas*, 268.
45. Cf. Whitehead, *Adventures of Ideas*, 265.
46. Deleuze, *Fold*, 128.

to—Charles Sanders Peirce, who, it could be said, is *the* chief expositor of chance within the natural world (his term for chance is "tychism," note), noting that there is an absolute, irreducible "chanciness" (my wording) inherent within the world as we know it. Indeed, Peirce's cosmology is postulated against the framework of his universal categories—Firstness, Secondness, and Thirdness.[47] These three universal categories are explanatory of the interplay of chance, action, and law in (macro-)evolution. Chance predominates in *tychistic* evolution. As such, *tychism* is the condition of blind change, which Peirce associated with Darwinian theory. In contrast, law dominates in *anancastic* evolution. Taken individually, both *tychism* and *anancasm* are partially correct. However, Peirce's own view—*agapasticism*—embraces both of the first two forms of creativity in a synthesis by which they are both conditioned and transformed. As such, *agapasticism* affirms the interweaving of chance and law in a process which includes spontaneity and is directed toward an end.[48]

Creative growth is the principal factor within evolution that points toward the need for *agape*. In fact, creative growth is the presence of spontaneity and the introduction of unpredictable yet intelligible novelty into the process of evolution. This kind of creative growth includes what has been referred to as "radical creativity."[49] Peirce's trifold set of hypotheses regard *tychism*, *anancasm*, and *agapism*, which are also known as Firstness, Secondness, and Thirdness.[50] It should be pointed out that Peirce's account of scientific creativity is, at root, novel.

Peirce divided scientific inquiry into three types of reasoning: abduction (also called a hypothesis), deduction, and induction. Of these three types of reasoning, Peirce states that only two are synthetic: abduction and induction. Synthetic scientific creativity, then, must begin with one or the other. For Peirce, induction "classifies," abduction "explains."[51] Induction, then, develops what is *already* known, whereas abduction introduces *newness*. Therefore, to find originality in scientific inquiry, one must look closely into abduction, for an abductive guess is "a bolder and more perilous step"

---

47. Hausman, "Eros and Agape in Creative Evolution," 11–25, esp. 14.

48. See Peirce, *Collected Papers*, 6:287–317.

49. Garry Wills, "Radical Creativity," 1019–28.

50. In a pertinent note, I plan on expositing Peirce's concept of *tychism* in a future monograph, as well as his other two categories—*anancasm* and *agapism*—in attempting to construct a plausible and palatable modern (or contemporary) model of the evolutionary advancement of nature, and God's involvement—if at all!—within the process known as "macroevolution." Cf. Peirce, *Collected Papers*, 1:46.

51. Peirce, *Collected Papers*, 2:632.

than inductive inference.[52] In what follows, I shall attempt a demonstration of this abductive process in Peirce. I contend that abduction is the source of scientific creativity, as well as that pure multiplicity is an affirmation of the "game" that follows no pre-existing set of rules, along with no pre-established harmonies. Instead, what Faber refers to as the "divine game" is an affirmation of "unrepeatable" creativeness, comprised of a singularity.[53] Thus, the game of creativity is innovative.

SPIRIT'S NATURE AS CREATIVE

Faber notes that one can discern that humanism means, simply, that humans are self-creative. Moreover, Whitehead says that everything is self-creative. For postmodern people, however, this is an illusion, because one is a subject of the power structures which give rise to them.[54] After all, because there is always the element of creativity according to Whitehead, correlatively, there is always something new—and therefore we cannot successfully reduce the synthesis of elements to the analytic elements that constitute it. Therefore, one cannot stabilize it. Traditionally, we think we have a ground first, then things emerging from it. Whitehead, in a paraphrase, states that within philosophic theory there is an ultimate which is actual in virtue of its instantiations. In fact, only in the actualization of accidents is there a real ultimate. So then, Whitehead calls *that* creativity—which means that becoming never stops at any point.[55]

Faber notes that Whitehead claims Ultimate Reality is only immanent to the process.[56] Beyond that, Ultimate Reality is merely an abstraction. As such, something like creativity is only an abstraction of the process. Indeed, for Whitehead, the search is not for an eternal or universal principle, but for the conditions under which something new is created, which is known thereby as creativeness or creativity.[57] Further, according to Faber's Whitehead, creativity is the principle of novelty.[58] Indeed, creativity introduces novelty into the content of the many. The elements of the universe are finite—even in a very huge way with numbers, there is no other way than repetition at a certain point. But in Whitehead, everything becomes uniquely

---

52. Peirce, *Collected Papers*, 2:632.
53. Peirce, *Collected Papers*, 2:632.
54. Faber, "Whitehead and Postmodernity," Oct. 3, 2018.
55. Faber, "Whitehead and Postmodernity," Oct. 3, 2018.
56. Faber, "Whitehead and Postmodernity," Oct. 3, 2018.
57. Faber, "Whitehead and Postmodernity," Oct. 10, 2018.
58. Faber, "Whitehead and Postmodernity," Oct. 17, 2018.

one only once and nothing can be repeated in this way. For Whitehead, further, creativity as a principle is not finite—there's no beginning; it just spreads out instead.[59]

God's nature, as it is pictured within the Process tradition, is nothing short of "creative-responsive love," which is based upon, fundamentally, an infinitely *relational* God, who is redemptively present in everything that happens, from beginning to end.[60] Indeed, Whitehead's unique solution to the problem of the bifurcation of reality is none other than God himself, who is present with us at all times,[61] through the being of the Spirit (I add). For Whitehead, creativity is the activity of becoming and perishing, which describes the pure happening of the moving quality of the universe as the emergence of new happenings in perpetuity.[62] Indeed, he notes, with regard to creativity, that unity is always an integration (or synthesis) that simply happens. It is not, Faber contends, that this particular unity emerges from within the universe; instead, the universe itself as a moving "whole" becomes *within* this unity.[63] In a sense, then, a unity emerges as creative novelty out of multiplicity. Or, one might say, this unity is relativized into one unity among many in a universe that precisely thereby is creatively renewed. Hence, Whitehead's universe is an ecological process of integration and relativization, and a *process of processes*.

In Whitehead's ecological doctrine of God, God is the "Poet of the World" that encompasses all that is processual, that is, the creatively formative process in a full sense.[64] While the world requires creative form and deliverance *in* and *through* God, it is God who happens as event Godself, that is, who gives Godself to the world and takes it up as reality. From Whitehead, Faber contends that the creative process throughout the universe is the *form* of the unity which comprises it; that God constitutes the universe as process by offering to it various possibilities for realization; that it is as the creative power of the universe in which truth is actualized; and that God is the salvific "poet" of the world.[65] Faber further avers that Process theology is perichoretic, representative of God's creative dance *within* the world, insomuch as he is the ground of its novelty, as well as its constant companion. It is in this sense that Whitehead refers to the world process thoroughly and

59. Faber, "Whitehead and Postmodernity," Oct. 24, 2018.
60. Faber, *God as Poet of the World*, 13.
61. Faber, *God as Poet of the World*, 23.
62. Faber, *God as Poet of the World*, 24.
63. Faber, *God as Poet of the World*, 24.
64. Faber, *God as Poet of the World*, 25.
65. Faber, *God as Poet of the World*, 15.

completely as "creativity."⁶⁶ Creative events at once receive their ground of the arising "newness" of an entity, but also at the same time the ground of the efficacious influence of the old.⁶⁷ In view of this assertion, creativity refers to the principles of both spontaneity and causality, as it is at once also the pure activity of becoming—without even the hint of passivity—while it refers to the shaping principles inherent in the process of an event that has already become, that is, the power of events to bring themselves forth.

Whitehead calls this aspect "immanent creativity" (or spontaneous self-creativity) and "transitory creativity," because it is causally potent to produce other events.⁶⁸ As a ground of an event, creativity is moored by nothing "in and of itself," for it is beyond the actualization of events, as it is only real "in" them. It is in this sense, further, that creativity is (1) inherently immanent, while also (2) spontaneous and transitory, in part because it causally produces other events.⁶⁹ As "ground," creativity is truly nothing in and of itself, for it is only real in the actualization of events. Faber points out that creativity refers to the power of "pure self-giving,"⁷⁰ a contention which resonates nicely with my (and Oord's) depiction of *kenosis* as "self-giving."

CONCLUSION: MUTUAL IMMANENCE, UNCONTROLLING LOVE, AND THE CREATIVITY OF THE SPIRIT

The world and God, by the *kenosis* of the Spirit into the natural environ, are marked by mutual immanence: each is *interpenetrating* of the other. This mutual immanence is based upon pure divine love that itself is a process of *poiesis*—i.e., the weaving of a poem of the baseless fabric.⁷¹ Although Whitehead had contested the theistic conclusion that *poiesis* meant "immanent self-creativity," which is wrought with the world via eminent relationality,⁷² "becoming" is nevertheless a creative (self-driven) advance "into novelty."⁷³ In fact, if divine *poiesis* "has any meaning at all," it must be "subtracted from immanent self-creativity" as it is from creature or creator.⁷⁴ Self-realization

---

66. Faber, *God as Poet of the World*, 76.
67. Faber, *God as Poet of the World*, 76.
68. Faber, *God as Poet of the World*, 76.
69. Faber, *God as Poet of the World*, 76.
70. Faber, *God as Poet of the World*, 76.
71. Cf. Faber, *Divine Manifold*, 11.
72. Faber, *God as Poet of the World*, 130.
73. Whitehead, *Process and Reality*, 28; cf. Faber, *Divine Manifold*, 203.
74. Faber, *Divine Manifold*, 122; cf. 156.

is the ultimate fact of facts. As such, an actuality is self-realizing.[75] The world itself is self-creative, due to the *kenosis* of the Spirit into creation earlier alluded to, and the self-creating creatures pass into their function as partial creators of the world.[76] I contend that the above-referenced purely immanent self-creativity is nothing more or less than the *thoroughly immanent Spirit of God*.[77] The phrases "immanent creativity" and "self-creativity" both avoid the implication of a transcendent creator, which—although biblical—is entirely *insufficient* as a metaphysical position upon reality.[78]

Somewhat akin to Peirce, who said that we need a "thorough-going evolutionism or none,"[79] I contend that we need a (nearly) *thoroughly immanent* God or none at all. For Peirce, nothing less than this "thorough-going" evolutionism would provide the basis for an adequate cosmology. In fact, "a pseudo-evolutionism which enthrones mechanical law above the principle of growth is at once scientifically unsatisfactory, as giving no possible hint as to how the universe has come about."[80] I share Peirce's desire for a fully thorough-going evolutionism, understanding that it *alone* can fully explicate the magnificent journey of species over the last, roughly, 3.5 billion years. Peirce's account of developmental teleology applies to *all* growth, demonstrating thereafter how a *telos* develops during a creative process. In developmental teleology, the *telos* is partially indeterminate at the onset of the process, and is developed and specified in and through the process itself. I would like to appropriate this perspective in my model of creativity by the *kenosis* of the Spirit into nature. Here I would like to point out that considering the creative process as a sort of developmental teleology is a potent understanding of it, when thereafter applied to the modern theology and science conversation. This developmental teleology may be the basis of the thorough-going evolutionism of which Peirce speaks.

All in all, this chapter has contributed to a systematic theology of creation by constructing a theological synthesis between *kenosis* and the

---

75. Whitehead, *Process and Reality*, 222.

76. Whitehead, *Process and Reality*, 85.

77. Note that Whitehead recognizes that the relationality of the Godhead to the essentially *necessary* world is directly wrought by the divine *Pneuma*, that is, the Spirit of God, which means that God's relation, through the Spirit, with the crested world, is not arbitrary, but immanently present instead, for we cannot discover a transcendent God, but very well could an immanent one. Roland Faber discusses these Whiteheadian points elsewhere (Faber, *Divine Manifold*, 130–31).

78. Cf. Faber, *Divine Manifold*, 211.

79. Peirce, *Collected Papers*, 6:14.

80. Peirce, *Collected Papers*, 6:157.

evolutionary complexification of matter.[81] This theological synthesis is mediated by the *uncontrolling* love of God through the *creative* Spirit. Pointedly, I proffer that the existence—and especially the success thereof—of the evolutionary creative advance and the pursuit of novelty depend upon the primal kenotic (*in*-filling) act of the creative Spirit *pouring herself into* creation, which onsets the long and laborious process of prebiotic evolution. Thereafter, the shift to biological evolution toward increasing complexity occurs. So then, the complexification of matter has its ontological origin in and through the agency of the Spirit of creativity, who is present within the contingency of evolution, as well as in its lawful regularity.[82]

The kenotic creating Spirit, who *donates*[83] uncontrolling love to her creation, is present "in, with, and under" the processes of biological evolution and should be seen to act—exclusively perhaps (probably?)—through natural law and later human action.[84] One may accurately posit that creation therefore possesses the Spirit of creativity from its very origin,[85] a contention which holds much import for the relation of (post-)modern biological and theological sciences.[86] In summation, the creative Spirit is directly and inherently found within creation, which grants the proximity—immanently and eminently—to *influence* the incessant derivation of different (and often, but not always, "higher"[87]) entities in the (macro-)evolution of all things, but especially species.[88] That last statement is critical, in my

81. Bradnick and McCall, "Making Sense of Emergence," 240–57.

82. Polkinghorne, "Kenotic Creation and Divine Action," 90–106; quote from 96.

83. I especially appreciate Karol Wojtyla's depiction of love as self-donation, and I herein adopt it for my usage (Wojtyla, *Love & Responsibility*, 82).

84. Peacocke, *Theology for a Scientific Age*, 301–10; quote from 308.

85. Lucien, *Kenosis and Creation*, 33.

86. The Spirit could be seen, then, to be *embedded* within creation. I contend that this has application to the derivation of panpsychism.

87. Weber makes mention of this in passing, as he indicates that "telic causation" (i.e., eschatological causation) is understood to be the product of God's steady call for more intensive and valued experiences (Weber, *Whitehead's Pancreativism*, 159–60).

88. Cf. Peacocke, "Cost of New Life," 21–42; quote from 32. I should here point out that I have toyed with the idea since ca. 2007 that the primal *kenosis* of the Spirit *into* creation onset the panpsychist condition that the Whiteheadian tradition so eloquently writes about. Several papers that I have presented at various national and regional American Academy of Religion meetings, e.g., advocate a position near panpsychism, based on the *kenosis* of the Spirit *into* creation. I can definitely support—and even advocate—the position that Philip Clayton presented at the recent 2018 AAR annual meeting in Denver, wherein he indicated that he did *not* consider panpsychism a correct hypothesis per se, even though it was posited with good motives and intentions. Instead, he attributed a "quasi-panpsychist position" (my wording) to all entities more complex than the individual cell. I agree with Phiip.

opinion, for the future of the theology and science dialogue (which may be better termed a "trilogue"—composed of theology, science, and the mediating philosophy betwixt the two), of which I desire to be a part.[89] After all, one may not consistently ignore in one field what one finds convincing in another. May we all, therefore—much like Peirce and Whitehead—seek a thorough integration of all of our various data points, all the while realizing that the contemplation of such is forever beyond our understanding, as "the limitations of human intelligence" make this point necessary.[90]

---

89. In the foreseeable future, I shall be extending and further elucidating the positions introduced in this chapter as I continue to grapple with an evolutionary understanding of divine action within science's world, and particularly upon our planet, especially in view of the contemporary context of faith.

90. Whitehead, *Concept of Nature*, 73.

4

Derrida and Nonhuman Animals

An Exploration of Shared Animality[1]

INTRODUCTION

Throughout his life, Derrida's corpus explored the human animal/nonhuman animal (hereafter HA/NHA) binary. Indeed, in his writings, Western thought regarding the binary is examined, as well as its inherently anthropocentric framework. Derrida successfully, however, deconstructs its systems and highlights why the binary—largely—remains in place. He wrote more than eight hundred pages explicitly devoted to the animal, most of which has appeared in print only after his death, which thereby makes animality one of his central philosophical themes. One of his essays, "The Animal That Therefore I Am (More to Follow),"[2] in fact served as a catalyst for the emergent field of animality studies in the last generation. Cary Wolfe, after a short survey of the field of animal studies, claims that Derrida's above highlighted article is the "most important" event in the history of that movement.[3]

---

1. This article is forthcoming as McCall, "Derrida & Non-Human Animals: An Exploration of Shared Animality." Reprinted with permission.
2. Derrida, "Animal That Therefore I Am (More to Follow)," 370.
3. Wolfe, "Flesh and Finitude," 9.

The HA/NHA binary has a long philosophical history, going all the way back to Aristotle—who, in his *The History of Animals*, established a hierarchical HA/NHA opposition. Aristotle rightly attributes intelligence to animals, and he thought that this differs only in quantity when compared to human animals. Aristotle outlined some psychical characteristics of animals, including fierceness, courage, and timidity; "Besides he proposed that the animals lack reason and his thinking leads to the denial of human kinship with animals . . . [insomuch as this conceptualization of the] belief that human animals have dominion over nonhuman lower animals and minimized the ethical obligations to non-human animals by exaggerating the distance between human animals and non-human animals."[4] Indeed, Calarco notes that Derrida had written the following:

> Pro-animal theorists have noted that these critical reworkings of our basic ideas about human nature and ethics also call into question traditional ideas about the human/animal distinction and ethical relations with animals. They argue that a thought of differance, when pursued in view of its implications for animals, can generate an expansive notion of ethics that acknowledges the importance of human animals /non-human animals relations and that respects the singularity of animals.[5]

Derrida deconstructs the binary by dissolving the perceived superiority of HAs, in part through a critique of the attributes that HAs have historically been used to separate themselves from nonhuman animals.

Because of the volume of Derrida's work, it is an entry point for those interested in critical NHA studies within philosophy (*and* theology); likewise, it has been received and analyzed in many fields outside of philosophy. Derrida argues that the dominant relationship in the Western world with NHA in modernity has taken the form of a "disavowal," a "war," or a "sacrifice."[6] No one, he intimates, is exempted from the guilt of participating in this disavowal, but neither is anyone barred from remembering their roots—i.e., their lowly NHA origin. For the most part, Derrida challenges a multitude of ideas related to our contentions about kingdom *Animalia*. Thereby, he helps us approach NHAs differently. Rather than leading us from NHA to subjects of "greater importance," Derrida illustrates our need to reconsider our responsibly to *graciously* and *lovingly* consider NHA. Extending Derrida's critique, one could argue that by limiting the religious

---

4. Derrida, "Animal That Therefore I Am (More to Follow)," 38.
5. Calarco, *Thinking Through Animals*, 4.
6. Cf. Deane-Drummond, *Animals as Religious Subjects*, 28.

subject to HA, the study of religion has become complicit in both the "disavowal" of regard for animals and the "war" against them of which Derrida speaks.

With respect to the NHA, Derrida further deconstructs the foundations of Western metaphysics in challenging directly other prominent philosophers who have called humanism into question, but continue to nevertheless promote the NHA/HA binary opposition. Indeed, their arrogant anthropocentrism "ties them firmly to the humanist tradition they attempt to call into question."[7] They do not oppose the primacy of humanity; or in Derrida's terms, regarding the acceptability of putting NHA to death, "they do not sacrifice sacrifice."[8] It is my contention that the "disavowal" of NHAs highlights a fully existential hermeneutic; "war" brings a political hermeneutic, whereas the term "sacrifice" recasts structuralist themes, locating the HA/NHA relationship in the context of the Abrahamic traditions. One of the chief theses I defend throughout this chapter is that the HA/NHA distinction can no longer—and ought no longer—be maintained. In stating this, my opinion is in line with Matthew Calarco's views, particularly expressed in his *Zoographies*.[9] It is one of my overall contentions in this chapter is that Derrida would support the assertion that NHAs differ from HAs not in *kind*, but in *degree*.

FIVE ORIENTING POSITIONS FOR A THEORY OF DIFFERENCE AND SAMENESS IN HUMAN AND NONHUMAN ANIMALS[10]

In Derrida's "The Animal That Therefore I Am,"[11] he belies the Western tradition that separates NHAs from HAs by excluding them from things thought to be only proper to mankind: that is, thinking, laughing, perceptible suffering, and verbalization. Animals have traditionally been considered the absolute *other* of human beings, a view of otherness that has served as the rationale for their domination, exploitation, and slaughter. This type of "animal thinking" may help us to think of the world—or imagine the possibility of thinking about it—in a nonexclusively human fashion. Looking at a possible theoretical framework that draws on both Whitehead and Derrida,

---

7. Calarco, *Thinking Through Animals*, 187.
8. Derrida, "'Eating well', or the Calculation of the Subject," 96–119.
9. Calarco, *Zoographies*, 15–16.
10. This section is based on Moore, *Divinanimality*, 233–36.
11. Derrida, "Animal That Therefore I Am (More to Follow)," 373.

we may posit that it might consist of the following six ideas, some which are more Whiteheadian than others. For example:

NHAs Are *Concrescing* Subjects

They are subjects because they have feelings and beliefs that belong to them and not to others; they make decisions on their own, guided by their own subjective aims. These four elements—feelings, beliefs, decisions, and aims—coalesce into a single reality in the ongoing life of both the HAs and NHAs in their lived-out subjectivity. NHAs are concrescing subjects in the sense that as they make their decisions, they are responding to the influences (stimuli) they incorporate from their past experience as well as the present surrounding world. Moment by moment, they are constituted by *other* things in the world. These past experiences, as well as the other actualities in their surroundings, are part of the *many that become one* in their experience.[12]

Understanding NHAs Requires Imagination

When cognitive scientists undertake experiments with NHAs, and when philosophers reflect on NHAs, they are trying to comprehend the subjective manner of the individual entity. Typically, they are also interested in how this way might illustrate the general way of being in the world of the species to which the individual NHA belongs. Such understanding requires more than mere observation, Moore concludes in *Divinanimality*, for it also involves *imagination*, in the sense that a person tries to *imagine* himself inside the life of the NHA from the NHA's point of view. As such, one may say that understanding NHAs is *not* a simple *science* but an *art* instead.[13]

NHAs *Consciously* Experience the World

The consciousness that human beings *and other animals* possess, we might say, is a type of subjectivity, interiority, or the "feelings" that Whitehead advocates with reference to the HA. Most experience—with regard to NHA as well as HA—is nonconscious; that is, lacking in the quality of awareness.[14]

---

12. Moore, *Divinanimality*, 233.
13. Moore, *Divinanimality*, 233.
14. Moore, *Divinanimality*, 233–34.

But it is strongly likely that the higher taxa of NHAs have at least a semblance of *consciousness* that is somewhat alike unto HAs.

All NHAs Are *Individual*, Sovereign Entities which Experience the World in Different Ways

This position entails the claim that any given species of animal does *not* enjoy the exactly share the same kind of consciousness. Instead, NHAs are highly divergent from each other, in much in the same way that HAs are. For example, every instance of NHA subjectivity has its own unique qualities, none of which is reducible by HAs who might try to understand them.[15]

NHAs Are Carriers of a Spirit, *Generically* Defined

Whitehead's philosophical position is critical here; indeed, he calls the initial phase of the subjective aim of an emerging experience a God-given "*lure*" for satisfaction relative to the conditions at the moment. This spirit, I contend, is alike unto to the breath, or *ruah*, that the Bible speaks of often.

> Taking all of the preceding notions together, we can conclude that NHA deserve ethical "respect," if not downright deference. Regarding the ethical actions that NHAs deserve,

Derrida's positive project employs is to bring animals within the scope of ethical and political considerations. If one of the overarching dogmatisms of the ontotheological philosophical tradition has been that animals are incapable of ethics and politics and thus fall outside the scope of ethical and political concern, then one of the main advances of Derrida's thought is his attempt to develop an idea of ethics and politics that avoids repeating these standard theses.[16]

> From the above statement, it is clear that the major motifs within Derrida's work from the mid-1980s forward (writings on democracy, the gift, hospitality, friendship, etc.) are *not* intended to exclude NHAs from their scope. Indeed, Derrida explicitly extends these *infrastructures* to include NHAs, thus bringing them within the area of ethics, and also insists that NHAs "have the capacity to interrupt one's existence and inaugurate ethical."[17]

15. Moore, *Divinanimality*, 235.
16. Calarco, *Zoographies*, 252.
17. Calarco, *Zoographies*, 252.

To Derrida, there is no rational justification in creating a rigid distinction between HAs and NHAs because both of them have more or less similar attributes. So, our inclination to mistreat our fellow HAs may be originated from our maltreatment of NHAs.[18]

THE HUMAN ANIMAL/NONHUMAN ANIMAL BINARY EXPLAINED

Derrida forcefully deconstructs the HA/NHA binary—but not in the same way that he has previously deconstructed other hierarchical binary oppositions. After Darwin, there is nothing novel in the arbitrariness by which the HA/NHA opposition is characterized. Hence, Derrida's declaration: "Everything I'll say will consist, certainly not in effacing the limit, but in multiplying its figures, in complicating, thickening, delinearizing, folding, and dividing the line precisely by making it increase and multiply"—a process he calls "limitrophy." Derrida is *less* interested in questioning the human-animal distinction than in complicating it infinitely and indefinitely. "Beyond the edge of the so-called human . . . there is already a heterogeneous multiplicity of the living . . . a multiplicity of organizations of relations between living and dead."[19] In my opinion, the HA-NHA distinction of yesteryear is no longer useful to scientists or philosophers. This is not to deny obvious species-related differences, but rather to critique the now-antiquated binary that is supporting a metaphysically laden hierarchy of privilege for HAs. In revealing the incoherence in "capacities"-based differentiation, the deep-seated notion of HAs as ontologically superior and in fact as NHAs themselves becomes seriously questioned.[20] Consideration for NHAs is often *not* given to them by HAs due to this lack of commonality. In part because HAs possess a well-developed language, they have deemed it as a significant indicator of the binary line. Unlike Heidegger, Derrida contends that language is *not* an inherent signal of the superiority of HAs; rather, it's a only *construct* of HAs.

The words "human" and "animal" are mere placeholders, not firm ontological signifiers. Regarding this assertion, Derrida writes:

> Animal is a word that men have given themselves the right to give. are found giving it to themselves, this word, but as if they

---

18. Derrida, "Animal That Therefore I Am (More to Follow)," 29.
19. Derrida, "Animal That Therefore I Am (More to Follow)," 413.
20. Naas, *End of the World*, 24–25.

received it as an inheritance. They have given themselves the word in order to corral a large number of living entities within a single concept: "The Animal," they say.[21]

Language affords HAs with a tool to create and uphold binaries and hierarchical oppressions. An HA-created language also allows for HAs to lump all other entities—which do not share in the language—into one homogenous category. Consideration is not necessary for the subordinate side of the binary. This flawed reasoning gives HAs the effective power to disregard and/or destroy all entities that are not HAs which fall into the kingdom of *Animalia*. Derrida recognizes that there are vast differences between HAs and NHAs, but those differences may not be so concrete as to definitively separate the two species. HAs and NHAs differ in *degree*, *not* in kind. Thus, there is not a single line of demarcation that creates such an expansive division that all traces of relation and similarity are gone. Neither language, consciousness, social structures (insofar as they exist at all), nor relation to death can serve the task of drawing the line between HAs and NHAs. Of this concept, Derrida writes,

> Beyond the edge of the so-called human, beyond it but by no means on a single opposing side, rather than "The Animal" or "Animal Life" there is already a heterogeneous multiplicity of the living.[22]

Humanity cannot reflect on these relations without viewing the interweaving of NHA life with its own. The interwoven hints of our NHA relation and animality are key to Derrida's essay entitled "The Animal That Therefore I Am (More to Follow)"; such relations are the intersections of HAs and NHAs, and not indivisible lines. Likewise, such intersections are attempts to demonstrate the illusory status of the binary; HAs and NHAs are *not* divisible—we are completely and thoroughly *interwoven* into the same division of reality. This contention dismantles the binary of either HAs vs. NHAs. HAs, however, have separated themselves from NHAs based on a flawed view of differences. The dividing line—lack of common language—seems to be unbridgeable. Agamben disagrees in writing:

> It is not language in general that marks out the human from other living beings—according to the Western metaphysical tradition that sees man as *zoon logon echon* (an animal endowed with speech)—but the split between language and speech, between semiotic and semantic (in Benveniste's sense), between

---

21. Derrida, "Animal That Therefore I Am (More to Follow)," 33.
22. Derrida, "Animal That Therefore I Am (More to Follow)," 31.

sign system and discourse. Animals are not in fact denied language; on the contrary, they are always and totally language ... Animals do not enter language, they are already inside it.[23]

Derrida strongly suggests that it is possible to connect HAs and NHAs through other means and similarities, such as their inevitable relationship to death. The word Derrida uses to explain his position with respect to his cat is "naked," which literally means down to one's hairs.[24] Due to the pointed nature of his words, we know the cat is a real cat, an actual feline. The gaze directed at him by this little entity invites Derrida to deconstruct the boundary line between HAs and NHAs using language.[25] Derrida does not interest himself in whether NHAs are capable of using language in the HA-like sense. Instead, his answer to this question instructs us to broaden our thinking of the meaning of language, so that the gaze of his cat may become equivalent to his thought. This analysis of the cat's behavior can be done without forcing upon the NHA an image of the HA, as he does not want to transform the NHAs into a virtual puppet for HAs, for doing such would belie the integrity of the NHA, in this instance, his cat.

Historically, NHAs have been denied of having self-awareness or consciousness. Peter Singer is one of, if not the, most influential living philosophers to promote a utilitarian approach to NHA ethics. Singer thinks that we should treat *all* NHAs as well as we treat cognitively similar HAs. According to Singer,

> Nor can we say that all human beings have rights just because they are members of the species *homo sapiens*—that is speciesism, a form of favoritism for our own that is as unjustifiable as racism. Thus if all HAs have rights, it would have to be because of some much more minimal characteristics, such as being living creatures. Any such minimal characteristics would be possessed by nonhuman as well as by human animals.[26]

Further, by concentrating on his own theory of HA subjectivity and the HA gaze, Derrida puts the homogenizing concept of NHAs (popular throughout the history of the NHA species) in question. By referring to the politics of speciesism, he points to the contemporary problem of marginalization which is present in all other fields of critical theory. Indeed,

---

23. Agamben, *Infancy and History*, 51–52.
24. Malle, "Animal That Therefore Derrida Is," 97.
25. Malle, "Animal That Therefore Derrida Is," 97.
26. Singer, "On Racism, Animal Rights, and Human Rights."

"Although Derrida has always insisted that such notions as 'differance',[27] the trace, ex-appropriation, and so forth circulate and function well beyond humanity, many of his best and most loyal readers have missed this aspect of his thought."[28]

In *Zoographies,* Calarco argues that Derrida's work on HAs "consists of three main aspects": 1) a kind of "proto-ethical" imperative that gives rise to 2) a concrete "ethicopolitical" position, on the one hand, and 3) a thorough "reworking of the anthropocentric" thrust of the Western philosophical tradition, on the other.[29] Derrida questions the meaning of subjectivity and he goes beyond the anthropocentric aspects of the metaphysics of subjectivity.[30] Derrida's neologism "carnophallogocentricism" is—according to Mishra[31]—composed of the following ideas: sacrificial (*carno*), masculine (*phallo*) and speaking (*ogo*). In writing this, he points out how NHAs are excluded from the status of being full subjects. In this way we can include various minority groups who have been denied the basic traits of subjectivity. Derrida thinks there have been other—many, in fact—subjects among HAs who have been denied the status of being a proper subject (we can find an example today in the status of the disabled [of which I am one] in that they are often marginalized, neglected, and ignored). Unfortunately, many NHAs receive—today perhaps more than ever—the same kind of violence typically directed at HA minority groups.

Derrida's work consistently posits the idea that there is not a single attribute that distinguishes between HAs and NHAs; thus, humanity is not as unique as has often been postulated. Thus, the attempts at categorizing NHAs in separate groups are not crystal clear. For Michael Naas, "Derrida quickly moves to the other side of the question in order to contest not the fact that animals do not have such a capacity or attribute but the principle by which philosophers have claimed that human animals do."[32] Here Derrida deconstructs not by eliminating NHA taxonomies or cognitive capacities of NHAs that have been established by HAs, but instead challenges why humanity has chosen to uphold the assumption that its own set of attributes (a potent mix of consciousness, language, relation to death, etc.) is where the division should be drawn.

27. Derrida, "'Eating Well', or the Calculation of the Subject," 116.
28. Cf. Calarco, *Zoographies*, 251.
29. Calarco, *Zoographies*, 255.
30. Calarco, *Zoographies*, 131.
31. Maiti, "Animal That Therefore Derrida Is," 97.
32. Naas, "Derrida's Flair (for the Animals to Follow)," 231.

Likewise, the assumption that all of humanity possesses such attributes and thus fits properly on the HA side of the binary is flawed when one begins to consider the disabilities and/or lack of attributes on the part of many HAs. From here, the binary continues to weaken when one considers the flawed assumptions of using several binary signifiers (language, consciousness, etc.) when not all of humanity possesses such attributes (e.g., persistent vegetative comatose patients in long-term care facilities, or severely handicapped people, e.g., Downs syndrome). But Derrida's deconstruction clearly challenges the NHA/HA binary as laid out above. Indeed, deconstruction serves as a method of renegotiating and reconsidering the status quo of humanity and the constructs, binaries, and hierarchies that have been created. Deconstructing the position of language as the binary division line between HAs and NHAs aids in destroying the supposed and commonly accepted boundary between them. Indeed, by employing his method of deconstruction, Derrida definitively demonstrates the *untenable* status of language as a binary line.

IS LANGUAGE THE DELINEATING ATTRIBUTE BETWEEN NONHUMAN AND HUMAN ANIMALS?

Humanity's concept of language is also limited. Indeed, we are under the assumption that language is an exclusive trait that belongs only to HAs. Derrida recognizes this not only as flawed, but also as a manifest desire for power by HAs over NHAs. Regarding the problem of the lack of language in NHAs, he writes, "Indeed, the most difficult problem lies in the fact that [the NHA] has been refused power to transform those traces into verbal language, to call to itself by means of discursive questions and responses, denied the power to efface its traces."[33] By withholding the potential of language for NHAs, humanity thereby disregards them and concludes that they *not* worthy of ethical consideration. With language as *the* trait for our binary division, those seeking to dismantle the binary must find ways to deconstruct it and diminish its power. There are countless examples one may employ to demonstrate how HAs are not so far removed, nor wholly distinct, from NHAs. In other words, one could demonstrate just how close HAs are to some other animals (e.g., nonhuman great apes); this will cause a slight shift in categorical groupings so that some animals now join HAs on one side of the ledger. What is problematic in this reasoning, scholar Cary Wolf notes, is that if HAs extend consideration to some NHAs based on their likeness to HAs, still other NHAs will be excluded and thus the new

33. Derrida, "Animal That Therefore I Am (More to Follow)," 50.

categorical grouping continues to decline consideration to the majority of NHAs.[34]

These somewhat artificial borders appear to be restrictions, but they are subjectively made, and thus could be objectively surpassed; it is possible for humanity to deconstruct these limitations. Humanity has conceptualized borders, such as the HA/NHA binary, perhaps to *distance* itself from its own animality. And yet, such hierarchies nevertheless echo throughout humanity and place certain entities in subordinate positions: woman, handicapped, non-white, etc. Withholding the capacity for concepts is akin to upholding other oppressions based on arbitrary reasons.[35] In view of the foregoing, there is an extreme response that we should ever be mindful of: that is, the response that gives NHAs the same physical, spiritual, and mental properties that HAs possess, and thus we show identical compassion to NHAs as we do to HAs since we and NHAs form a continuous supra-species. The other response, which is also insufficient, consists in reducing NHAs to a type of machine; doing so requires no compassion from us since in this view NHAs are a species that is separate from us.[36] Additionally, it is essential to note that the traditional HA/NHA opposition is also reductive of the rich diversity of HAs. If we characterize what is essentially HA as having language, rationality, or moral agency, then those HAs who lack such will be seen as *less* than an HA.[37] This outcome is clearly not the intended one, but it is the logical result of such a contention. Likewise, if we overemphasize identity and homogeneity among HAs, we will tend to dismiss—as totally unimportant!—the intrahuman differences everywhere present in the natural world. Difference theorists would insist that there are many intrahuman differences (for example, sexual differences) worth both attending to and allowing to flourish.[38]

REFLECTIONS ON DERRIDA'S POSITION ON NONHUMAN ANIMALS

Further, in dismantling traditional forms of the HA/NHA distinction, theorists of animality try to undercut the notion that there is a *single* barrier separating human beings from NHAs. This is highly pertinent, in part, for many of the capacities that have been considered proper to the HA alone

34. Wolfe, *Animal Rites*, 192.
35. Craig, "Rationality, Animality, and Human Nature," 3.
36. See Haraway's "A Manifesto for Cyborgs," 7–46.
37. Calarco, *Thinking Through Animals*, 38.
38. Calarco, *Zoographies*, 252.

in fact turn out to be found among NHAs in variant degrees. Particularly, as one looks closely at various markers of the HA, many of them turn out to be things of which human beings themselves have complex expressions. Traditional markers of HA uniqueness include awareness of death, self-consciousness, and language; these, however, are not straightforward abilities that we control ourselves.[39] These are complex, *emergent* properties and behaviors, insomuch as they are received from others even as they are constituted by ourselves. The thrust here is that markers of HA uniqueness are not distributed in the distinct manner that is sometimes hoped for, and definitely not as much as such is claimed. But we should be careful to note that the blurring of the HA/NHA boundary does not lead to its full collapse into HA-NHA identity. As such, Calarco then examines the ethical aspects of the thought of difference in view of its implications for NHAs.[40]

Derrida's worry here—which is a concern shared by many theorists who work within the *same* model as he—is that eliminating the HA/NHA distinction will lead to the flattening out of *differences* among HAs *and* NHAs rather than to their *thickening* and multiplication. If we were to set aside the project of establishing an anthropological difference (or anthropological differences), does such a stance necessarily lead us in the direction of homogenizing HAs and NHAs? Or might it be the case that leaving aside the project of establishing anthropological differences clears the way for other kinds of heretofore-unnoticed differences to emerge in isolation? The approach that Calarco covers in this book—i.e., the indistinction approach—offers us a veritable glimpse of how thought and practice might proceed to *thinking through NHAs* without the guidance of any difference(s).[41] If debates over the animality of HAs and NHAs threaten to send the concept to its ruin, discussions over the HA/NHA distinction would appear to make good upon this threat. In the last couple of decades, the traditional HA/NHA distinctions—such as the posit that a radical discontinuity between HAs and NHAs exists—have been relentlessly attacked from multiple perspectives. In biology, Darwinism has had the effect of undermining HA/NHA dichotomies in the name of the gradualist evolutionary paradigm. A similar displacement has occurred in the humanities, wherein traditional marks of the HA (knowledge of death, consciousness, etc.) have been shown either to exist in a similar form among NHAs or not exist among HAs in the way that people had originally thought.

39. Calarco, *Thinking Through Animals*, 38.
40. Calarco, *Thinking Through Animals*, 38.
41. Calarco, *Thinking Through Animals*, 46–47.

The vast majority of Derrida's texts about NHAs and animality regard the ways in which philosophers and others have tried to definitively separate HAs from other NHAs using traits, characteristics, etc.[42] Entire essays have been devoted to a deconstruction of traits often thought to be present only in HAs such as "the hand,"[43] spirit,[44] and awareness of death,[45] while other traits such as language, reason, and technology are discussed only in passing. Throughout these texts, it is clear that Derrida is abundantly suspicious of classical formulations of the HA/NHA distinction and therefore seeks to rethink differences between human beings and NHAs in a nonbinary way.[46] Stated in very basic terms, Derrida's thesis seems to be that wherever among life forms we find something like an identity, there is the play of difference, affect, inheritance, and response at work (typical "HA" traits). From this perspective, there is no clear separation between HAs and NHAs inasmuch as both "kinds" of beings are irreducibly caught up in the "same" network forces that make up their existence. Derrida's work as a whole tends to focus critically on these kinds of glaringly problematic binary oppositions. As Derrida expounds, such binary oppositions are typically riddled with horrendous ethical implications. Indeed, "In a classical philosophical opposition we are not dealing with the peaceful coexistence of a vis-à-vis, but rather with a violent hierarchy. One of the two terms governs the other (axiologically, logically, etc.), or has the upper hand."[47] This kind of gradation is evident in the HA/NHA distinction.

Derrida's thinking regarding the application of the term NHA is nearly equivalent to the concepts of postmodern HA theorists, as he proposes to eradicate the HA/NHA strict binary. Derrida's main intention in "The Animal That Therefore I Am" is to map the history of philosophical "logocentrism,"[48] a history that has consistently expressed a thesis regarding the NHAs, while the NAs position or presupposition is maintained from Aristotle to Heidegger, from Descartes to Kant, Levinas and Derrida. According to Krishanu Maiti, Derrida keeps himself on the same side with the critics of speciesism, who broaden the critiques of racism, sexism, etc. to include NHAs.[49] He argues that *not* to extend the same rights as HAs to

42. Calarco, *Zoographies*, 105.
43. Cf. Derrida, "Geschlecht II: Heidegger's Hand," 161–96.
44. Derrida, "Of Spirit: Heidegger and the Question," 6.
45. See e.g., Derrida, *Aporias: Dying—Awaiting (One Another at) the Limits of Truth*.
46. Calarco, *Zoographies*, 253–54.
47. Derrida, *Positions*, 41.
48. Derrida, "Animal That Therefore I Am (More to Follow)," 27.
49. Maiti, "Animal That Therefore Derrida Is," 95–96.

NHAs is immoral and worthy of consternation. In *Animal Rites: American Culture, the Discourse of Species, and Posthumanist Theory*,[50] Cary Wolfe challenges the NHA/HA binary opposition by:

- His advocation of posthuman NHA studies rejects the modernist tendency that places HAs above all other NHAs.
- His emphasizing the structural importance of NHA question in philosophy.

And his intention in this instance is to *trace* the classical opposition between human and NHAs that stems ultimately from Aristotle and thereafter to *break* this binary of perpetual problems.[51] Indeed, "Although Derrida has always insisted that such notions as 'differance',[52] the trace, ex-appropriation, and so forth circulate and function well beyond humanity, many of his best and most loyal readers have missed this aspect of his thought."[53] As aforementioned, Calarco argues in *Zoographies* that Derrida's work on NHAs consist of three main aspects: (1) A kind of "proto-ethical" imperative that gives rise to (2) a concrete ethicopolitical position, on the one hand, and (3) a thorough reworking of the basic anthropocentric thrust of the Western philosophical tradition, on the other.[54] These points are undoubtedly present throughout Derrida's corpus, as any cursory reading will show.

Derrida disputes both the *Cartesian* view that NHAs are machines who merit no compassion (i.e., metaphysical separationism), as well as the *animal rights* view that they should be shown the *same* compassion as HAs (i.e., biological continuism).[55] While it is necessary and important to support NHA rights, the approach is problematic because it reduces HAs to NHAs or elevates NHAs to HA-like existence: if one raises NHAs to the level of HAs, or if one lowers HAs to the level of NHAs, one ignores the difference that requires living beings to be treated multifariously.[56] Compassion in terms of pity and pathos has failed to establish an ethics of duty or obligation to NHA justice or NHA rights. The solution for Derrida is

---

50. Wolfe, *Animal Rites*, 113.

51. My italics, note.

52. For one example among many, see Derrida, "'Eating Well', or the Calculation of the Subject," 116.

53. Cf. Calarco, *Zoographies*, 251.

54. Cf. Calarco, *Zoographies*, 251.

55. Matthews, "Compassion, Geography and the Question of the Animal," 125.

56. Lawlor, "Animals Have No Hand: An Essay on Animality in Derrida," 45.

deconstruction, and the scrutiny of how we think and construct our lives, as well as for what purpose.[57]

CONCLUSION

Through his deconstructive analysis of the nonhuman animal, as well as his reflection on an encounter with his cat, which models the HA/NHA relation, Derrida contends that religion would do well to revise its understanding regarding the study of certain dimensions of human life. Specifically, Derrida claims that we have excellent reasons to revise our understanding of religious entities, making both NHAs and HAs able to participate in the phenomenon known as religion, as well as society and culture. A "turn to the animal"[58] occurred in the humanities beginning in the mid 1980s, the most evident of which is in between philosophy and cultural studies. Derrida did not let this proverbial revival of animality escape him. Nay, Derrida notes that "The question of the living and of the living animal ... will always have been the most important and decisive question. I have addressed it a thousand times, either directly or obliquely, by means of readings of all the philosophers I have taken an interest in."[59] In sum, Derrida remains unconvinced that all NHAs deserve to be categorized under the kingdom *Animalia*. From a biological standpoint, there is no question that HAs belong to the kingdom *Animalia*. But we run the risk of slipping between the border of biology and ontology. For example, it is common to find in genetic research the use of something like a model organism (usually an insect of some sort) that can represent many if not all other NHAs, as well as HAs. For much of the twentieth century, the standard organism used for such reflections was the fruit fly (*Drosophila melanogaster*), but more recently the roundworm (*C. elegans*) has been the archetypal animal due to its sequenced DNA and clearly defined developmental pattern. In psychology, too, we can look to the usage of rats and chimpanzees to map and understand the behavioral and neurological functioning of HAs. The use of such model organisms is a separate issue entirely from what Heidegger means by the essence of animality, but they do provide something of a glimpse at why it might be problematic to lump all NHAs together.[60]

This chapter has had as its aim to discuss the deconstructionist Jacques Derrida's contribution to the contemporary critical NHA studies. He is

57. Derrida, "Animal That Therefore I Am (More to Follow), 418.
58. Cederholm, Björck, Jennbert, and Lönngren, eds. *Exploring the Animal Turn*, 16.
59. Derrida, "Animal That Therefore I Am (More to Follow)," 370.
60. Buchanon, *Onto-Ethologies*, 67–68.

concerned with a critical thinking that starts with a dismantling of the distinction between the HA and the NHA, in part by questioning the hierarchical position of nature that belies the HA/NHA relationship. By concentrating on his own theory of animality, Derrida puts the homogenizing concept of NHA into question. The set of questions triggered by the thought *of* and *on* members of *Animalia* is timely; humanism seems to have exhausted itself and is giving way to posthumanism—ecological disaster looms large. Two interdisciplinary fields of inquiry have recently emerged to try to address these issues: ecocriticism and NHA studies. Derrida's two long lectures on the "autobiographical NHA" given in 1997 and later collected after his death in "The Animal That Therefore I Am" played a groundbreaking role in the NHA studies. In 2007, the *Oxford Literary Review* published a special issue on "Derridanimals"[61] that highlighted philosophy, literature, and cognitive sciences to help frame questions in the wake of Derrida's work.[62] The posthumanist Derrida directly challenges the *privileged* position of the HA because HAs are not distinct from NHAs, for HAs *themselves* also belong to the same kingdom: *Animalia*. This realization would perhaps have humbled him to be kinder to the other members of the kingdom *Animalia*. We can only speculate if that is the case, however.

61. Badmington, "Derridanimals," v–vii.
62. Berger and Segarra, "Thoughtprints," 3–22. Paragraph based on p. 3.

Part 3

Theological Perspectives on Evolution and Divine Involvement (Activity)

5

The God of Chance and Purpose[1]

INTRODUCTION

The thirteenth-century Christian philosopher Thomas Aquinas insisted that a perfect universe must contain randomness to allow humans their autonomy.[2] In the present paper, I will argue that ontological randomness is genuine. God does not determine the outcome of every scientifically random event, but instead controls randomness by setting broad boundaries, such as the range of possible outcomes of a random event and the probability of each outcome. God then allows particles, systems, and organisms to interact according to natural laws within these boundaries, producing a wide range of beautiful and complex results. So then, we live in a world of chance and randomness. But how much is truly random? This chapter looks at how, through paleontological examination, randomness and chance, which are inextricably linked, shape the world from the bottom up.[3] While I appreciate Brendan Sweetman's distinction between the two terms—that

---

1. This article originally appeared as McCall, "God of Chance and Purpose," 133–42. Reprinted with permission.
2. Aquinas, *Summa Contra Gentiles*, bk. 3, ch. 74, para. 3.
3. Sweetman, *Evolution, Chance, and God*, 110.

an event came about by *chance* means it could have been otherwise, whereas *randomness* refers to there being no goal toward which an event strives—I do intentionally highlight that even he admits the two terms are tightly linked with one another.

However, this is not the end of the story. Indeed, the phenomena known as convergence, which this paper also explicates with reference to dagger-like canines in animals and several examples of the multiple convergences in camera-like and compound eyes in animals, indicates that evolution through natural selection may proceed along various paths, but the destinations are few. So then, there is a dichotomy: randomness is constrained within pattern. Constraint in evolution is central in determining what might never be possible as against the very likely, perhaps even inevitable. In fact, Conway Morris contends that when one looks at either the functionality of biological solutions or the roads taken in evolution, the choices are indeed restricted, if not inevitable.[4] Convergence theory is important because it is central to the study of evolution due to its confirmation of the power of adaptation acting upon historical contingencies. It brings into focus the tension that is present within the rule of organization for any entity and the radical contingency of historical pathways in the paleontological record.[5] Convergence is ubiquitous across the scale of life; although the number of possibilities in evolution is more than astronomical, the ones that actually work are merely a small subset of the potential number.[6] Convergence opens up new ways to picture evolution by natural selection.

But in order to understand the events and generalities of life's pathway, we must go beyond principles of evolutionary theory to a paleontological examination of the contingent pattern of life's history on our planet—the single actualized version among millions of plausible alternatives that did not occur. Such a view of the history of life is highly contrary to both the conventional deterministic models of Western science and to the deepest social traditions of Western culture for a history culminating in humans as life's most magnificent expression.

In his magnum opus, *The Structure of Evolutionary Theory*, Stephen Jay Gould emphasizes the importance of recognizing both the reality of structural constraint and that structures have historical origins. In so doing, he helps unite insights from both sides of the age-old debate between functionalist and formalist biologists. The functionalists—such as Darwin and Jean-Baptiste Lamarck—typically stressed that features of organisms existed

4. Morris, *Runes of Evolution*, 31.
5. Morris, *Runes of Evolution*, 5.
6. Morris, *Runes of Evolution*, 21.

for utilitarian reasons (they were adaptations to their environments), and formalists—such as Étienne Geoffroy Saint-Hilaire and Johann Wolfgang von Goethe—stressed the structural unity of type common across similar organisms. A formalist often denied the possibility of evolution because they believed that only superficial change, not fundamental change, was possible. This division was permanently undermined when Darwin showed that structures had evolved through natural selection, although after their emergence, these structures may indeed constrain the evolutionary pathways available to organisms. In this, Darwin fundamentally reoriented the functionalist-formalist debate by adding a new dimension to the functional (active adaptation) and formal (constraints of structure) dichotomy: historical contingencies.[7]

Three features of the paleontological record stand out in opposition to the conventional view of the history of life as a broadly predictable process of gradually advancing complexity through time: the constancy of modal complexity, the concentration of major events in short bursts interspersed with long periods of stability, and the role of external impositions—primarily mass extinctions—in disrupting patterns of "normal" times.[8] These three features, combined with the more general themes of chaos and contingency, require a rethinking of the oft-accepted framework for conceptualizing the history of life.

GOD OF CHANCE

According to Gould, the history of life is not progressive, necessarily, and it is certainly not predictable. The Earth's biota has evolved through a series of fortuitous events. *Homo sapiens*, for example, did not appear on the Earth in one glorious moment of time; humans arose, rather, as a contingent outcome of thousands of linked events, any one of which could have occurred differently and thereby led evolutionary history on a pathway that possibly could not have led to the derivation of consciousness. To mention just four examples among many: 1) If a member of our Chordate phylum, *Pikaia*, which shows its relation to humans by its possession of a notochord, had not been among the survivors of the initial radiation of multicellular animal life in the Cambrian explosion circa 520 million years ago, then it is unlikely that vertebrates would have inhabited the Earth at all. 2) If a small group of lobe-finned fishes had not evolved with a radically different limb skeleton, with a strong central axis perpendicular to the body, capable of

---

7. Gould, *Structure of Evolutionary Theory*, 251–60.
8. Gould, *Richness of Life*, 212.

bearing weight on land, then vertebrates possibly would never have become terrestrial. 3) If a meteorite had not struck the Earth circa 65 million years ago, then dinosaurs would probably still be dominant today and mammals would still be small creatures living within the dinosaurs' world. 4) If a small lineage of primates had not evolved upright posture on the African savannas just two million years ago, then our ancestry might have wound up as a line of ecologically marginal apes.[9] We are an item of evolutionary history, and not an embodiment of general evolutionary principles.

Toward the end of the twentieth century, Gould published *Wonderful Life: The Burgess Shale and the Nature of History*, perhaps the most successful book on a paleontological subject since Darwin's *The Origin*. Although seemingly a historical account of the discovery of the Burgess Shale invertebrates, which are found high in the Canadian Rockies, Gould uses the book to advance a number of claims about the very nature of evolution. According to Gould, Charles Doolittle Walcott misinterpreted the fossils that he first found in the Burgess Shale in 1909, due in large part because of his conventional view of life that insisted that evolution was marked by a steady, progressional rise of complexity. *Wonderful Life* promotes the notion that Walcott committed a cardinal error by "shoehorning" the Burgess Shale fauna into existing phyla and classes.[10] Walcott's interpretations of the Burgess fossils remained uncontested for more than fifty years until a group spearheaded by Harry Whittington at Cambridge University in 1971 published a monograph that not only reexamined Walcott's conclusions, but also radically reinterpreted the Burgess Shale fauna, and with it the view of life, even our own evolution. *Wonderful Life* recounts the reinterpretation of the Burgess Shale fossils, and of the ideas that emerged from this work by Whittington's group. Three paleontologists dominate the center stage in *Wonderful Life*, as they did the bulk of the technical work in anatomical description and taxonomic placement: the aforementioned Harry Whittington, the world's leading expert on trilobites, and two men who began their careers as his understudies and then built their careers on the Burgess fossils[AW colon]—Derek Briggs and Simon Conway Morris.

Gould employs the fossils of the Burgess Shale to further his arguments for the importance of historical contingency relative to natural selection and adaptation in the history of life. Indeed, Gould makes three primary arguments. First, rather than the "cone of increasing diversity"—which he indicates is the primary iconography of evolution—the fauna of the Burgess Shale supports a model of rapid increase in morphologic disparity, a

9. Gould, "Evolution of Life," 3.
10. Gould, *Wonderful Life*, 108.

Christmas tree pattern, followed by elimination of many lineages and diversification of the successful lineages, noting that the morphologic disparity was a primary feature of the Cambrian explosion, and not a consequence of the subsequent evolutionary history.[11] He avers that the familiar accounts of evolution are meant to reinforce a comfortable view of human inevitability and superiority, arrived at after a ladder of progress. However, he contends, "Life is a copiously branching bush, continually pruned by the grim reaper of extinction, not a ladder of predictable progress."[12] So then, in Gould's view, evolutionary innovation was primarily focused in the events of the Cambrian, with later history largely "generating endless variants upon a few surviving models."[13] He refers to this pattern as "decimation," because he can combine the literal and vernacular senses of the term to suggest the two cardinal aspects stressed throughout the book: the largely random sources of survival or death, and the high probability of extinction.

Gould suspects that in the great majority of cases the traits that enhance survival during an extinction event do so incidentally, and are not related to the causes of their evolution in the first place. While animals evolve their sizes, shapes, and morphologies under natural selection during normal times and for specific reasons, when a mass extinction comes along, what may have been advantageous before could turn out to be deleterious, whereas a trait without particular significance before the mass extinction event might attain one afterward. He asserts that there can be no causal correlation in principle between the derivation of a trait in that circumstance and its new usage. After all, a species "cannot evolve structures with a view to their potential usefulness millions of years down the road—unless our general ideas about causality are markedly awry, and the future can control the present."[14] With regard to randomness, Gould notes that "decimate" comes from the Latin *decimare*, "to take one in ten," which referred originally to the standard punishment for members of the Roman army who were found to be guilty of mutiny: one soldier out of every ten was selected by lot and put to death. With regard to the probability of extinction, he

---

11. For the general pattern of the Christmas tree, see Raup, Gould, Schoff, and Simberloff, "Stochastic Models of Phylogeny and the Evolution of Diversity," 525–42; Raup and Gould, "Stochastic Simulation and Evolution of Morphology," 305–22; Gould, Raup, Seposki, Schoff, and Simberloff, "Shape of Evolution: A Comparison of Real and Random Clades," 23–40; and Gould, Gilinsky, German, "Asymmetry of Lineages and the Direction of Evolutionary Time," 1437–41. We may interpret this bottom-heavy pattern in many ways; Gould sees it as "early experimentation and later standardization" (Gould, *Wonderful Life*, 304).

12. Gould, *Wonderful Life*, 35.

13. Gould, *Wonderful Life*, 47.

14. Gould, *Wonderful Life*, 307.

points out that "decimate" connotes how most—say, 90 percent—of the individual entities in the Burgess fauna were extinguished without leaving any significant lineage. Stereotypy, the cramming of most species into a few anatomical plans, is the mark of modern life forms.[15]

The model of maximal increase in morphologic disparity early in the history of Metazoa as a whole leads to the second major argument of *Wonderful Life*, which is Gould's thought experiment of replaying the tape of life over. The Burgess pattern of decimation shows that groups may prevail or die for reasons that are not related to Darwinian selection processes. This leads him to stipulate that if it were possible to "replay the tape" of evolution, the outcome would almost certainly be very different, both in detail and in general. Gould's argument represents the culmination of his fight against overly adaptive storytelling and inferred evolutionary progress:

> Any replay of the tape would lead evolution down a pathway radically different from the road actually taken. But the consequent differences in outcome do not imply that evolution is senseless, and without meaningful pattern; the divergent route of the replay would be just as interpretable, just as explainable *after* the fact, as the actual road. But the diversity of possible itineraries does demonstrate that eventual results cannot be predicted at the outset. Each step proceeds for cause, but no finale can be specified at the start and none would even occur a second time in the same way, because any pathway proceeds through thousands of improbable stages. Alter any early event, ever so slightly and without apparent importance at the time, and evolution cascades into a radically different channel.[16]

For Gould, this is the essence of contingency. Occurrences in the history of macroevolution *just happened*—they were not necessary, certainly not predictable, and every one of them could have been different. In fact, a number of other possible events may have happened in their stead. Importantly, Gould is keen to highlight that each event has its own cause, but these causes were not necessary. In postulating this, both Gould and I differ from Brendan Sweetman.[17] Sweetman seemingly does not grant the fact that Gould concedes that each event has a cause, for he queries us, "do we mean that the mutation has no cause?," when referring to Gould and Dawkins.[18] Gould's third argument in *Wonderful Life* builds from the pattern of

15. Gould, *Wonderful Life*, 49.
16. Gould, *Wonderful Life*, 51.
17. Sweetman, *Evolution, Chance, and God*, 101.
18. Sweetman, *Evolution, Chance, and God*, 107.

disparity and the import of contingency to conclude that natural selection and adaptation play a less significant role in evolution than acknowledged by most evolutionary biologists. We do not know why most of the early experiments were failures, with only a few surviving to become modern phyla. It is tempting to say that the victors won by virtue of greater complexity, better fitness, or some other predictable feature of the conventional Darwinian struggle.[19] But nothing in particular unites the victors, and a radical alternative must be considered: that each early experiment received little more than a proverbial ticket in the largest "lottery" ever played on our planet—and that the surviving lineages, including our own phylum of vertebrates, survived more by the luck of the draw than by any intrinsic merit.[20]

The transforming power of the Burgess message can be seen in its affirmation of history as the chief determinant of life's direction, and it shows that the fantastic explosion of early disparity is followed by decimation, largely based in terms of what can be pictured as a lottery. Gould concedes that the origin of life on Earth was virtually inevitable, given the early chemical composition of oceans and the atmosphere, along with the nature of self-organizing systems. While the laws of nature impact the general forms and functions of organisms, the channels are so broad that the details are left to chance. The physical channels do not specify "arthropods, annelids, mollusks, and vertebrates, but, at most, bilaterally symmetrical organisms based on repeated parts."[21] In fact, Gould states, "I suspect that given the composition of early atmospheres and oceans, life's origin was a chemical necessity. Contingency arises later, when historical origin enters the picture of evolution."[22] Much less do they specify the essential answers related to our own origin, such as why mammals evolved, why primates moved from land to the trees, and why the fragile lineage of *Homo sapiens* emerged and survived in Africa. This evidence suggests that God does not determine the outcome of every scientifically random event, which I herein define as being referent to events that are not calculable in anticipation of their occurrence, but instead controls randomness by setting broad boundaries. God thereafter allows organisms to interact according to natural laws within these boundaries, producing a wide range of beautiful and complex results. Sweetman, who argues explicitly for determinism, even admits that this definition of randomness works well within the discipline of biology. I disagree with

19. Gould, *Richness of Life*, 217.
20. Gould, *Wonderful Life*, 239.
21. Gould, *Wonderful Life*, 290.
22. Gould, *Wonderful Life*, 309.

Sweetman, one may surmise, when he further stipulates that it is the "simple fact that it is not true that the cause (or more accurately causes) of any event in the universe could have been different than they in fact were . . . In short, we are looking at a completely deterministic universe."[23]

GOD OF PURPOSE

Perhaps the most sustained critique of Gould's contingency argument has come from Simon Conway Morris. Conway Morris is Professor of Evolutionary Palaeobiology at the University of Cambridge. He notes that in the phenomena known as convergence, similar patterns appear in widely divergent groups. He has compiled manifold amounts of examples of convergence in nature and has employed them to argue that despite the apparent contingency, evolution is far more predictable than admitted by Gould.[24] He writes, however, that "the likelihood of exactly the same cognitive creatures—with five fingers on each hand, a veniform appendix, thirty-two teeth, and so on evolving again if, somehow, the Cambrian explosion could be rerun is remote in the extreme."[25] But what about the emergence of more general features in evolutionary epic?

A few overarching themes emerge from the literature on convergence. The most obvious is that convergent features arise in response to similar processing demands. Convergence operates at all levels of biological organization. Conway Morris writes,

> To paraphrase much of this book, life may be a universal principle, but we can still be alone. In other words, once you are on the path it is pretty straightforward, but finding a suitable planet and maybe getting the right recipe for life's origination could be exceedingly difficult: inevitable humans in a lonely Universe. Now, if this happens to be the case, that in turn might be telling us something very interesting indeed. Either we are a cosmic accident, without either meaning or purpose, or alternatively . . .[26]

The central theme of *Life's Solution* depends upon the realities of evolutionary convergence: the recurrent tendency of biological organization to arrive

---

23. Sweetman, *Evolution, Chance, and God*, 113.
24. Morris, "Predictability of Evolution," 1313–37; cf. Morris, *Life's Solution*; and Morris, *Crucible of Creation*.
25. Morris, *Life's Solution*, xii.
26. Morris, *Life's Solution*, xiii.

at the same "solution" to a particular "need." Within it, there are four conclusions: First, what we regard as complex is usually inherent in simpler systems: the real unanswered question in evolution is not novelty per se, but how things are put together. Second, the number of evolutionary end points is limited, meaning that in no way is everything possible. Third, what is possible has usually been arrived at multiple times. Finally, all this takes billions of years to become increasingly inevitable.[27] Convergence tells us at least two things: that evolutionary trends are real, and that adaptation is not some occasional component in the organic machine, but is central to the explanation of derivation of life.

It is surprising in light of the high probability for novelty to find, even in similar niches, high morphological similarity in distinctly different genetic lines. Evolution is indeed constrained, if not bound. Despite the immensity of biological hyperspace, Conway Morris argues that nearly all of it must remain forever empty, not because our chance drunken walk failed to wander into it, but because the possibilities were from the beginning unavailable. This implies that it matters little what our starting point may have been, as the different routes will not prevent a convergence to similar ends, and that we may be on the verge of glimpsing a deeper structure to life.

Conway Morris gives an example from the world of predator-prey relationships. The dagger-like canines, in both placental cats (the sabre-tooth cats) and a group of South American marsupials known as the thylacosmilids,[28] independently evolved. In fact, the evidence suggests that even within the placental cats the sabre-tooth habit evolved at least three times: in the primitive nimravids, the barbourofelids, and the machairodont felids.[29] Although as a group the marsupials are best known as kangaroo and wombat species, they tend to be regarded in some generalized sense as inferior to the placentals.[30] Interestingly, Kirsch suggests that the marsupium, that is, the pouch in which the young develop, actually arose several times independently within the marsupials, an argument that presupposes that primitively this group of mammals lacked the pouch. So too, the rich, but now largely extinct, diversity of South American marsupials is widely regarded as having been competitively inferior to the placental mammals

---

27. Morris, *Life's Solution*, xii–xiii.

28. See, for example, Turnbull, "Another Look at Dental Specialization in the Extinct Sabre-Toothed Marsupial Thlyacosmilus," 319–414. Conway Morris is quick to point out, however, that the identity between the thylacosmilids and sabre-toothed cats is not exact because "Convergence is never precise" (Morris, *Runes of Evolution*, 54).

29. See, e.g., Turner and Antón, *Big Cats and Their Fossil Relatives*; cf. Morris, *Runes of Evolution*, 54–55.

30. Kirsch, "Six-Percent Solution," 276–88.

that surged south when the Panamanian isthmus was formed several million years ago.[31] In contradistinction to the prevailing notion, the sabre showed a number of design advantages when compared with the placental equivalents in the marsupial thylacosmilids, including the possession of a protective flange, a self-sharpening mechanism, and a deeper insertion into the skull that presumably afforded a more secure housing for the canine. Despite this manifest convergence, neither group escapes its hallmark of phylogenetic history, which is marked in the specific structure of the teeth.[32]

Not only are the dagger-like canines convergent, but also other features are in nature. For example, cats see through the dilated pupils of their camera eyes, whereas the mosquito sees through its compound eyes. Not only have both these types of eye— camera and compound—evolved several times, but even the neural architecture underlying the sight mechanism has shown multiple convergences. The existence of camera and compound eyes reminds us that solutions to biological evolution need not be unique, but are simply very strongly constrained. When considering convergences between camera eyes, it is almost inevitable that comparisons will be drawn between the camera eyes of vertebrates and those of the advanced cephalopods, notably the squid and octopus. Of course, there are well-known differences; most notable are those between the relative position of the light-sensitive layer, the retina, which arise as a result of the different embryologies in vertebrates and mollusks. In mollusks, the retina is derived from the ectoderm (the outer layer); as it involutes to make the eyecup, the associated nerve cells extend into the body to make their connection with the brain. The vertebrate retina, in contrast, is effectively an outgrowth of the central nervous system. The net result of this process is that in the vertebrates the nerve cells overlie the retina. The exit point of these nerves to the optic tract, which then leads to the brain, results in a 'blind spot' in the retina. The arrangement of nerve cells and retina in mollusks and vertebrates is reversed, however, with the cephalopods having arguably the better design of nervous layer beneath sensory retina.

These differences are important, but it is still the case that the similarities between the human eye and those of a cephalopod are very striking. What is less well known is that a similar camera eye has evolved independently in several other groups; for instance, the most notable is in a group of marine annelids (alciopids), which are close relatives of the more familiar

31. See Lessa and Farina, "Reassessment of Extinction Patterns among the Late Pleistocene Mammals of South America," 651–62.

32. See Koenigswald and Goin's remarks on enamel structure in "Enamel Differentiation in South American Marsupials and a Comparison of Placental and Marsupial Enamel," 129–68.

earthworms.[33] These eyes are strikingly similar to those of the vertebrates and cephalopods, and because the annelids are also relatively closely related to the mollusks, the retina has the same arrangement as in the latter group.[34] There is, moreover, another convergence in the alciopid eye: the so-called accessory retinas, which are light-sensitive patches located nearer to the front of the eye; these are convergent on similar structures found in some deep-sea fish and cephalopods. Returning to the mollusks, considering this time the gastropods (snails), we find that in this group a camera-like eye seems to have evolved independently at least three times.[35] Wald and Raypart remark, "The presence of accessory retinas in alciopid eyes offers a prime instance of the phenomenon of evolutionary convergence."[36] They suggest that they could thus be used to judge depth.

Nor does the list of convergently evolved camera eyes quite end there; there are two more examples that Conway Morris recounts, each in their own way surprising.[37] The first example comes from the primitive cubozoans, which are a type of jellyfish renowned both for their highly toxic stings and for their remarkable eyes. The eyes are similar in construction to other camera eyes, with a large lens located in front of the retina.[38] Cubozoan jellyfish belong to a primitive group of animals, the cnidarians, which also includes the sea anemones and corals. While primitive eyespots are known in other cnidarians,[39] at first sight the sophistication of the cubozoan eyes, which typically total eight arranged around the margin of the swimming bell, is quite surprising. What is particularly interesting is the relative simplicity of their nervous system, which consists of a nerve net linked to a series of four pacemakers, a neural architecture that is effectively imposed by the jellyfish body plan. There is no brain. Yet there are complex eyes and sophisticated behavior. So then, even considering rudimentary forms of life, the pattern of convergence dominates, suggesting that there is a God of purpose behind it all, wooing, if you will, creation forward in complexity.

33. Morris, *Life's Solution*, 152.
34. Wald and Raypart, "Vision in Annelid Worms," 1434–39.
35. Wald and Raypart, "Vision in Annelid Worms," 1439.
36. Wald and Raypart, "Vision in Annelid Worms," 1437.
37. Morris, *Life's Solution*, 154.
38. Pearse and Pearse, "Vision of Cubomedusan Jellyfishes," 458.
39. See the work by Blumer, von Salvini-Plawen, Kikinger, and Buchinger, "Ocelli in a Cnidaria Polyp," 221–27.

CONCLUSION

So what does the preceding analysis of Gould's and Conway Morris's postulates mean? I suggest two things. First, there is ontological randomness in nature. God uses this randomness in order to achieve the maximum population of creation by maintaining dynamic equilibria in complex systems. But this ontological randomness does not preclude the derivation of propensities toward the expression of similar form, even among widely divergent evolutionary lines. These findings strengthen the case that mechanical optimization can drive evolution, contributing to the longstanding debate over the evolutionary roles of randomness versus physical constraints that limit the solutions that are feasible in living creatures. In sum, quantifying physical properties that underlie biological phenomena could help us recognize when an optimal mechanical solution is likely to drive convergent evolution.

6

Augustine's Theolog(ies) of Creation

Simultaneous Creation, "Seminal Seeds," and Genesis 1–3

INTRODUCTION

Andrew Brown has rightly noted that Augustine's *Literal Meaning of Genesis* is the apex of works on Genesis within the Patristic Period, holding sway thereafter as well through the medieval and Renaissance periods, from Lombard to Aquinas, from Luther to Calvin, etc.[1] But is Augustine's views of creation still relevant today, post the scientific revolution, and especially post-Darwin?[2] Surely, much of his interpretation cannot withstand the onslaught of modernity and its concomitant increase in scientific knowledge. Can it? Perhaps not, but we can still learn from Augustine. It is a modern myth that the scientific revolution alone forced the church Catholic to come up with interpretations that were amenable to the science of their time. Augustine is a prime example of this "wrestling with the Divine." However, we should not go to Augustine with the hopes of settling the debate on origins

---

1. Brown, "Augustine's View of Creation and Its Modern Reception," 36.

2. Whitehead once said that Western philosophy is a series of footnotes to Plato; similarly, one might say that Western theology is a series of footnotes to Augustine (Cf. Williams, "Significance of St. Augustine Today," 4).

and scriptural interpretation. Not simply *should not*, but in fact *cannot*. Augustine erred mightily when he sought to use the Bible as a proverbial science textbook. I say this for the following reason: he tried to use scripture to explain *how* the heavens and the Earth were made. *How*, however, is not a theological category, but a scientific one instead. *Why*, on the other hand, would be an apropos question for theology to answer. But this Augustine did not seek. Indeed, he writes, "For now it is our business in the account of Holy Scripture *how* God made the universe, not what He might produce in nature or from nature by His miraculous power."[3]

Although we can lift interpretive principles from Augustine's approach to scripture, we cannot, however, strike the balance between literality and figurative interpretations based on review of his work(s), for in fact Augustine himself does *not* reach such a balance, though apparently that's what he sought after (as will become clear later). He is, rather, a walking contradiction, a muddled mess, one might say. In his first commentary of Genesis 1–3, he strikes an allegorical interpretation, and then moves later to a "literal" one. Indeed, in his mature work, written in his mid-fifties, Augustine claims that his interpretation of Genesis 1–3 is "literal," and not metaphorical, figurative, or allegorical.[4] But then he spiritualizes the meaning of the text? While he admits that the interpretive process of Genesis is fraught with difficulties, he nevertheless takes stands on his interpretations. Confuddled thinking, I assert, is demonstrated by Augustine in his interpretation(s) of Genesis 1–3! This paper will make such a statement of my own clearer. Herein, I will stipulate that Augustine's theology of creation is highly convoluted, a muddled mess, and even confused—in fact, impenetrable to the contemporary mind. Indeed, Augustine himself admits as much, later, in his *Retractationes*, stating, "Let those, therefore, who are going to read this book not imitate me where I err, but rather when I progress toward the better. For, perhaps, one who reads my works in the order in which they were written will find out how I progressed while writing."[5] We would be wise to take heed to his instructions.

Indeed, after recalling what he wrote at the beginning of the second book of Augustine, *A Refutation of the Manichees*, he continues, "Now, however, it has pleased the Lord that after taking a more thorough and considered look at these matters, I should reckon (and not, I think, idly) that I am able to demonstrate how all these things were written straightforwardly

---

3. Augustine, *Confessions*, 47. Italics added.
4. Young, "Contemporary Relevance of Augustine's View of Creation," 62.
5. Augustine, "Retractationes," 5.

in the proper, not the allegorical mode."[6] Here, Augustine admits that he could not offer a literal interpretation though he wanted to in *De Genesi contra Manichaeos*. But *now* he is equipped and able to interpret the text in a proper and literal sense. He views the ability to interpret the creation stories literally as progress. I view it as a backwards movement, in contradistinction to him. Along with McMullin, I contend that Augustine's *original* interpretation of the Genesis event was indeed the most proper and most accurate one; of this other, nonliteral interpretation of the Genesis account, McMullin notes that it was "one that was gradually more or less lost from sight, but one, as it happens, that would have made the appearance of Darwin's *Origin of Species* seem more culmination, perhaps, than surprise."[7] So then, Augustine *was* on the right track. But . . .

BRIEF OVERVIEW OF AUGUSTINE'S CORPUS

Augustine's theologies of creation and the Trinity were significantly influenced by his exegesis of Genesis 1, John 1:1–3, Wisdom of Solomon 11:20[8] and other scriptures, and his ideas resonate with the *hexaemeral* works of Basil and Philo of Alexandria.[9] Augustine's theology of creation is developed in dialogue with both Manichean and Platonic accounts; indeed, within his theologizing one finds the shadow of both Manichee and Plato (or, rather, Plotinus's Neo-Platonic development of Plato's theses).[10] Augustine wrote commentaries on the Genesis creation narratives nearly throughout his life. In fact, according to Christian, few other passages of scripture intrigued Augustine as much as the first three books of Genesis.[11] His first attempt was a short work wherein he defends Genesis against the Manichees. Indeed, circa 388, after returning to Africa and before his ordination to the priesthood, he composed *A Refutation of the Manichees*, which was his first biblical commentary. In this work, Augustine interpreted the

---

6. Augustine, *Literal Meaning of Genesis* (trans. Hammond), 349 (*De Genesi ad litteram*, bk. 8).

7. McMullin, "Darwin and the Other Christian Tradition," 291–92.

8. Interestingly, Curtis notes that "every reader of medieval Latin texts knows that few Bible phrases were so often quoted and alluded to as the phrase from the Wisdom of Solomon, 11:20" (Curtis, *European Literature and the Latin Middle Ages*, 504).

9. Kim, *Augustine's Changing Interpretations of Genesis 1–3*, 147.

10. For this point, see Crouse, "*Paucis Mutatis Verbis*: St. Augustine's Platonism," 37–50.

11. Christian, "Creation of the World," 315. Christian further notes that Augustine's prolific output with regard to the opening chapters of Genesis reflect the fecundity of his mind, and assertion with which I heartily agree.

creation stories largely in an allegorical manner, "for the weaker brethren and the little ones among us."[12] Apparently, the "weaker and little ones" were referent to the Manichees, who posited an ultra-strictly literal interpretation of Genesis 1–3.[13] In a reflective moment, Augustine later admits that he could not—at that time!—interpret the first chapters of Genesis in a literal fashion.[14] Further, about his views he presented earlier in his *A Refutation of the Manichees*, he states:

> Now at that time it had not yet dawned on me how everything in them could be taken in its proper literal sense; it seemed to me rather that this was scarcely possible, if at all, and anyhow extremely difficult. So in order not to be held back, I explained with what brevity and clarity I could muster what those things, for which I was not able to find a suitable literal meaning, stood for in a figurative sense. Bearing in mind, however, what I really wanted but could not manage, that everything should first of all be understood in its proper, not its figurative sense.[15]

However, about five years later, circa 393, Augustine did just that in *De Genesi ad litteram liber unus imperfectus*. In this work, Augustine tries to offer a literal interpretation of Genesis 1, not according to its allegorical meaning, but according to its historical signification instead.[16] It is most interesting to realize that Augustine abandoned this work after one book, "under the weight of so heavy a load," for he seemingly could not—yet—affirm a literal interpretation of Genesis 1–3.[17] Indeed, he stopped this work at Genesis 1:27. Thirdly, Augustine presents a figurative interpretation of the first chapter of Genesis in his last three books (i.e., 11–13) of *The Confessions* (ca. 401), an attempt that combines literal and allegorical interpretations into a seamless argument.

Fourthly, between 401 and 416, Augustine wrote the completed version of *The Literal Meaning of Genesis*, in which he interpreted the creation stories, "not according to the allegorical significance, but according to historical events proper."[18] In this work, Augustine achieves his goal of interpreting the opening chapters of Genesis literally. In fact, according to Edmund Hill, this work is a kind of Augustinian summa on the subject

12. Augustine, "Refutation of the Manichees," 39.
13. Kim, *Augustine's Changing Interpretations of Genesis 1–3*, 4.
14. Augustine, "Retractationes," 17.
15. Augustine, *Literal Meaning of Genesis* (trans. Hammond), 349.
16. Kim, *Augustine's Changing Interpretations of Genesis 1–3*, 4.
17. Augustine, "Retractationes," 76.
18. Augustine, "Retractationes," 168–69.

of creation, although Augustine himself noted that this work poses more questions than it answers, and does not solve any questions, per se. Further, for whatever answers it gives, not many can be held to be certain.[19] Finally, Augustine turns again to the creation narratives in books 30–33 of *The City of God*, written circa 417. Why did Augustine spend so much time on the Genesis creation narratives? Apparently, he viewed the creation narrative to be of primal importance to Christianity. His writings contradict each other, however, and reflect an ongoing wrestling with the divine through science, reason, and the text of scripture.

Augustine is convinced that the sacred scripture is written to nourish our souls and that truth is consistent, yet perhaps recondite. In fact, "truth had to be one if it was truth."[20] Augustine's interpretative framework, though not his resolution of problems per se, provides a useful approach for us today as we seek to meet the challenges of science and faith. Indeed, Augustine interweaves biblical interpretation,[21] an appeal to "right reason," and a knowledge of contemporary science in his theological reflections concerning creation, which can be summarized as follows:

- God brought everything into being at a specific moment.
- Part of the created order takes the form of embedded causalities which emerge or evolve at a later stage.
- The image of a dormant seed is an appropriate but not exact analogy for these embedded causalities.
- The process of generation of these dormant seeds results in the fixity of biological forms.[22]

AUGUSTINE AND *RATIONES SEMINALES*

In or about the year 400, Augustine described a view of creation in which "seeds of potentiality" were established by God, which then unfolded through time in an incomprehensibly complicated set of processes. Of

---

19. Jaki, *Genesis 1 Through the Ages*, 85.
20. Jaki, *Genesis 1 Through the Ages*, 85.
21. For a hearty examination of Augustine's approach to these topics, see Lienhard, "Reading the Bible and Learning to Read," 725. In a related note, "Augustine's 'spiritual exegesis' permits him to take extraordinary liberties with what is often the most obvious meaning of the Scriptural text, something of which he seems at times uncomfortably aware" (O'Connell, *St. Augustine's Early Theory of Man*, 156).
22. McGrath, *Fine-Tuned Universe*, 107.

particular interest here, art least interpretatively, is Augustine's suggestion that God created by potencies (dormant seeds) *and* by process. Augustine's interpretation of scripture led him to conclude that God created not by producing ready-made plants and animals but by potencies and process. He uses the analogy of seeds—not as literal objects but as a way to wrestle with "the theologically difficult notion of a hidden force within nature through which latent things are enacted."[23] The most famous aspect of Augustine's partial dependence on metaphor, notes Paul Allen in *Augustine and Science*, is his advocacy of a quasi-evolutionary interpretation of the six days of creation.[24] Indeed, derived from his nonliteral interpretation of scripture is his idea of the *rationes seminales*, that is, the idea that God made everything in the beginning, but nevertheless allowed all things—especially species, if you will—to develop in their own due time—from "seed."[25] McMullin summarizes Augustine's claims, in fact, in this way:

> Nature is whole and entire in its own right; the "seeds" of all natural kinds are implanted at the beginning—Augustine argues that the six days of the Genesis account have to be understood as metaphor—and the corresponding kinds appear when conditions are right. God's purposes are brought about not by intervening (that is by overriding natural causality), but by ensuring that the desired result comes about naturally.[26]

McMullin stipulates, based upon Augustine's theological enterprise, that:

> When conflict arises between a literal reading of some Bible text and a truth about the nature of things which has been

---

23. McGrath, *Fine-Tuned Universe*, 102.

24. Allen, "Augustine and the Systematic Theology of Origins," 13. Caiazza, however, is not comfortable with the assertion that Augustine's views were in any way a precursor to modern evolutionary theory. Rather, Augustine's context was theological, not scientific, and his motives were theological (Caiazza, "Augustine on Evolution, Time, Memory," 115–16). Further, Caiazza notes that due to his heavy dependence on and agreement with Neoplatonist ideas regarding the immutability of forms, a true evolutionary interpretation—with animals and plants truly changing through time perhaps even into other entities—would have never occurred to Augustine (Caiazza, "Augustine on Evolution, Time, Memory," 120).

25. Allen, "Augustine and the Systematic Theology of Origins," 13. Christian would seemingly agree in noting that not all things were created "visibly and actually," but only "potentially or causally" in these "hidden seeds" (Cf. Christian, "Creation of the World," 329). It is from these "seeds," hidden to the naked eye, that the creative activity of God brings forth things from the water according to their own kinds; as such, this creator of seeds is the creator of all things (Cf. O'Toole, *Philosophy of Creation in the Writings of St. Augustine*, 15).

26. McMullin, "Cosmology and Religion," 587.

demonstrated by reliable argument, the Christian must strive to reinterpret the biblical text in a metaphorical way. Since real conflict is impossible between the two sources of truth, revelation and our tested knowledge of the world, the presumption will be that when we are sure of our natural knowledge, the apparent conflicting text of the bible must be read in a way which will eliminate the conflict.[27]

McMullin adds that these seed principles: "function . . . to explain how one can say *both* that God made all things at the beginning and that the various kinds of things made their appearances only gradually over the course of historic time. And the warrant for it is almost entirely theological."[28]

These *rationes seminales* resemble "seeds" not because of their form, but because of the potentialities contained within them.[29] As such, *rationes seminales* represent the latent powers of natural development in created things. These "seeds'" development, however, are not wholly natural, but governed by God's providential work.[30] Augustine's "seed principles" (or "seminal principles") are ontological aspects of creatures that he implies are given through Trinitarian acts of creation. However, the seminal principles are the cause of the development or growth of a creature and the propagation of creatures and species.

The *rationes seminales* are not simply germ cells or seeds in a literal sense, however, but they are like seeds insomuch as they "causally explain the positive transformation of things, the actualization of the latent potentialities that exist throughout nature."[31] They are physical in the sense that they are somehow contained in material things, but they are not understood to be discrete physical units with material forms all their own. Augustine writes, in comparing causal formulae to seeds,

> So let us consider the beauty of any kind of tree you like, in its trunk, its branches, its leaves, its fruits. This admirable sight did not of course suddenly spring into being in its full stature and glory, but in the order with which we are also familiar. Thus it rose up from its roots, which the first sprig had fixed in the earth, and from there grew all these parts in their distinct forms and shapes. That sprig, furthermore, came from a seed; so it was

27. McMullin, *Evolution and Creation*, 2.
28. McMullin, "Cosmology and Religion," 595.
29. Kim, *Augustine's Changing Interpretations of Genesis 1–3*, 148.
30. In this respect, then, they somewhat differ from Plotinus's naturalistic emanation.
31. Spiegel, "Augustine, Evolution, and Scientific Methodology," 197–98.

> in the seed that all the rest was originally to be found, not in the mass of full growth, but in the potentiality of its causative virtue... Does anything, after all, sprout or hang from that tree which has not been extracted and brought out from the hidden treasure of that seed?[32]

Causal formulae are similar to seeds in that they contain potentiality within them; however, they are dissimilar in that they do not have bodily forms—they are invisible. However, "Seeds do indeed provide some sort of comparison with this, on account of the growths to come that are bound in with them; before all seeds, nonetheless, are those causes."[33]

Spiegel points out that Augustine borrows the concept of *rationes seminales* from the Stoics, by way of Plotinus.[34] Augustine's reason for this adoption of the terminology from the Stoics was apparently to massage his interpretation of Genesis 1–3. Indeed, he had to proverbially square the biblical datum of creation with certain facts of the physical world as then understood. After all, the creation narrative climaxes with God's *rest*, not his activity. Are we then to presume that God ends his creative activity? Are things that have been derived from creation since then, *not* themselves, then, God's creation, because they were not immediately generated by God's creative activity? For example, if God totally rested his creative activity on the sixth day of creation, is my to-be-born offspring *not* God's creation too?

We seem, then, to be forced to either deny the ongoing emergence of new creatures or deny that God indeed "rested" on the sixth day. Augustine apparently understood the irrationality of such a thought, so his way out of the dilemma was to distinguish between "two moments of creation: one in the original creation when God made all creatures before resting from all His works on the seventh day, and the other in the administration of creatures by which he works even now."[35] Notably, theologians today also divide the creation(s) of God into two similar categories: "divine creation" and "divine providence,"[36] thereby affirming that God created things once at the beginning, but also that things which *continue* to be created are also "created by God." It is in this later case that Augustine's terminology of the "administration of creatures" applies, and it is thus necessary for him to introduce *rationes seminales* so as to give God the (proper?) credit also for the creation of things subsequent of the six days in Genesis 1–3. Indeed,

32. Augustine, *Literal Meaning of Genesis* (trans. Hammond), 299.
33. Augustine, *Literal Meaning of Genesis* (trans. Hammond), 307.
34. Spiegel, "Augustine, Evolution, and Scientific Methodology," 195–96.
35. Augustine, *Literal Meaning of Genesis* (trans. Hammond), 162.
36. Spiegel, "Augustine, Evolution, and Scientific Methodology," 197.

"According to the division of the works of God described above, some works belonged to the invisible days in which He created all things simultaneously, and others belong to the days in which He daily fashions whatever evolves in the course of time from what I might call the 'primordial wrappers.'"[37]

Augustine develops the *rationes seminales* idea in *The Literal Meaning of Genesis*, and to a lesser degree in *The Trinity*, and though he mentions it somewhat substantially in these works, the notion is sufficiently vague so as to allow multiple interpretations. It is important to note there is no exact English equivalent with the term *rationes seminales*. It is often translated as "seminal reasons," "causal reasons," "causal principles," "causal formulae," "seminal reasons," or even "seminal principles." The term *rationes* itself is a variant of the term *ratio*, which means to reckon or calculate, whereas *seminales* refers directly to seeds or germinal sources.[38] In fact, "seminal principles" is Blowers's terminology for Augustine's *rationes seminales*. As Blowers explains these principles, they are about the "propagation" and "historical unfolding" of creatures in "actual creation" (not initial creation).[39] But I prefer the terminology of "seeds."[40] Nevertheless, according to Blowers, Augustine's discussions of the seminal principles and the capability "to emerge and develop" are "closely associated" with Augustine's references to Wisdom of Solomon 11:21 and the measure, number, and weight given to creatures by God.[41] So then, the essential idea is that of inherent powers of development with which God endowed creation, so that over the course of time certain immutable and eternal forms are sequentially and subsequently realized and actualized through natural processes. Augustine explains these *rationes seminales* under several "aspects":

> Under one aspect these things are the Word of God, where they are not made but eternally existing; under another aspect they are in elements of the universe, where all things destined to be were made simultaneously; under another aspect they are in

---

37. Augustine, *Literal Meaning of Genesis* (trans. Hammond), 183–84.
38. Spiegel, "Augustine, Evolution, and Scientific Methodology," 196.
39. Blowers, *Drama of the Divine Economy*, 156–159.
40. I prefer the notion of seeds for semantic reasons, mostly. Indeed, the imagery of seeds accurately captures the potency of the "action," as well as the necessity for some sort of concursus on behalf of the other. Seeds themselves may contain within them the "ability" to produce a mighty oak tree, for example, but lest there is a concursus on behalf of nature, i.e., the other, there will be nothing "grown." I submit that the same idea applies to the "seeds" of creation, insomuch as if God did not constantly accompany creation throughout the evolutionary process, the potential of these "seeds" would never materialize or become actual.
41. Blowers, *Drama of the Divine Economy*, 156.

things no longer created simultaneously but rather separately in its own due time, made according to their causes which were created simultaneously . . . under another aspect they are in seeds, in which they are found again as quasi-primordial causes which derive from creatures that have come forth according to the causes which God first stored up in the world.[42]

McGrath describes Augustine's theological movements here as follows: "Augustine's basic argument is that God created the world complete with a series of dormant multiple potencies, which were actualized in the future through divine providence . . . God must be thought of as creating in that first moment the potencies for all the kinds of living things that would come later, including humanity."[43] This process of development, Augustine contends, is governed by fundamental laws, which reflect the will of their creator; indeed, "God has established fixed laws governing the production of kinds and qualities of beings, bringing them out of concealment into full view."[44] Augustine saw three phases of creation: the "unchangeable forms in the Word of God," "seminal seeds" created in the instant of creation, and a later "springing forth" in the course of time.

It is important to point out that Augustine was not some kind of a pre-Darwinist. He thought, for example, that species were immutable and were not the product of common descent. What is striking about him, however, is his insistence on understanding and incorporating the best available non-theological thinking into our religious views. His thinking changed in some ways in the process, and his writings are somewhat contradictory, confusing, and—dare I say—even confused at points. Over the years he fluctuated—or, rather, vacillated—between allegorical interpretations and literal views. He believed, in the end, apparently that God created everything in an instant and that he described it for us as being completed in six normal days for the sake of our comprehension.

AUGUSTINE, FORMLESS MATTER, AND SIMULTANEOUS CREATION

According to Rowan Williams in *Augustine Through the Ages*, any contention that God made the world out of preexistent formless matter is inadequate,[45]

---

42. Augustine, *Literal Meaning of Genesis* (trans. Hammond), 189.
43. McGrath, *Fine-Tuned Universe*, 102.
44. Augustine, *Literal Meaning of Genesis* (trans. Hammond), 191.
45. R. Williams, "Creation," 251–54.

and "no sense" can be made out of the suggestion—in view of Augustine's writings found in such titles as *The Confessions*, *De fide et symbolo* (2.2), and *De Genesi adversus Manichaeos* (1.55–57)—that God makes "creation" out of preexistent formless matter. When God "creates," he dissipates darkness and inaugurates light, but he does not use an "eternal, uncreated abyss of disorder."[46] Instead, the "formlessness" of Genesis 1:2 refers not to an imposition of form on shapelessness—for to be entirely and completely without forma means to have no existence at all—but instead to the "setting in being of a living system destine to grow toward beauty and order."[47] Hannah Arendt agrees: "As Supreme Being, God is the quintessence of Being, namely self-sufficiency, which needs no help from the outside and actually has nothing outside itself . . ." In fact, "God needs no assistance from anything else in the act of creation as though he were one who did not suffice himself."[48]

Since being is "immutable," it is simultaneously the ultimate limit of both the farthest removed past and the most distant future. The creator remains forever identically the same, independent of his creation and whatever may happen within it. His eternity is not a different temporal mode, but, strictly speaking, no-time. Even his "operations" cannot be temporally understood "in intervals of time," except that one may say that they are all happening "at the same time" (*simul*).[49] The universe seen as God's creation must be understood as containing all things simultaneously, for "God created all things at once," and they exist in a hidden way just as all those things which in time grow into a tree are invisibly in the very seed and in this sense simultaneous with the whole of creation.[50] Indeed, Augustine takes an unexploited idea from Ambrose, and argues that in reality the seven days of creation constitute one day recurring seven times:

> The more likely explanation, therefore, is this: these seven days of our time, although all the seven days of creation in name and in numbering, follow one another in succession and mark off the division of time, but those first six days occurred in a form unfamiliar to us as intrinsic principles within the created. Hence evening and morning, light and darkness, that is, day and night, did not produce the changes that they do for us with the motion of the sun. This we are certainly forced to admit with regard to

---

46. R. Williams, "Creation," 251.
47. Williams, "Creation," 252.
48. Arendt, *Love & Saint Augustine*, 21.
49. Arendt, *Love & Saint Augustine*, 55–56.
50. Arendt, *Love & Saint Augustine*, 58.

the first three days, which are recorded and numbered before the creation of the heavenly bodies.

Why, then, does the Genesis narrative recount six days of creation and one day of rest? Augustine answers, "The reason is that those who cannot understand the meaning of the text, *He created all things together*, cannot arrive at the meaning of scripture unless the narrative proceeds slowly step by step."[51] So then, one may surmise that the seven-day scheme in scripture pertains to the frailty of human understanding; that is, it is an accommodation,[52] and not to be taken literally. Indeed, it is the manner in which scripture speaks "with the limitations of human language in addressing men of limited understanding, while at the same time teaching a lesson to be understood by the reader who is able."[53] This is an example of the muddled thinking that I earlier alluded to with regard to Augustine's interpretation of Gen 1–3. Indeed, he herein exposits that the whole of creation took place in one simultaneous instance, contradicting his own claim to not be specific with regard to his interpretations. In fact, "There can be no mistake that Augustine teaches that God created everything simultaneously in the beginning."[54] Some things, according to Augustine, were made immediately in full form, whereas others were made in potential form.

AUGUSTINIAN VIEWS OF CREATION IN *DE GENESI AD LITTERAM*

Moreover, in *De Genesi ad litteram*, Augustine develops this idea in that he uses the terms, alternately, of *rationes causales* and *rationes seminales*. These terms, however, refer to an unfolding of potentiation that was already there—from the beginning. It is not a true "evolution," per se. Indeed, these *rationes* specify the manner in which things—already upon Earth—may be acted upon by God. Indeed, McGrath notes that perhaps the most significant aspect of Augustine's theology of creation rests upon his usage of the terminology of *rationes seminales* and *rationes causales*.[55] The idea behind Augustine's postulations of the *rationes* is that God created the world with

---

51. Augustine, *Literal Meaning of Genesis* (trans. Hammond), 192.
52. Jaki, *Genesis 1 Through the Ages*, 86.
53. Augustine, *Literal Meaning of Genesis* (trans. Hammond), 196.
54. Young, "Contemporary Relevance of Augustine's View of Creation," 65.
55. McGrath, *Fine-Tuned Universe*, 101. Cf. McMullin, *Evolution and Creation*, 1–58, for a particularly illuminating account of these important Latin terms.

a series of dormant potencies, which were only actualized in time (i.e., the future) through continued divine providence.

So then, in Augustine's view within his mature work on the literal interpretation of Genesis, God did not fully create the world with mature plants and animals ready-made, as it were. Augustine flatly rejects such a postulation as being inconsistent with scripture. Rather, Augustine posits in his mature literal interpretation of Genesis that God created in the primal moments the potencies for all kinds of living things that would come (or, as I say, "evolve") later, including humanity. Augustine illustrates this principle in mentioning the case of a tree growing from a germinal seed:

> In the seed, then, there was present invisibly everything that would develop in time into a tree. And we must visualize the world in the same way, when God made all things together, as having all things as having all things that were made in it and with it . . . includ[ing] also the beings which the earth produced potentially and causally before they emerged in the course of time.[56]

Notably, Augustine herein does not suggest that these "seeds" are to be understood as physical entities that were embedded within the original creation, unlike the how the actual tree seeds lie in the ground. Rather, he seems to have perceived the m to be dormant "virtual" potencies, which enabled the world to emerge in its own way and in its own time. So then, according to the mature Augustine's *Literal Interpretation of Genesis*, God's creation extends from actualities to potentialities, of which all were "bestowed" into the primal act of creation and origination.[57] Indeed, Augustine writes that "These were made by God in the beginning, when he made the world, and simultaneously created all things, which were to be unfolded in the ages to come. They are perfected . . . They have, however, just begun, since in them are the seeds, as it were, of the future perfections that would arise from their hidden state, and which would be manifested at the appropriate time."[58] These processes of development are governed by fundamental laws, for Augustine, which reveal and reflect the will of their creator.

---

56. Augustine, *Literal Meaning of Genesis*, 5.23.45.
57. McGrath, *Fine-Tuned Universe*, 103.
58. Augustine, *Refutation of the Manichees*, 6.11.18.

AUGUSTINIAN VIEWS OF CREATION IN *THE CONFESSIONS*

In *The Confessions* 12.6–13, Augustine interprets the first verse of Genesis to mean that God, in all his majesty and glory, creates by establishing the two extreme cases of creaturely reality. Before God created in the "days" of creation, in fact, the Bible tells us that he established the heavens and the Earth. So then, independent of temporal succession, apparently, God brings into existence the maximally endowed level of reality, the "heaven of heavens," which is essentially an "intellectual sphere," and the Earth, which is essentially something approaching pure potentiality or formlessness.[59]

For Augustine, an allegorical approach to the seven days of creation is first employed in his early writing *On Genesis Against the Manicheans*. In this early title, Augustine seeks to bypass Manichean objections to the literal sense of Genesis 1–3, as well as the overtly (overly?) anthropomorphic presentation of God therein. He does this by laying out the seven days of creation as an allegory of the redemptive history of mankind, running from Adam to Noah, Noah to Abraham, Abraham to David, David to the exile, and thereafter to the advent of Christ.[60] He did this, presumably, because "words can in no sense express how God made and created heaven and earth and every creature."[61] This early work shows that Augustine cannot—yet!—concur with a literal interpretation of the text (more on this later). Indeed, "I wanted to see what I could accomplish in the laborious and difficult task of literal interpretation; and I collapsed under the weight of a burden I could not bear. Before completing even one book, I gave up a task that was too much for me."[62]

Earlier in this work, Augustine deflects the Manichean skepticism about how it is possible to have days "pass" without a veritable sun to mark them (note the sun was created on the third day, according to the Genesis account). Augustine notes, "we are left with the interpretation that in that period of time the divisions between the works were called evening because of the completion of the work that was done, and morning because of the beginning of the work that was to come. Scripture clearly says this after the likeness of human works."[63] Indeed, for he also writes, "how could there be

---

59. Williams, *Augustine Through the Ages*, 253.
60. Brown, *Days of Creation*, 46.
61. Augustine, "Refutation of the Manichees," 66.
62. Augustine, *Retractationes*, as quoted by Taylor, in Augustine, *Literal Meaning of Genesis*, 2.
63. Augustine, "Refutation of the Manichees," 69. This statement is akin to a modern interpretation regarding Genesis known as the "day-age theory," but it is not

days before there was time, if time began with the course of lights, which Scripture says were made on the fourth day? Or was this the arrangements set forth according to what human frailty is used to and by the law conveying exalted things to the humble in a humble fashion?"[64]

Earlier, in *A Refutation of the Manichees* (ca. 388 CE), Augustine utilizes the seven days as an allegory of the Christian's spiritual journey. In this text, allegory is utilized as an interpretive device, for it unlocks a richness of meaning that transcends the literal narrative.[65] Further, Augustine even employs the imagery of formless matter in this early text. Indeed, he writes: "So then, the first thing to be made was basic material, unsorted and unformed, out of which all the things would be made which have been sorted out and formed; I think the Greeks call it chaos. This, you see, what we read in another place, as said in praise of God: You have made the world from unformed materials" (i.e., Wis 11:17).[66] In this early text, he expounded why the unformed material spoken of in the opening verses of Genesis could nevertheless be called "heaven and earth," by invoking Jesus of Nazareth, noting that "the Lord also talks in this way of speaking, when he says: *I will not call you slave any longer, because a slave does not know what his master is doing; but I have called you friends, because I have made known to you everything I have heard from my Father* (Jn 15:15) . . . not because this had already been done, but because it was most certainly going to be done . . . So too the material world could be called heaven and earth, from which heaven and earth had not yet been made, but nonetheless was not going to be made from anything else."[67]

According to McKeough, all creatures were contained potentially in this formless matter; the inherent powers in the formless matter acted under the laws of nature in accordance with the divine command.[68]

In *The Literal Meaning of Genesis* (ca. 415), Augustine confronts the literal understanding of the Genesis account once more, flirting at first with a plainly literal understanding of creation in six ordinary solar days,

---

an exact parallel. Nevertheless, it is remarkable that Augustine thought such a millennium before the age of "uniformitarianism" in geology was onset, which means that the laws we can discern today in effect to change the Earth also were in effect in yesteryears (Cf. Hutton and Lyell for this point). Indeed, in uniformitarianism, "the present is the key to the past." Augustine was, undoubtedly, ahead of his time in this regard (Cf. Fergusson, *Creation*, 10).

64. Augustine, *Literal Meaning of Genesis* (trans. Hammond), 43.
65. Brown, *Days of Creation*, 46.
66. Augustine, "Refutation of the Manichees," 47.
67. Augustine, "Refutation of the Manichees," 46.
68. McKeough, "Meaning of the Rationes Seminales in St. Augustine," 23.

considering the first three days of creation in the sun's absence to be explicable perhaps by means of an intermittent or orbiting light source, much like that which was put forward by his predecessor, Basil.[69] However, he dismisses such, for it seemingly is indefensible, noting: "As for material light, it is not clear by what circular motion or going forth and returning it could have produced the succession of day and night before the making of the heaven called firmament, in which heavenly bodies were made."

Augustine's reading of the Latin version of the Bible—particularly of *Ecclesiasticus* 18:1, which reads, "He who remains for eternity created all things at once," as well as the seemingly "suddenness" of creation in his Latin version of Psalm 32:9—seemingly reinforced Augustine's instinctive (Neo-?)Platonist[70] inclination toward an idealist understanding of the term "day" in Genesis.[71] Indeed, Augustine states further,

> In this narrative of creation Holy Scripture has said of the Creator that He completed His works in six days, and elsewhere, without contradicting this, it has been written of the same Creator that He created all things together. It therefore follows that he who created all together also created these six or seven days—or rather the one day, repeated six or seven times. So why then was there any need for six distinct days to be set forth in the narrative one after the other? The reason is that those who cannot understand the meaning of the text, He created all things together, cannot understand the meaning of the Scripture unless the narrative proceeds slowly in this stepwise manner ... For this Scripture text that narrates the works of God according to the days mentioned above, and that Scripture text that says God created all things together, are both true.[72]

Importantly, it seems as though Augustine "hardened" in his interpretation of Genesis over time. Henry Chadwick would seemingly agree with this point, noting that at first, "Like most ancient writers, Augustine

---

69. Notably, Basil held that on the first six days, God did not truly create various beings, but created the power to generate them instead (Kim, *Augustine's Changing Interpretations of Genesis 1–3*, 146; cf. McKeough, "Meaning of the Rationes Seminales in St. Augustine," 22).

70. Henry Chadwick describes Augustine's conversion to Christianity as a marriage of Neo-Platonism and Christianity, with the latter transforming elements of the former (Chadwick, *Augustine*, 25–29). Christian would seemingly agree with Chadwick, noting that there are not "two Augustines," so to speak (i.e., the Neo-Platonist and the Christian dogmatist), but only one Augustine instead (Christian, "Creation of the World," 323).

71. Brown, *Days of Creation*, 47.

72. Augustine, *On Genesis*, 4.33.52.

assumes that even matter-of-fact narratives are polyvalent."[73] However, within the *Literal Meaning of Genesis* text, Augustine notes that the ideal outcome of interpretation is to identify "the meaning intended by the author. But if this is not clear, then at least we should choose an interpretation in keeping with the context of Scripture and in harmony with our faith."[74] Not only this, but understanding that in the conceptual world in which Augustine inhabited with his Alexandrian forebears, mathematics reveals the structure of reality, and the number six was ideal for expressing the perfection of creation: indeed, "God created all His work in six days because six is a perfect number."[75] So then, in some sense, Augustine views the narrative in Genesis 1–3 as a literary device to portray eternal truths. Even this, however, is a little confuddled in Augustine's works. Indeed, he at once seemingly views the "days of creation" as figurative, but then views the creation of Adam and Eve, and the approximately six-thousand-year-old Earth (now, note, not then!) as literal. It is muddled indeed. Moreover, at the onset of the *Literal Meaning of Genesis* text, Augustine decides to explain Genesis 1–3 as "a faithful record of what happened," as well as "according to the plain meaning of the historical facts, not according to future events which they foreshadow."[76] But how can this be a literal interpretation—that is, of what really happened, to put words in Augustine's mouth—if in fact he spiritualizes the meaning of "days" in the text itself?[77] It's a muddled mess. So then, Augustine's usage of the terminology of "literal" stretches the meaning of the term to where it is unrecognizable, minimizing historical reality. Augustine says as much, seemingly, noting that "Whoever, then, does not accept the meaning that my limited powers have been able to discover or conjecture but seeks in the enumeration of the days of creation a different meaning, which might not be understood in a prophetical or figurative sense, but literally and more aptly, . . . let him search and find a solution with God's help."[78] Greene-McCreight, then, rightly refers to the "slippage" in Augustine's usage of the terminology "literal."[79]

---

73. Chadwick, "Augustine," 67.

74. Augustine, *On Genesis*, 1.21.41. McGrath agrees, noting, "Augustine understood the term "literal" to mean something like "in the sense intended by the author" (McGrath, *Fine-Tuned Universe*, 98).

75. Augustine, *On Genesis*, 4.7.14. It is interesting to note, in fact, that the number six is the smallest number that is a sum of all its factors (i.e., 1+2+3=6).

76. Augustine, *On Genesis*, 1.17.34.

77. For this point of spiritualizing the meaning of the text away, see Caiazza, "Augustine on Evolution, Time, Memory," 119.

78. Augustine, *On Genesis*, 4.28.45.

79. For the meaning of literal interpretation in *De Genesi ad litteram*, see

Augustine's use of the key terms for hermeneutics and exegesis such as *ad litteram, historia, similitudo, allegoria,* and *figura* is most erratic and inconsistent, which causes immense difficulty in studying his exegesis.[80] Augustine does not offer a consistent definition of literal and figurative interpretation. Also, his view on distinction and relationship between literal and figurative interpretation changes from his earlier to later commentaries. In *A Refutation of the Manichees,* Augustine does not give a clear explanation of what he does mean by literal interpretation. He seems to have a very strict definition of literal interpretation.[81] He considers a literal interpretation as "tak[ing] everything that is said here absolutely literally."[82] His understanding of figurative interpretation is quite comprehensive. At first, he seems to regard figurative interpretation as almost synonymous with spiritual interpretation.

Indeed, to interpret the image of God as referring to the internal man where reason and intelligence are found is a spiritual or figurative interpretation, since "in the Catholic school of doctrine the faithful who have a spiritual understanding do not believe that God is circumscribed in a bodily shape."[83] That is, figurative interpretation includes dealing with spiritual or incorporeal things beyond what the letter sounds like. Figurative interpretation also means to interpret a text as prefiguring something to come. For example, to interpret the seven days of creation as prefiguring the seven ages of human history is a figurative interpretation.[84] Augustine writes, "If, however, no other way is available of reaching an understanding of what is written that is religious and worthy of God, except by supposing that it has all been set before us in a figurative sense and in riddles, we have the authority of the apostles for doing this, seeing that they solved so many riddles in the books of the Old Testament in this manner."[85]

In *De Genesi ad litteram imperfectus,* Augustine writes,

> So about these words, In the beginning God made heaven and earth, one may inquire whether they are only to taken in an historical sense, or whether they also have some figurative meaning, and how they agree with the gospel, and what the cause is of this book's beginning in this way. As regards the historical

---

Greene-McCreight, *Ad litteram,* 32–49.

80. For Augustine's usage of these terms, see Bernard, "*In figura.*"
81. See Teske, "Introduction," in Augustine, *On Genesis,* 17.
82. Augustine, "Refutation of the Manichees," 72.
83. Augustine, "Refutation of the Manichees," 57.
84. Augustine, "Refutation of the Manichees," 62–67.
85. Augustine, "Refutation of the Manichees," 72.

sense, we ask what in the beginning means; that is, whether it is in the beginning of time, or in the beginning, in the very Wisdom of God, because the Son of God actually called himself the beginning.[86]

In *De Genesi ad litteram*, Augustine presents a different view on literal and figurative interpretation. He writes,

> So if we take it like this, the making of evening would seem to signify the sin of rational creatures, while the making of morning would mean their restoration. But this is an interpretation on the lines of prophetic allegory, which is not what we have undertaken in this work. We undertook, you see, to talk here about the scriptures according to their proper meaning of what actually happened, not according to their riddling, enigmatic reference to future events.[87]

According to the later Augustine, Genesis is a historical book like 1 and 2 Kings. Thus, to interpret the opening chapters of Genesis in a literal sense is to take the text as history, that is, what actually happened. Stressing the historicity of the account of paradise, he continues,

> So then they should pay very close attention to where this assumption of theirs is leading them, and try hard with us to take all these primordial events of the narrative as actually having happened in the way described. Is there anyone, after all, who would not support them as they turned their minds next to working out what lessons these things have for us in their figurative meaning, whether about spiritual natures and experiences or even about events to come in the future?[88]

In this passage, Augustine contends that the literal meaning should be sought first and then the figurative meaning may be drawn. In a similar way, he writes, "What first has to be demonstrated about all the things that are written here is that they actually happened and were actually done, and only after that, if need be, should any lessons be drawn about their further significance."[89] So then, what he emphasizes is the order of interpretation, that is, literal interpretation first and then figurative interpretation. In these passages, Augustine means by figurative meanings lessons about spiritual nature or events to come in the future.

---

86. Augustine, "Unfinished Literal Commentary on Genesis," 116.
87. Augustine, *Literal Meaning of Genesis* (trans. Hammond), 183.
88. Augustine, *Literal Meaning of Genesis* (trans. Hammond), 348.
89. Augustine, *Literal Meaning of Genesis* (trans. Hammond), 252.

One may inquire whether they are only to be taken in the historical sense, or whether they also have some figurative meaning, and how they agree with the gospel.

Augustine further notes,

> The whole Old Testament Scripture, to those who diligently desire to know it, is handed down with a four-fold sense—historical, aetiological, analogical, allegorical. Don't think me clumsy in using Greek terms, because in the first place these were the terms I was taught, and I do not venture to pass on to you anything else than what I have received. You will notice also that amongst us Latins, there are no words in common use to express these ideas. If I were to attempt a translation of them I might be even clumsier. If I were to use circumlocutions I should be less speedy in my exposition. This only I ask you to believe that, however I stray, I write nothing merely in the interests of a proudly inflated style. In Scripture, according to the historical sense, we are told what has been written or done. Sometimes the historical fact is simply that such and such a thing was written. According to the aetiological sense we are told for what cause something has been done or said. According to the analogical sense we are shown that the Old and New Testaments do not conflict. According to the allegorical sense we are taught that everything in Scripture is not to be taken literally but must be understood figuratively.[90]

In this chapter, we have seen a presentation of Augustine's theolog(ies) of creation through examining his views of "seminal seeds," simultaneous creation, and his interpretive acrobatics with regard to Genesis 1–3. As a concluding thought, I would like to quote Augustine extensively, and note that whereas his initial persuasion on this matter was sound, he nevertheless contradicted it in his own writings, to our corporate detriment. If only he had in truth adhered thoroughly to the comments that follow . . .

> There is knowledge to be had, after all, about the earth, about the sky, about the other elements of this world, about the movements and revolutions or even the magnitude and distances of the constellations, about the predictable eclipses of moon and sun, about the cycles of years and seasons, about the nature of animals, fruits, stones and everything else of this kind. And it frequently happens that even non-Christians will have knowledge of this sort in a way that they can substantiate with scientific arguments or experiments. Now it is quite disgraceful and

90. Augustine, "Unfinished Literal Commentary on Genesis," 115.

disastrous, something to be on one's guard against at all costs, that they should ever hear Christians spouting what they claim our Christian literature has to say on these topics, and talking such nonsense that they can scarcely contain their laughter when they see them to be *toto caelo*, as the saying goes, wide of the mark. And what is so vexing is not that misguided people should be laughed at, as that our authors should be assumed by outsiders to have held such views and, to the great detriment of those about whose salvation we are so concerned, should be written off and consigned to the waste paper basket as so many ignoramuses. Whenever, you see, they catch out some members of the Christian community making mistakes on a subject which they know inside out, and defending their hollow opinions on the authority of our books, on what grounds are they going to trust those books on the resurrection of the dead and the hope of eternal life and the kingdom of heaven, when they suppose they include any number of mistakes and fallacies on matters which they themselves have been able to master either by experiment or by the surest of calculations? It is impossible to say what trouble and grief such rash, self-assured know-alls cause the more cautious and experienced brothers and sisters. Whenever they find themselves challenged and taken to task for some shaky and false theory of theirs by people who do not recognize the authority of our books, they try to defend what they have aired with the most frivolous temerity and patent falsehood by bringing forward these same sacred books to justify it. Or they even quote from memory many things said in them which they imagine will provide them with valid evidence, *not understanding either what they are saying, or the matters on which they are asserting themselves* (1 Tim 1:7).[91]

---

91. Augustine, *Literal Meaning of Genesis* (trans. Hammond), 186–87.

7

Nondualistic (Macro-)Evolution

An Exercise in Mystical Immanence and Divine Involvement in an Evolutionary World

INTRODUCTION

Whether Ultimate Reality is to be conceived as a personal God or an impersonal principle somehow at work in the world is an issue which tends to divide major world religions into opposing camps. Furthermore, even within a given religion philosophers and theologians may differ on how God or Ultimate Reality is to be conceived. It is a commonplace that while Asian philosophy is nondualistic, the West, because of its uncritical reliance on Greek-derived intellectual standards, is dualistic. Dualism is a deep-seated habit of thinking and acting in all spheres of life through the prism of binary opposites, which leads to paralyzing practical and theoretical difficulties. In general, Asian philosophy can provide assistance for the future a Christian nondualism, even though the West finds Asian philosophical nondualism, especially that of Mahayana Buddhism, nihilistic. However, postmodern thought may deliver us from the dualisms embedded and embodied in modernity.

The West already contains within one of its more marginalized roots, that of ancient Hebrew culture, a prephilosophical form of nondualism which makes possible a new form of nondualism, one to which the West can subscribe. This new nondualism, directly inspired by Buddhism but not identical to it, is an epistemological, ontological, metaphysical, and praxical middle way[1] both for the West and also between East and West.[2] Many scholars, seemingly, think it to be true that the Western mindset is necessarily committed to dualism, and by extension, dualistic theism. But Paul Tillich demonstrates that the natural world can have no being itself without the underlying ground of being, that is, God (the Spirit). Indeed, the infinite is precisely the finite, for if it were not, it could not be infinite in truth. As Thatamanil says, the infinite is precisely what it is: not other than the finite.[3]

The definition of mysticism, as used in this chapter, is based upon Ralph Inge's comments that it is "the attempt to realize the presence of the living God in the soul and in nature."[4] A critical component in this definition is the following: in order to know God, mankind must partake of the divine nature itself. If this definition is accepted, among many other feasible and possible ones—notes Julio Savi[5]—the goal of mysticism is the same as the purpose of human life described by Baha'u'llah: "to know [one's] Creator and to attain His Presence."[6] I would like to expand this concept to the entirety of the natural world in what follows, particularly pneumatologically.

GENERAL CHARACTERISTICS OF MYSTICISM

The assumptions of mysticism, as described by Inge, and those of the Baha'i faith, according to Julio Savi, are the same: human beings have a divine nature whose development through practicing the love of God allows their inner vision to become acuter, leading thereby to perceive the presence of God. This perception of the presence of God is usually referred to by mystics and students of mysticism as "mystical experience."[7] The world religious literature is rich in descriptions of mystical experience. Based on these descriptions, scholars have listed a number of its characteristics as follows:[8]

1. Cf. Yong, *Pneumatology and the Christian-Buddhist Dialogue*.
2. Cf. Scarborough, *Comparative Theories of Nonduality*.
3. Thatamanil, *Immanent Divine*, 184.
4. Inge, *Christian Mysticism*, 5.
5. Savi, "Baha'i Faith and the Perennial Mystical Quest," 5.
6. Effendi, *Gleanings from the Writings of Baha'u'llah*, 70.
7. Savi, "Baha'i Faith and the Perennial Mystical Quest," 7.
8. Note that I am indebted to Savi for this list, and I acknowledge such forthrightly, even though I have "massaged" it for my own purposes. See Savi, "Baha'i Faith and the Perennial Mystical Quest," 10–11.

1. A consciousness of the oneness of everything
   Walter Terence Stace describes this consciousness as arising from the exclusion of "all the multiplicity of sensuous or conceptual or other empirical content . . . so that there remains only a void and empty unity."[9] In this condition, the mystic "attains to complete communion with the Absolute Order, and submits to the inflow of its supernal vitality,"[10] and thus experiences what Nicholas of Cusa called *"coincidentia oppositorum"*[11] or "coincidence of contradictories."[12]

2. Timelessness
   Frank C. Happold explains that during a mystical experience the relationships between events "are not capable of being adequately described in terms of past, present, and future, or earlier than, later than. These experiences have a timeless quality."[13]

3. A sense of objectivity or reality
   Happold writes that mystical experiences "are states of knowledge,"[14] a knowledge characterized by a high degree of certitude.

4. Feelings of blessedness, joy, peace, happiness, etc.

5. A feeling that what is apprehended is holy, sacred or divine, including:

   - Ineffability: Mystical experience resembles a feeling and "it is not possible to make a state of feeling clear to one who has not experienced it."[15]

   - Paradoxicality: Mystics frequently feel an urgent need to share their experience with others, and they try to overcome its ineffability through such "linguistic devices as simile, metaphor and paradox, however inadequate these may be for the task."[16]

   - Transience: Mystical experience, with its feeling of timelessness, is seldom prolonged. And yet, some mystics are wholly immersed in their spiritual condition, so that their mystical experience "can become so frequent, so much a way of life, that, in the words of

---

9. Stace, *Mysticism and Philosophy*, 79.
10. Underhill, *Mysticism*, 432–33.
11. Nicholas of Cusa, "Apologia Doctae Ignorantiae," 2.15.
12. Hopkins, *Nicholas of Cusa's Debate with John Wenk*, 470.
13. Happold, *Mysticism*, 47–48.
14. Happold, *Mysticism*, 45.
15. Happold, *Mysticism*, 45.
16. Gilbert, *Elements of Mysticism*, 89.

St. John of the Cross, "the soul has it in its power to abandon itself, whenever it wills, to this sweet sleep of love."[17]

- Passivity: The mystics perceive themselves as the object of their own experience, as deprived of any will, as being seized by an outward power.

- Nonreality of the ordinary self: Usually there is a strict connection between the perception of the self, on the one hand, and sensory perception, awareness of time, and the feeling of being willingly active, on the other. In a mystical experience all of that disappears and, in the words of Rudolf Otto, the mystic perceives "the self . . . the personal 'I', as something not perfectly or essentially real, or even as mere nullity."[18] The perception of the self expands and brings the individual closer to her inner self, a reality that mystic Meister Eckhart calls "*scintilla animae*" (the spark of the soul).[19]

- Side phenomena: That is, "special altered states—visions, locutions, raptures and the like—which admittedly have played a large part in mysticism but which many mystics have insisted do not constitute the essence of the encounter with God."[20]

Many scholars agree with Dom Cuthbert Butler—whose text on Western mysticism has been described as "a masterly exhibition of the religious and psychological normality of the Christian contemplative life, as developed by its noblest representatives"[21]—on the opinion that:

> "Essential mysticism should not be identified with occasional accidental concomitants, as visions, revelations, raptures, or other psycho-physical phenomena', and that 'the title mystical' should not be given 'to curious experiences and manifestations bordering on those of Spiritism; to intimations, second sight, telepathy; or religious 'queer stories'. For all such phenomena there is an accepted scientific term: they are 'psychic' not 'mystic.'"[22]

"True mysticism" seems here described as a state of communion between a believer and the soul of the manifestation of God that conveys the Spirit of God unto him or her, bringing "such ecstasy of joy that life becomes

---

17. Happold, *Mysticism*, 55.
18. Otto, *Idea of the Holy*, 21.
19. Eckhart, *Passion for Creation*, 277.
20. McGinn, *Foundations of Mysticism*, xvii–xviii.
21. Underhill, *Mysticism*, xi.
22. Butler, *Western Mysticism*, lxii.

nothing." This communion is so important as to be identified with "the secret, inner meaning of life" and with "the core of religious faith."[23] Through their studies of the descriptions of the mystics, scholars have inferred that many factors may contribute to bringing about mystical experience:[24]

- A personal predisposition, which may also be ignored by the subject.
- An act of will on the part of the subject, which may express itself as an active search for God before her experience begins.
- Specific stimuli, whose nature depends on the mystic's personality, upbringing, and religious, social and cultural background. These stimuli are synthesized by Robert Andrew Gilbert as follows: aspects of nature (commonly water, trees, flowers and their scent, sunrise and sunset), music; poetry; creative work; sexual love; natural beauty; sacred places; prayer, meditation and worship; the visual arts; literature in various forms; and personal relationships.[25]

IMMANENCE, TRANSCENDENCE, AND NONDUALITY

Gilles Deleuze and Félix Guattari, in *What Is Philosophy?*, state: "Immanence can be said to be the burning issue of all philosophy because it takes on all the dangers that philosophy must confront, all the condemnations, persecutions, and repudiations that it undergoes."[26] Immanence and mysticism, seemingly, go hand in hand. Or, rather, nonduality and mysticism do. Or, perhaps, a decidedly *nondual* version of immanence and mysticism do. I will, for lack of better terminology, still hesitantly employ the term "immanence" in this chapter, but let the reader understand that I am employing it 1) reluctantly, and 2) guardedly. This chapter asserts that the processes of (macro-)evolution itself are a mystical experience, as they exhibit and manifest the profundity of (God) the Spirit's creativity within the physical realm through my newly coined terminology of "divine involvement."

I will, in the course of this chapter, assert a radical panentheistic immanence, bordering upon pantheism. But it is not truly pantheism, for, as Tillich says, God is neither alongside things nor even "above" them; rather, he is nearer to them than they are to themselves; "He is their creative

---

23. Savi, "Baha'i Faith and the Perennial Mystical Quest," 16.
24. Cf. Gilbert, *Elements of Mysticism*, 87–88.
25. Gilbert, *Elements of Mysticism*, 87.
26. Deleuze and Guattari, *What Is Philosophy?*, 45.

ground, here and now, always and everywhere."[27] Tillich is an important conversation partner herein because his theology "amounts to a twentieth-century distillation of the history of Christian mystical theology."[28] It is more accurate therefore to speak of the "reality of God," which points to his true nature as being-itself. This insight, says Tillich, enables us to take a first step towards solving the problem of the transcendence and the immanence of God, for "as the power of being, God transcends both every being and also the totality of being. Being-itself infinitely transcends every finite being. There is no proportion or gradation between the finite and the infinite."[29] Indeed, within Tillich's corpus, one can discern the footprints (or shadow), or even voices, of such great historical mystics as Meister Eckhart and Nicholas of Cusa, who themselves propagated and "kept alive a radical sense of divine presence."[30] Therefore, Tillich's theology incorporates one of, if not the, most robust accounts of divine immanence on tap today.

I assert that *creatio ex deo*, creation out of God, can be made consistent with a nondual, panentheistic perspective upon divine involvement in an evolutionary world. This *creatio ex deo* removes the stumbling block of the seemingly unbridgeable chasm between God and the world, particularly in and through the work of the Spirit. As a Process theologian, I assert that this panentheistic concept of divine involvement in an evolutionary world envisions a God and natural world relationship that is not based upon duality. Thus, this chapter avers that God's Spirit is everywhere present and pervasive within the natural world, but also exceeds it, though this is no duality, for the reality of God's Spirit is supraspatial (i.e., God's Spirit is beyond spatiality) and supranatural (i.e., God's Spirit is beyond naturality).[31] As such, the natural world is not external to the divine reality, in any wise. Rather, God's reality is determined by his sic relation to the natural world

---

27. Tillich, *Systematic Theology*, 2:7.
28. Thatamanil, *Immanent Divine*, 9.
29. Tillich, *Ultimate Concern*, 263.
30. Thatamanil, *Immanent Divine*, 9.
31. Note that whereas Tillich uses the term "supranatural" to refer to what is ordinarily called "supernaturalism," I use the term as being referent to what is beyond nature but not wholly outside of it. In fact, Tillich claims that the entire and "basic intention of my doctrine of God" is to go beyond the naturalism and supranaturalism (again note his distinctive meaning for supra-) (Tillich, *Systematic Theology*, 2:5). Indeed, according to Tillich, whatever conception of divinity that portrays God as intervening from the outside into causal networks within the world is "supranatural" (Tillich, *Systematic Theology*, 2:5). This supernaturalism, as I refer to it (but supra- according to Tillich) is problematic because it is not only contra science, but also because it pictures God as regularly disrupting the "inviolability of the created structures of the finite" (Tillich, *Systematic Theology*, 2:6).

insomuch as his involvement (or activity) therein is based upon being the very ground of creativity and *being* itself. And that itself *is* mystical. Tillich again is useful here, in part because he understands being-itself to be a "dynamic creative power" that "gives rise to what it grounds."[32] Giving rise to what it grounds, I submit, is an apt metaphor for how God "creates" (if I may use such a loaded word) through the processes of macroevolution and also permeates the natural world thereafter.

TILLICHIAN NONDUALITY

The focus of Christian nondualism is on bringing the human closer to God and realizing a "oneness" with the divine.[33] According to David R. Loy, the concept of nonduality is usually associated with various kinds of absolute idealism, or mystical traditions in the East—and as a result, many modern philosophers are poorly informed on the topic. Increasingly, however, nonduality is finding its way into Western philosophical debates.[34] Loy in fact distinguishes five different conceptions of nonduality:[35]

1. The negation of dualistic thinking in pairs of opposites. The Yin-Yang symbol of Taoism symbolizes the transcendence of this dualistic way of thinking.

2. *Monism*, the nonplurality of the world. Although the phenomenal world appears as a plurality of "things," in reality they are "of a single cloth."

3. *Advaita*, the nondifference of subject and object, or nonduality between subject and object.

4. *Advaya*, the identity of phenomena and the Absolute, the "nonduality of duality and nonduality."

5. *Mysticism*, a mystical unity between God and mankind.

John J. Thatamanil seizes upon Tillich's idea of ecstatic experience as the closest one gets to mending the gap between immanence and transcendence. An important characteristic of the ecstatic experience is an "inbreaking" of the divine into existence—not vice versa. Tillich's vision, dynamic as it is, denies that Ultimate Reality is an unchanging absolute that resists

32. Thatamanil, *Immanent Divine*, 11.
33. Charlton, *Non-Dualism in Eckhart, Julian of Norwich and Traherne*, 2.
34. Loy, *Nonduality: In Buddhism and Beyond*, 6.
35. Loy, *Nonduality: A Study in Comparative Philosophy*, 17–25.

change—nay, is incapable of it!—and leads one to an immanence that might itself be called nondual.[36] A dualistic conceptioning of God is at least problematic for, if not devastating to, twenty-first-century theology because it "transforms the infinity of God into a finiteness which is merely an extension of the categories of finitude."[37] What Tillich means by this is that using a dualistic notion of God subjects God to the categories of time and space, along with substance ontology.[38] Indeed, the God of dualism is an entity that has his "home" in heaven above, but nevertheless acts within time, interacts with other beings causally, and is merely one substance among others, which is a self-defeating proposition to the very idea itself, and amounts to much dastardly consequences. "Such a God is just one item in a universe that proves to be more encompassing than God is."[39] This is the unlaudable conclusion that pushes Tillich to claim that God is the creative ground of being. This antidualistic character of Tillich's thought is underappreciated, to be sure.

So then, is naturalism the choice for Tillich, in view of such? Not in any manner! A strict naturalism merely "identifies God with the universe, with its essence or with special powers within it."[40] Although Tillich views naturalism as the preferable option over and above supernaturalism (what he terms supra-), it is nevertheless problematic in part because it "denies the infinite distance between the whole of finite things and their infinite ground, with the consequence that the term 'God' becomes interchangeable with the term 'universe' and therefore semantically superfluous."[41] Tillich indicates that God's life is life as spirit. He notes that humanity in their theologizing have always distinguished between the abyss of the divine and the fullness of its content, that is, between divine depth and divine *logos*. The first of these, divine depth, has historically been applied to the Father, and the second of these—divine *logos*—is generally assumed to be the Son. Indeed, the first principle makes God be "God," as it is the rudiment of his:

> "majesty, the unapproachable intensity of his being, the inexhaustible ground of being in which everything has its origin . . . The classical term *logos* is most adequate for the second principle, that of meaning and structure . . . Without the second principle the first principle would be chaos, burning fire, but it

36. Thatamanil, *Immanent Divine*, 23.
37. Tillich, *Systematic Theology*, 2:6.
38. Thatamanil, *Immanent Divine*, 19.
39. Thatamanil, *Immanent Divine*, 19.
40. Tillich, *Systematic Theology*, 2:6.
41. Tillich, *Systematic Theology*, 2:7.

would not be the creative ground . . . As the actualization of the other two principles, the Spirit is the third principle. Both power and meaning are contained in it and untied in it. It makes them creative."[42]

I follow Thatamanil in his development of a thorough Christian nondualism by applying his insights from the human predicament, using Tillich, to the concepts of immanent creativity and macroevolution. Tillich is clear that the meaning of transcendence must be conceived differently in our modern era, since God does not inhabit a spatiotemporal realm that is different than the natural world in which we live. Indeed, I assert that the Spirit, who is manifest by immanent creativity in the macroevolutionary process, already participates in the natural world, all of the time, meaning there is not a time when the Spirit is not embedded and embodied within this natural world. In fact, for Thatamanil, the divine life necessarily includes human life insomuch as God (the Spirit) is the creative ground of human life.[43] I agree with this sentiment, but would like to expand it to the entire temporal and natural world, not just human beings per se. As such, the Spirit is not alien to the natural world; rather, it is the very depth of the natural world, the depth to which the Spirit inhabits. Further, then, God as Spirit does not stand over against the natural world; rather, Tillich is quite explicit in stating that God is infinite because he has the finite within himself united with his infinity.[44]

So, therefore, the Spirit is never—ever!—separate from the finite natural world. Indeed, the infinite power of the creative Spirit is forever and always present to the natural world, driving it toward greater complexity in and through the processes of macroevolution. Thus, there is within the natural world an infinite drive toward self-transcendence, whether that "self" be atomic nuclei, atoms, electrons, elements, bacteria, cats, dogs, mushrooms, or people (and so forth, as it were). Entities are never at rest; they are never content with being what they are for the present moment; instead, they forever "strive" to become more than they are through macroevolution, and this in and of itself testifies to both the presence and power of the infinite within the finite, whether that finite entity be atoms or animal species. However, Tillich is not enough to flesh out my nondual interpretation of mystical immanence being expressed in macroevolutionary processes in and

---

42. Tillich, *Systematic Theology*, 1:250–51.

43. What Thatamanil here applies to God generically, I would like to—as indicated by my parenthetical addition—apply to the Spirit specifically. Cf. Thatamanil, *Immanent Divine*, 147.

44. Tillich, *Systematic Theology*, 1:252.

within the natural world, because Tillich himself retains a residual dualism. Thus, there is need to look elsewhere, for example, to the nonsubstantialist theological ontology of one Joseph Bracken, in which Ultimate Reality is perceived to be an overriding activity (or, in my language, "involvement") versus being a substance. Tillich's work has made the path easier to arrive at this mystically immanent, nondualistic macroevolution, for he has set forth the thesis of an internal relationship between being-itself and other beings, and he appeals to Paul the apostle's pneumatology.

In Romans 8:26, divine immanence is experienced as an immanently ecstatic event accomplished by the work of the Spirit that grasps and prays through us when we know not how to pray. I would like to extend this thought to "creation" in general and macroevolution in particular by claiming that it is the Spirit who is the immanent principle of creativity throughout the natural world. In Tillich's theology of Spirit, God approaches humans when they are "grasped" by the power inherent in being-itself and thereafter driven beyond themselves into ecstatic union with divinity.[45] The result of this endeavor is the "mutual immanence" that Tillich so eloquently speaks of in his third volume of *Systematic Theology*.[46] I would like generalize this Tillichian idea and extrapolate it to all of reality.

Instead of the conceptual terms "causality" and "substance," Tillich prefers "a more directly symbolic term, 'the creative and abysmal ground of being.' In this term both naturalistic pantheism, based on the category of substance, and rationalistic theism, based on the category of causality are overcome."[47] "Ground," for Tillich, serves to incorporate the best elements of both causality and substance, but at the same time rejects their literal adequacy. In a sense, then, God can be imagined as a substance inasmuch as beings cannot exist without and apart from God, just as brick mortar cannot exist apart from sand granules. But at the same time, God cannot literally be a substance, or the natural world (and other beings) would not be marked by freedom. Similarly, God can be imagined as a cause amongst other causes, since it is the activity or involvement of God that causes the natural world and hence other beings to be, but God cannot literally be thought a cause because of the freedom of the natural world and other beings. However, God (the Spirit) indeed is the ground of being as well as its depth of being. God (the Spirit's) involvement as the ground of being is neither contingent nor provisional, for, as Tillich himself states, "There is

---

45. Cf. Thatamanil, *Immanent Divine*, 11.
46. Tillich, *Systematic Theology*, 3:114.
47. Tillich, *Systematic Theology*, 1:238.

no divine nature which could be abstracted from his eternal creativity."[48] Indeed, for Tillich, the ground is the very source from which everything emerges: "The ground of being has the character of self-manifestation; it has *logos* character. This is not something added to the divine life; it is the divine life itself."[49] Tillich's God, then, cannot be thought apart from the world.[50]

As Bracken states, "the grounding activity is not an entity, and the entity is other than the grounding activity. At the same time, they are not two since only together, namely, as grounding activity and that which exists in virtue of the grounding activity, are they one concrete reality. This grounding activity, moreover, is infinite because it serves as the ontological ground for literally everything that exists . . . it transcends them all since it is their common ground or source of existence and activity. Whereas entities are inevitably limited or defined by their relations to one another, this grounding activity is strictly unlimited and therefore infinite."[51] Within Bracken's thought, the being of being-itself is *becoming* itself.[52] Thatamanil suggests that the way forward, building on and perhaps correcting some of Tillich's contentions, is to go the route proffered by Bracken: infinite reality must be understood as activity and not as a substance.[53] I agree with such a sentiment. In fact, Thatamanil argues along with Bracken that viewing being-itself as ontological creativity is a wise move, theologically.

This has direct implications for the immanence versus transcendence of God debate, for God cannot be transcendent if by that one means that there is a separation between God and the world. Assuming this latter point, Tillich thus redefines the terminology of "transcendence" insomuch as it is purged of its supranaturalistic overtones, which, by using the term "supranatural," Tillich seemingly means what I ordinarily attribute to the term "supernatural." As such, there is no antagonism between God's transcendence and immanence, so God's immanence does not come at the price of his transcendence, nor vice versa. William Placher rightly calls such a dynamic the "contrastive" account of the debate between transcendence and immanence, one that makes "divine transcendence and involvement in the world into a zero-sum game."[54] Placher analyzes the history of the transcendence versus immanence debate back to the fundamental error of thinking God to

---

48. Tillich, *Systematic Theology*, 2:147.
49. Tillich, *Systematic Theology*, 1:157–58.
50. Thatamanil, *Immanent Divine*, 145.
51. Bracken, "Infinity and the Logic of Non-Dualism," 41.
52. Thatamanil, *Immanent Divine*, 188.
53. Thatamanil, *Immanent Divine*, 188.
54. Placher, *Domestication of Transcendence*, 111.

be one being among others. He contends that "If God were one of the things in the world—as implied by the contrastive account of transcendence—then it would be natural to ask where God is located—in the world or outside it?"[55] And, as Thatamanil notes, either answer militates against the other. Tillich denies this sort of duality and the reified concept of divinity that it necessitates. It is my assertion that nondualistic macroevolution rejects the contrastive account of the transcendence versus immanence debate. Tillich's God does not need to intervene in nature or history to be present there, for in his theology, symbolically speaking, God *is* the power of being in everything, and as such is "the source of all particular powers of being."[56] The volcano, the earthquake, the rogue nation, the nation championing justice, the sinner and the saint—all are ultimately empowered by the source of all being, which is God's creative power. It is in this sense that God can be spoken of as "Almighty."[57] Indeed, for Tillich, all power, understood as "the eternal possibility of resisting non-being," ultimately comes from God. Therefore, "since God as *the* power of being is the source of all particular powers of being, power is divine in its essential nature."[58]

CONCLUSION

Tillich's theology of transitory dualism contains the proverbial seeds of a Christian nonduality. It is my contention that a Christian nondualism in which God is understood to be all in all, a vision in which the correlate is that for God to be anything less than that is no God at all, is a potent vision for twenty-first-century theology, especially with how it is applicable to a mystical understanding of macroevolution. Christian nondualism both asserts and achieves a deep coincidence between immanence and transcendence. Tillich contributes to this view of Christian nondualism by explicating how traditional theism yields impoverished and inadequate views of transcendence and immanence. In their stead, Tillich proffers a vision of God in which he is at once qualitatively transcendent in power, yet also, at the same time, radically immanent by being the ground of being itself.

Several Process-oriented thinkers, myself included, are quite content to think of God not as an entity but as a unifying activity immanent within the cosmic process. Bernard Meland, for example, refers to God not as a

---

55. Placher, *Domestication of Transcendence*, 112.
56. Tillich, *Systematic Theology*, 3:385.
57. Tillich, *Love, Power, and Justice*, 110–11.
58. Tillich, *Systematic Theology*, 3:385.

transcendent person but as "the Efficacy within relationships."⁵⁹ Similarly, Bernard Loomer identifies the world with God in the following passage:

> The world is God because it is the source and preserver of meaning; because the creative advance of the world in its adventure is the supreme cause to be served; because even in our desecration of our space and time within it, the world is holy ground; and because it contains and yet enshrouds the ultimate mystery inherent within existence itself.⁶⁰

In a more recent publication, Gordon Kaufman likewise refers to God not as a world-transcendent entity but as a "serendipitous" creativity (i.e., that which I designate "activity" or "involvement") at work in our own lives and in the around us.⁶¹ Indeed, within *In Face of Mystery*, Kaufman proposes the concept of "serendipitous creativity" as a metaphor more appropriate for thinking of God today than such traditional image/concepts as creator, lord, and father. In another essay,⁶² Kaufman more fully elaborates and more carefully nuances that concept. It is no longer possible, he argues, to connect today's scientific cosmological and evolutionary understandings of the origins of the universe and the emergence of life (including human life and history) with a conception of God constructed in the traditional anthropomorphic terms in an intelligible way. However, the metaphor of serendipitous creativity—directly implied in the idea of evolution itself—has resources for constructing a religiously pertinent and meaningful (late-)postmodern conception of God. Indeed, it is apropos for naming God because it preserves—and even indeed emphasizes—the ultimacy of the *mystery* that God is, even while it connects God directly with the coming into being of the new and the novel. As brain scientist Terrence Deacon has observed in his book *The Symbolic Species: The Co-Evolution of Language and the Brain*, "Evolution is *the* one kind of process able to produce something out of nothing ... [A]n evolutionary process is an origination process ... Evolution is the author of its spontaneous creations."⁶³

In sum, affirming nonduality does *not* amount to eviscerating transcendence.⁶⁴ Indeed, Thatamanil states that is possible, in nonduality, to have immanence without forgoing transcendence. For me, God and the natural world are thoroughly interdependent as manifest in the processes of

---

59. Meland, *Fallible Forms and Symbols*, 152.
60. Loomer, "Size of God," 42.
61. Kaufman, *In Face of Mystery*, 390–401.
62. Kaufman, "On Thinking of God as Serendipitous Creativity," 409–25, esp. 410.
63. Deacon, *Symbolic Species*, 458. Italics added.
64. Thatamanil, "Ecstasy and Nonduality," 19–24; Cf. 21.

macroevolution. God *is* the (serendipitous) creativity everywhere expressed by and within the macroevolutionary process. Because God is the creativity of the macroevolutionary process, God is forever linked with entities, both inanimate and animate, while they advance in complexity. Bracken agrees in saying, "The One and the Many are fully interdependent. Only thus, as I see it, does one avoid the pitfalls of monism and dualism in thinking through what is meant by Ultimate Reality."[65] In this Christian nonduality, God is both encountered and experienced through the processes of macroevolution. If this be not mysticism, what else could it be?

---

65. Bracken, "Non-Duality and the Concept of Ultimate Reality," 146.

8

Evolutionary Christology

Adoptionism and Jesus of Nazareth

INTRODUCTION

In the present chapter, one will find a highly suggestive conclusion, one that is quite provocative, to be blunt, and generally not in keeping with orthodoxy.[1] Nevertheless, each part of this chapter suggests an overall thesis that the Spirit is the immanent presence of the Godhead upon the Earth, which

---

1. Crisp and Sanders attempt to be "orthodox," yet also try to address new concerns in Trinitarian thinking. Classical theologians of the past were for the most part engaged in expounding and making sense of doctrine and dogma by appealing to authoritative documents such as the Bible, creeds, and confessions. That way of doing theology is no longer tenable in a twenty-first-century context, since it has largely done away with the primacy of authority as constitutive of truth, and has been impacted greatly by a post-Darwinian mindset. In its place, we should conceive of the task of the theologian as one of imaginative construction (Crisp and Sanders, eds., *Advancing Trinitarian Theology*, 13). Crisp and Sanders contend that this need for both theological exposition and construction is nowhere clearer or more needed than in the work that has been done on the doctrine of the trinity (Crisp and Sanders, eds., *Advancing Trinitarian Theology*, 14). While I do not agree with their conclusions, I nevertheless heartily agree that constructive theology needs to be extended in the twenty-first century; I will attempt such in this essay.

has historically designated the Sons of God through the imbibification[2] of his divinity, as most pronouncedly seen in the life of Jesus of Nazareth, culminating in his approval as the Son of God at his baptism.[3] I have coined the term "imbibification" in order to refer to the process by which the Spirit once imbibed the natural world with herself, and now continues to imbibe the world with her very being, by which the advancement of species is made possible and effected. By adding the suffix "-ation" to the end of the verb "imbibe," I am effectively making it into a noun that has reference to an activity; and while suffixes often change the meaning of the term from its original intent, I intend this newly coined term in its original sense of absorption or assimilation. So then, the term "imbibification" is a word coined by me to refer to the descent of the Spirit into the Son (and primally into matter at "creation," which causes the Spirit to be embedded within nature, and thereby be embodied within it as well). In this capacity, the Spirit of God is ever before the Son, wooing him to his divine appointments. I will argue that via the *kenosis* of the Spirit's beingness *into* Jesus of Nazareth, the poor Palestinian peasant became the Son of God.[4] Building upon Bradford McCall's and Thomas Jay Oord's usage of the term *"kenosis"* to refer

---

2. In biology, specifically botany, it is important to note that the term "imbibe" is used with reference especially of seeds absorbing water into ultramicroscopic pores. This is the sense in which I intend my coining of the word "imbibification."

3. Thus, the baptismal voice was rendered anticlimactic, and the spelling out of its original implications came to be branded "adoptionism" (Robinson, *Jesus*, 211). It should be noted at the outset of this essay that I adhere to what may be called a Spirit Christology, deeming it true that it is the Spirit who designates the Son of God through "descending upon him, as if a dove," at his baptism according to the biblical witness. I agree with Del Colle, who insists that what is distinctive in Spirit Christology is that on the level of theological construction and doctrinal interpretation, it proposes the relationship between Jesus and God and the role of Christ in redemption cannot be understood unless you do so pneumatologically (Cf. Del Colle, *Christ and the Spirit*, 4). In a very real sense, then, I propose that through the adoption wrought by the descent of the Spirit, Jesus *becomes* godly royalty.

4. It should be noted that I am quite hesitant when it comes to affirming the historical reliability of the Gospels. While I do affirm there was a miracle-working figure named Jesus in antiquity, it disturbs me that our closest recollection of him in written form was at earliest about twenty years post his death (the book of James tangentially, and the Gospel of Mark directly). Stories have the tendency to become marked by verbosity (amongst other things) over such a period of time. In saying this, I largely agree with Bart Ehrman, who, in *Jesus Before the Gospels*, states that "During the intervening years—and even in the years after our Gospels were written—stories about Jesus were in oral circulation, starting with tales told by those who were eye- and earwitnesses to the things he did and said." He goes on, "I am deeply interested in how Jesus was being 'remembered' and 'misremembered' by those who were telling such stories . . ." (Ehrman, *Jesus Before the Gospels*, 6). I share Ehrman's "interest" in knowing how Jesus was remembered by those who merely heard of him prior to the written Gospels.

to an infilling, self-donated love, versus a self-emptying (since or about the year 2008),[5] I here apply that meaning to the "adoption" of the Son of God at his baptism. While I did not originate the terminology of love as "self-donation"[6]—which is a principle upon which my contention of "kenotically donated love" is based—I coopt its usage in this chapter.

Neither did I originate the terminology of "self-giving, uncontrolling love."[7] However, this kenotically donated love onsets an evolving fertility, which most proximately is a result of the panentheistic relationship of God and world. This panentheistic relationship was initially wrought by the kenotic donation of God's very self *into* chaotic matter eons ago, and is now continually sustained and upheld by the repetitive impartation of his very self—through imbibification of the Spirit—into the natural world. It should be noted, then, that I do not dispute the *kenosis* of the Son into humanity, only redefine what the term is referent unto instead. In noting that the love of the creating Spirit is kenotically donated, I mean to draw attention to the idea that she not only gives us love itself, but also *her-self* in the very act of love. Further, in characterizing love as self-giving, I intend to once again draw attention to the fact that the creating Spirit gives of herself (liberally) to her creation and the creatures of creation. She, in fact, imparts part of herself to it and them, both, in a kenotic manner. Hence, I say the creating Spirit's love is kenotically donated.

Within early Christianity, there were at least four views regarding the divinity of Jesus: that he is divine, but not human (Docetism); human, but not divine (Ebionites); that he is divine/human as two figures in one person (Alexandrian: unity in differentiation; or Antiochian: differentiation in unity); and that he is fully divine *and* fully human as one figure in one person. The latter option won the day and became orthodoxy; I stipulate that such a contention is unthinkable in a scientifically literate society, like the twenty-first-century context. The position described in the previous paragraph above—that is, the infilling of the Son by the Spirit—has historically been referred to as adoptionism, or even more precisely, as dynamic monarchianism. Through this self-giving act of kenotically donated love, the Spirit imparts to Jesus of Nazareth an empowered ministry to the lost and destitute of this Earth, and he becomes also thereby the duly appointed Son

---

5. For McCall and Oord's usage of term *kenosis* as "self-offering," an "in-filling," a "self-donation," and a "self-giving" action, see McCall, *Kenosis of the Spirit into Creation*; and Oord, *Defining Love*, 32. For an elaboration of *kenosis* as "self-donation," I point you to McCall, *Thomistic Personalism in Dialogue with Kenosis*, 21–32; also see, more recently, McCall "Necessary, Kenotically-Donated, & Self-Giving Love."

6. Karol Wojtyla did this in *Love and Responsibility*, 82.

7. Oord did in the book by the same name: *Uncontrolling Love of God*.

of God, insomuch as the fullness of the deity is bestowed upon him through a process of imbibification. Although the term "imbibification" is my own—a noun used by me to refer to the process of imbibing—the sense in which I use it can be found in the notes of Bart Ehrman. He brings forth evidence for Christianity changing its mind with the view called adoptionism. He attributes this view to the Ebionites (second century) and the Theodotians (third century). Each of these groups is said to have believed that Jesus was a mere man who was "adopted by God at his baptism." In fact, Ehrman reports that "In terms of their Christological views, the Ebionites do indeed appear to have subscribed to the perspective of the first Christians."[8] As such, it is my contention that the Son of God is definitively constituted by the primordial self-donating *kenosis* of the Spirit, which thereby also means that the Son is pneumatologically derived. Pneumatology, then, becomes central to the story of God's work upon the Earth during the biblical era through the Son, who is himself empowered by the Spirit, as well as in the contemporary era wherein the Spirit has free reign.

The second century CE was a particularly messy one.[9] It was, by all accounts, a transitional—even formative—century in the life of the church, a moment in time when she was vulnerable to what had often been deemed wrong-headed thinking. The doctrine of Christ was probably the most contentious of all doctrines debated in this century—that is, the desire to develop a coherent Christology. Is Jesus of Nazareth divine insomuch as he is not, therefore, at all a man? Or was he a man, exalted to the position of God by his spotless life and death? Is he a mix of God and man?[10] These questions, at least indirectly, I seek to address in this chapter.

Larry Hurtado's response to the aforementioned questions is rather clear; he stipulates that Christianity had a very early "high Christology," going back to perhaps even the first few months of the post-Easter Christian community. According to him, Jesus was purported to be instrumentally related to Yahweh from the beginning of the Christian movement. In fact, Hurtado categorizes seven categories of evidence for this "high" christological devotion, though he concedes that such did not develop during Jesus' lifetime: first, there was a "well-established pattern of prayer in which Jesus figures prominently"; second, there was invocation and confession of the type Paul gave in Aramaic in 1 Corinthians 16:22–23: "If anyone has no love for the Lord, let him be accursed. *Marana tha!*" (my translation); third, the "redefinition of the Shema" is evidence for a distinctive Jewish Christian

---

8. Ehrman, *How Jesus Became God*, 290.
9. Wagner, *After the Apostles*, 1.
10. Kruger, *Christianity at the Crossroads*, 134.

confession of Jesus as kingly royalty; fourth and fifth, there was baptism in the name of the Jesus and communion done in his name, which are both in their own way rituals focused on Jesus as kingly royalty, and are "comparable to pagan rites given to their pagan deities;" sixth, there were many hymns sung to Jesus, which "celebrated Christ's identity and work;" and finally, there is the attribution of "prophecy" to Jesus, which is directed by God the Spirit.[11] Crispin Fletcher-Louis offers an eighth point to Hurtado's above list: the church offered the physical gesture of prostration to Jesus—and in the Bible, physical prostration accompanies the praise of a deity or divine ruler.[12] Together, Fletcher-Louis contends, these points make a strong case for an exceedingly *high* original Christology late in the first century CE.[13] But I am not so sure.

Many divisive points were registered with reference to the aforementioned questions of theology. Much of the presumed wrong-headed thinking, historically, has been referred to as "heresy," which apparently was a word first coined by Bishop Ignatius in the latter part of the first century.[14] However, there would have been no heresy without orthodoxy, while there also would be no orthodoxy without heresy.[15] In fact, it is the case that the heresies themselves caused, spurred onward, and generated the formulation and reformulation of "catholic" (i.e., universal) doctrine in the first few centuries of the Christian experiment.[16] But do not the "winners" of history get to deem the heresies? As such, is it not possible that potentially palatable and possibly potent views of various doctrines get swept under the proverbial rug by the winners?

According to Harold Brown, there is no doubt that many, if not most, of the first heretics were indeed heretical; it is less clear that they should ever be called Christian.[17] However, with the rise of the monarchians (which includes both modalists and adoptionists), particularly in its adoptionist form, we have an appearance of *believers* who ascribed to alternate realities that could still feasibly be called Christian. Brown further notes that with these monarchians, its adherents were truly and devoutly trying to understand Christ aright, but that nevertheless the rest of the church grew

---

11. Cf. Hurtado, *One God, One Lord*, 83–124.
12. Fletcher-Louis, *Jesus Monotheism*, 18–19.
13. Fletcher-Louis, *Jesus Monotheism*, 21.
14. O'Grady, *Early Christian Heresies*, 5.
15. O'Grady, *Early Christian Heresies*, 4.
16. O'Grady, *Early Christian Heresies*, 7.
17. Brown, *Heresies*, 95.

to call them heretics.[18] These monarchians rejected the duality, or even the plurality, of gods taught by Marcion and the various Gnostic groups. In their stead, they countered that Jesus was a man of the best and noblest variety, one who was specially adopted due to his unique fulfillment of God's goals for his life; but he was *not* uniquely God from birth. Instead, he was either adopted into the deity (i.e., adoptionism), meaning that there was a time when he was not,[19] or he progressively was manifested to be the Son in a different mode, aspect, or form of a singular God (i.e., modalism). Let us try to understand why positions such as the monarchians held were important in the second century, and are still relevant to us in the twenty-first century.

In the second century, various Gnostic groups had grown to be a formidable force in the embryonic quasi-Christian context. The church was greatly split over the questioned orthodoxy and palatability of Gnostics viewpoints. Into this situation, the monarchians (which, again, included both modalists and adoptionists), found themselves trying to adhere to what they considered orthodox views on the deity of Christ. The multiple Gnostic groups claimed that there were at least two (if not more) divine beings: a good God and an evil anti-god. The somewhat nascent Christian movement was divided: would they take the considered "orthodox" route, or would they adopt and perpetuate the Gnostic viewpoint(s)? I propose that the monarchians were a response to the fledgling Gnostic movement within second-century Christianity. The response of the church to Gnosticism claimed that there is only one God, the creator, who is wholly and entirely good. But if there is only one God, what to do with Jesus of Nazareth?

Questions like that must have been at the forefront of the fledgling Christian movement. Is Jesus God? Surely he was more than a mere man, the early church must have thought. But is he God? If not, what was he? And if so, how could they still claim to be monotheistic believers? That is, how could they claim to believe in only one God? If God is in heaven above, and Jesus walked upon Earth, how is he nevertheless God? As we now know, this was the chief reason that Jesus was put to death: both his "self-understanding" and other people's claims for him to be the Son of God.

---

18. I will now coopt a statement from Keith Ward: these monarchians knew that "if something is completely incomprehensible it is just nonsense" (Ward, *Christ and Cosmos*, 293). I submit to the reader that perhaps the monarchians realized this fact, and thus sought to make the best sense they could out of the presumed deity of Jesus of Nazareth. Ward points out orthodoxy's lack of self-understanding, which has also repetitively been made manifest throughout the history of the movement.

19. Against the adoptionists, Origen insisted on the eternal generation of the Son and repudiated the notion that "there was a time when he was not" (Origen, *De principiis*, 1.2.9; 4.1.2; 4.4.1).

As we also now know, the "orthodox" answer from the church to this dilemma, in the middle of the second century from the likes of Polycarp and the latter half of the second century from Theophilus of Antioch, was the beginning of the formulation of the doctrine of the Trinity. That is, that the Godhead is comprised of the Father, the Son, and the Spirit, and these three are nevertheless one. This means that God the Son *became* man in the person of Jesus of Nazareth. The Christian response to this quagmire, indeed, was to emphasize both the unity and oneness of God in contrast to the inherently dualistic approach of the multiple Gnostic groups. But this response called into question the formulation(s) of other doctrines concerning the God of Israel. What to do? It seemed there was no way to maintain oneness while also affirming multiplicity. Into this situation stepped both modalism and adoptionism.[20]

Modalism, which was alone designated as monarchianism by contemporaries, tended to blur the distinctions between Father, Son and Spirit, and was a posit of the priest located in or about Rome named Sabellius (notably, Praxeas and Noetus had similar ruminations before Sabellius, though less developed). Succinctly, this position held that both Jesus and the Father are merely different names for the same underlying reality, that is, the same individual. Notably, these believers were also known as patripassionists, for they contended that the Father suffered upon the cross along with Jesus of Nazareth. This modalist position contrasted with that of the adoptionists. Indeed, the latter group emphasized the unity of God against the Gnostics, noting that Jesus of Nazareth was essentially especially blessed by God, but was *not* himself God by origin (i.e., he was not "Light from Light, true God from true God," etc., as the Nicene Creed stipulates). As such, they denied the notion of Jesus' inherent divinity, adhering instead to a Christology of sorts that averred Jesus was especially blessed by God and that the Spirit of God dwelt within him as no other. These people are also known as dynamic monarchians, for they spoke of a *dynamis* or power that descended upon Jesus at either his baptism or his resurrection when he was "adopted" by the Father (more about this later). The classification of both as forms of monarchianism stems from the assumption, despite different starting points and motives, that they were united by a concern for the divine unity, or *monarchia*.[21]

But these were by no means the only options present within the embryonic church of the mid-second century. Indeed, a third "heresy"—in

20. This paragraph is loosely based upon the account of these events given by Hogan, *Dissent from the Creed*, 57–66. This title is notable because it contains the "imprimatur" of the Roman Catholic Church, indicating that it is *entirely* free from error.

21. Kelly, *Early Christian Doctrines*, 115.

addition to adoptionism and modalism—known colloquially as Arianism, bears some resemblance to adoptionism: it denies both the eternality and the absolute deity of Jesus. This heresy holds that Jesus—the Son—is *not* of the same divine essence as the Father. As such, Arianism teaches that the Son had been begotten at some point in time.[22] Only in this sense is he the "Son of God": Christ is not divine by nature, but was human in every sense of the term. Orthodox Christians opposed such Christologies because, for them, Christ has to be more than a "mere man" for his work of salvation to be effectual. He "must himself have been divine."[23] The problem which the fathers had to solve was not whether Jesus is God, but how, within the monotheistic system which the church inherited from the Jews—preserved in the Bible[24] and pertinaciously defended against the heathen—it was still possible to maintain the unity of God while insisting on the deity of one who is distinct from God the Father.[25]

VARIOUS ADOPTIONIST CHARACTERISTICS

Epiphanius, in his *Panarion*,[26] indicates that adoptionism began in Rome with a man known as Theodotus the Tanner (a leather seller from Byzantium),[27] who had originally renounced the notion that Jesus is the Son of God; however, he later began to actively proclaim that Jesus is *psilos anthropos*, that is, a mere man who received the Spirit of holiness from God in a special way at his baptism.[28] According to Hippolytus of Rome, Theodotus taught that Jesus of Nazareth was a man born of a virgin, as the contention from the council of Jerusalem stated, that he lived like other men of his day, and was highly pious; however, at his baptism in the Jordan River, "Christ" came down upon him in the likeness of a dove (cf. Luke 3:22), after which a voice thundered form heaven, "This is my beloved Son, of whom I am well pleased" (my translation).[29] Afterward, Jesus returned to

22. In fact, a couple centuries later, Arius taught that adoption is what is "common to us and the Son" (as cited in Peters, *God as Trinity*, 61).

23. Ehrman, *Orthodox Corruption of Scripture*, 19

24. This, of course, all the while there is quite a bit of "adoptionist" language in Hebrews—that is, language that speaks of Jesus as *becoming*, or being *begotten* or *appointed* to his status as the decisive intermediary between God and man during his life or in consequence of his death and resurrection (Cf. Dunn, *Christology in the Making*, 52).

25. Prestige, *God in Patristic Thought*, 76.

26. Epiphanius of Salamis, *Panarion of Epiphanius of Salamis, Book I: (Sects 1–46)*.

27. Bethune-Baker, *Early History of Christian Doctrine to the Time of Chalcedon*, 99.

28. Bracken, *God*, 9.

29. Sonship to God also characterizes Jesus' human solidarity with his fellow

Jordan, whereupon he was led into the wilderness. Thus, after the descent of the Spirit upon him, Jesus was enabled to do mighty deeds—wonders, even (*dynamis*)—but these wonders only manifested themselves *after* the Spirit's descent upon him, which constituted the moment of adoption of the Son by God the Father.[30]

Various views exist regarding the relations between the Father, the Son, and the Spirit. Amongst these various groups, one shall find the adoptionists, who somewhat base their thinking upon the Gospel of Mark, to the exclusion of the other Gospels.[31] It is theorized by adoptionist thinkers that Mark was written at a time in which the doctrines of the pre-existence of Christ and his virgin birth had not yet been ardently advocated, and hence the text of Mark does not represent that perspective, nor advocate such. However, by the time that the Gospels of Luke and Matthew had been written, Jesus is identified as the Son of God from the beginning of his life; this, of course, is not the most radical position, for the latter Gospel of John asserts that Jesus of Nazareth is the *pre-existent* Word of God, which existed in the beginning.[32] As adoptionism denies that Jesus eternally pre-existed his appearance upon Earth, and although it indeed explicitly affirms his deity subsequent to events in his life, its adherents view Jesus as currently

---

humans. What set him apart from all other humans was that he perfectly kept God's law and so was the most righteous man on Earth. As such, God chose him to be his Son and he determined to offer himself as a sacrifice for the sake of others (Bauckham, *Jesus and the God of Israel*, 281–82).

30. This is a synopsis of the points from Papandrea, *Earliest Christologies*, 45–51. Notably, I cannot—at the present time—support the position of antiquity that Jesus of Nazareth was God "incarnate." I see no feasible means by which Jesus could be born of a virgin, and hence I am more than hesitant to support it. However, I can definitely get behind an "exaltation" Christology, one that holds that Jesus of Nazareth, due to his upright life before God (perhaps even perfect life?), was designated the Son of God by adoption. This perspective greatly supports Jesus' solidarity with humans.

31. Traditionally, three lost "Jewish gospel" writings have been identified: *The Gospel According to the Hebrews*, *The Gospel of the Nazareans*, and *The Gospel of the Ebionites*. These lost gospels are preserved in patristic quotations and the marginal notes of certain texts of Matthew. It is assumed that one or more of these lost gospels come from an Aramaic version of the Gospel of Matthew. In general, the Jewish gospels promote an adoptionist Christology. From a Judaic perspective, notably, this is *not* low Christology; it is *true* Christology (Evans, ed., *Encyclopedia of the Historical Jesus*, 264; italics added).

32. Ehrman notes that it is important to point out that precisely when the Christians started saying such exalted things about Jesus is when the emperors were beginning to be worshiped throughout the Roman world. The emperor was the Son of God (because he was adopted by the preceding emperor); Jesus was the Son of God. The emperor was regarded to be divine; Jesus was divine. The emperor was a great ruler; Jesus was a great ruler. The emperor was lord and sovereign; Jesus was Lord and sovereign (Ehrman, *How Jesus Became God*, Kindle ed., pos. 3389).

divine—and he has been since his adoption by the Father—although he is in no manner equal to the Father (cf. Jesus' statements to the effect of "my Father is greater than I," John 14.:28).[33]

This dynamic monarchianism school found itself under attack by the various *logos* theologians, which included Tertullian, Hippolytus, Clement of Alexandria, and Origen. This persecution greatly increased post the pronouncement of *anathema* (heresy) by Pope Victor I in the mid-90s of the second century, who himself, oddly, was a certified monarchian of the modalist variety. Interestingly, the early Christian writing referred to as the *Shepherd of Hermas* taught that Jesus of Nazareth was a virtuous man filled with the Spirit of God, and thereafter was adopted by the Father. While for some time the *Shepherd of Hermas* was bound with the rest of the recognized scriptures, eventually it was removed from the codices that included the rest of recognized scriptures, and one may safely assume this was due at least in part to its "unorthodox" Christology—that is, its congruence with an adoptionistic Christology.

Adoptionism holds to the ideas that God is completely and totally one being, unitary, and above all else indivisible, and thus of one nature only. It seeks to avoid the problems latent within the doctrine of the Trinity, particularly with regard to Jesus not being coeternal with the Father, positing instead that the Son was granted godhood by the Father as a reward due to his spotless and perfect life. While different versions of this position of adoptionism have held that Jesus was adopted either at his baptism or at his resurrection, I contend that the first of those moments is more robust theologically, for it manifests a pneumatological constitution of the Son's deity (note that the "Spirit" was seen to be descending upon the Son at his baptism),[34] a position which is largely consonant with the theological position known as Spirit Christology.[35]

So then, while Christians of the first three centuries largely agreed that Jesus is the Son of God, they disagreed over what this sonship means and how it was brought about. For proto-orthodox believers, it entails a different level of existence from the rest of humankind; for them, Jesus is thoroughly divine. Other Christians, however, rejected this claim and argued that Jesus

---

33. Witherington, *What Have They Done with Jesus?*, 7.

34. In this way, Jesus could be called "God" because he would represent God functionally, but he would *not* be identical with God ontologically (Cf. Harvey, *Jesus and the Constraints of History*).

35. Jürgen Moltmann claims, "According to this [view], Jesus was adopted as Son of God through the Spirit, so that he might become the firstborn among many brethren. The strength of these Christologies lies in the fact that they bring out the force of the Spirit as subject in Jesus' life and ministry" (Moltmann, *Trinity and the Kingdom*, 132).

of Nazareth was a flesh-and-blood human being without remainder, a man who had been adopted by God to be his Son in order to bring about the salvation of the world.[36] To be sure, these representatives of adoptionism constituted no monolith;[37] they differed among themselves, for example, concerning the moment at which Jesus' adoption had taken place. But by the second century most adoptionists believed that it had occurred at his baptism. For the vast majority of believers, this form of Christology represented an error, for if Jesus were a "mere man," then the salvific efficacy of his work could be radically called into question.[38]

THE ORTHODOX RESPONSE TO ADOPTIONISM

It is my contention that adoptionism was one such "losing" doctrine, one that may not have been considered a heresy if given better conditions within which to flourish. As it is the case, dynamic monarchianism is the first of two movements that appealed to the "uniqueness of the first principle" (Greek: *monarchia*) in order to establish the principle of monotheism in the face of perceived movement toward polytheism, which was seen in the attempts to explicate a *logos* Christology by Justin Martyr, Tertullian, and other like-minded apologists.[39] Indeed, as Kärkkäinen notes, these two monarchian movements were attempts to reconcile the seemingly impossible equation between strict monotheism with the idea that there are three divine beings within the godhead.[40]

Generally deemed to be the first step toward Trinitarianism, the fathers of the second and third centuries accepted the prehuman existence of the (Platonic) *logos*. Then, at Nicaea in 325 CE, the *homoousios* view of the relation between Jesus of Nazareth and the Father was accepted, after which it was contended that is was just as immutable the Father. Later, the Spirit of God was accepted to be an ontologically equal third member of the Trinity, as seen especially in the teachings of the Cappadocian Fathers, among whom were Basil, Gregory of Nyssa, and Gregory of Nazianzus. Manifold generations later, a final step toward the modern-day Trinitarian understanding was taken insomuch as the *filioque* was added to the Nicene Creed by the Catholic Church in 1054 CE. Having established a brief time

---

36. Apparently, a merged patchwork savior of Christian dogma emerged, and the alternative views of Christ were quelled. Cf. Price, *Deconstructing Jesus*, 4.
37. Ehrman, *Orthodox Corruption of Scripture*, 169.
38. Ehrman, *Orthodox Corruption of Scripture*, 169–70.
39. Hultgren and Haggmark, *Earliest Christian Heretics*, 136.
40. Kärkkäinen, *Trinity*, 21.

line, I would now like to jump right into the debate regarding the adoptionist position on the deity of Christ.

In the book entitled *The Orthodox Corruption of Scripture*,[41] Bart Ehrman argues—quite persuasively in my opinion—that adoptionist theology may in fact date back almost to the time of Jesus. Ehrman notes that in the earliest gospel (Mark) there are some manuscripts which do not have the phraseology of "Son of God" with reference to Jesus of Nazareth in the first verse of the gospel. Ehrman advocates, based upon this omission, that the phrase "Son of God" was not applied to Jesus of Nazareth until after his baptism by John the Baptist. Thus, the earliest gospel reflects an adoptionist perspective.[42]

CHRISTOLOGICAL HERESIES

The term "heresy" originally referred to an "act of choice," most basically, and whereas for some time the word "heresy" did not contain a negative implication—simply meaning "party" or "sect" instead—at a rather early date in the history of Christianity, the term "heresy" was used as a term of derision and disparagement.[43] Indeed, at an early period within the fledgling Christian movement resulting from the life and death of Jesus of Nazareth, the charge of "heresy" began to be seen as the worst possible offense in which a Christian could become involved. In fact, at its height of condemnation in the early Middle Ages, a heresy was considered a capital crime. But heresies and the heretics who advance them are often in fact merely innovators, nonconformists, and protestors. As such, a case could be made that those convicted of heresy were the truest and best imitators of Christ, no matter how far-removed their teachings may have been deemed by their opponents in the majority.[44] So then, there may have been some instances when the term "heresy" was applied merely to the minority's position upon a doctrine that was being hammered out by the faithful.

---

41. Ehrman, *Orthodox Corruption of Scripture*, 74–75. The attainment of orthodox formulations of the Trinity in antiquity was a cumbersome process—long and drawn out.

42. It should be pointed out, in addition, that the earliest epistles—i.e., those written by the hand of Paul—do not explicitly mention the purported virgin birth of Jesus, but instead note that Jesus was "born of a woman, born under the law . . . as to his human nature a descendant of David" (Cf. Gal 4:4, which is one of the—if not *the*—earliest of all Pauline writings).

43. Brown, *Heresies*, 1–6.

44. Cf. Marjanen and Luomanen, *Companion to Second-Century Christian Heretics*, 1–4.

I contend that one such instance of the term "heresy" being misapplied to the minority's position is manifest in the history of and response to the adoptionist movement within Christianity. Whereas it is usually the case that orthodoxy owes its existence to a heresy, it has at times been the case that the "heretical" view may have been the most correct. This chapter therefore has presented a case for the orthodoxy (right doctrine) of the early adoptionistic viewpoint within Christianity. Far from being a phenomenon that appeared only in isolated cases in the third century, adoptionism is instead a tradition that existed from the earliest days of Christianity and was part of the Christian mainstream until the emergence of newer Christologies led to it being regarded as heretical and thus led ultimately to its large-scale demise. It should be noted that the fear(s) regarding adoptionistic doctrines were presumably soteriological in nature: if Jesus is not truly *the* Word, the union of the divine and human in Christ would be denied, and thereby traditional atonement theories could not account for salvation.[45] I see that contention as an overreaction, perhaps spurious, and even erroneous.

Though Theodotus professed to adhere to the Apostle's Creed, Pope Victor I excommunicated him in the mid-90s of the second century. Adolf von Harnack contends that Theodotus, in fact, was one of the—if not the—first *Christians* who were labeled a heretic *despite* the fact that they continued to profess belief in the rule of faith.[46] As such, his case proved the inability of the Apostle's Creed alone to deem one orthodox or not, and thus the leaders of the Christian movement were propelled to refine further their belief in both God and his presumed Christ. After all, much of the New Testament can potentially be read in a straightforward adoptionist manner, for the number of passages that clearly emphasize the ontological deity and pre-existence of Christ are few and far between. It should be pointed out that Christians of the second and third centuries generally—*regardless* of theological persuasion—claimed to espouse the views of Jesus' earliest followers. With regard at least to the adoptionists, modern scholarship has by and large conceded the claim. These Christians did not originate their views of Christ; adoptionistic Christologies can be traced to sources that predate the books of the New Testament.[47]

But this fact begs the question: did these conveners at the first ecumenical councils get it right? Did they, in other words, correctly contend that Jesus was divine from birth, and not adopted to be the Son of God? Reading the New Testament as averring that Jesus was an endowed human

---

45. Hultgren and Haggmark, *Earliest Christian Heretics*, 136.
46. Harnack, *Lehrbuch der Dogmengeschichte*, 1:730.
47. Ehrman, *Orthodox Corruption of Scripture*, 172.

is possible, and perhaps even favorable (?). Harnack didn't think the understanding of adoptionism to be incorrect, as he was one of the greatest liberal representatives of an adoptionistic Christology. Indeed, Harnack defended the second- and third-century adoptionists as the *true* critical thinkers of their day, for they—for example—used grammatical rather than allegorical exegesis.[48] Harnack also contended that the "easy" way for a Christian then was to be either a Platonic mystic or an Adventist, expecting the return of Christ to occur almost immediately after his death and burial. But the adoptionists were neither; instead, they were analytical Aristotelians.[49]

Later, during the first part of the third century, the adoptionist position experienced a notable revival in Paul of Samosata,[50] bishop of Antioch in the mid-third century. Paul maintained that only the Father is genuinely God, and thus that neither the Son nor the Spirit can properly be accorded the same rank of deity as the Father. Paul's teaching obviously owed much to the earlier adoptionists, but was (much?) more consistent. He held, apparently, that Christ was an earthly man, indwelt impersonally by divine influences, to which Jesus responded with obedience so complete that he was exalted to fellowship with God. His exaltation was the final stage in a moral progression.[51] Paul of Samosata, notably, was condemned by the Council of Antioch in 268 CE.[52]

DERIVATION METHOD OF THE ADOPTED JESUS

In this final section of the chapter, I would like to propose a new method of divine bestowal of divinity. Indeed, I posit that the adoption of the Son occurred due to a kenotic self-bestowal of divinity by the Father through the Spirit onto the Son at his baptism. One has previously described this kenotic action, in a different context,[53] as a *pouring out* of the divinity into creation.

48. Harnack, *Lehrbuch der Dogmengeschichte*, 1:711f.
49. Harnack, *Lehrbuch der Dogmengeschichte*, 1:711f.
50. González and González, *Heretics for Armchair Theologians*, 24.
51. There seems to be an early layer of exaltation Christology within the Christian movement in Palestine. But what, exactly, does this mean? It entails at least the following notions: that Jesus is an expansion of or included in Yahweh; that an exaltation Christology works backwards to pre-existence; that there seems to have always been both low and high Christologies; that the book of Daniel predicted that the Son of Man would inherit God's everlasting kingdom; and that the glory of God appears as human but is not a human in truth (Cf. Caragounis, *Son of Man*).
52. Prestige, *God in Patristic Thought*, 115.
53. Cf. McCall, "God of Chance and Purpose"; see also McCall, "Thomistic Personalism in Dialogue with Kenosis," 21–32; see further McCall, "Whitehead, Creativity,

In the same manner that the Spirit was poured out onto creation, thereby imbibing it with evolving fertility, I contend the same principle meaning has application to the adoption (or deification) of the Son into the family" of God by the Father, the declaration of which we are made privy to by the Gospels' accounting of Jesus' baptism.[54] In a sense, then, Jesus of Nazareth became the Christ precisely due to the imbibification of the Spirit into him. There in the story we encounter the Spirit of God kenotically descending upon the Son in the River Jordan. One has not to buy into the archaic language of the Gospel account to garner from the story that the Spirit in some manner was made manifest to the Son, and even bestowed his proverbial "blessing" onto him, which I here note by calling it a self-bestowal of divinity through *kenosis*.

CONCLUSION

After Julius Caesar's death in 27 CE, a venomous power struggle occurred between his supporters and his own family, especially with respect to which of his sons would succeed him as emperor. Michael Peppard's book *The Son of God*[55] indicates that in the Roman world an adopted child was given a greater, higher status than a child who was such by birth. The natural son was who he was more or less by accident; his virtues and fine qualities (or lack thereof) had nothing to do with the fact that he was born as the child of two particular parents. The adopted son, on the other hand—who was normally adopted as an adult—was adopted precisely *because* of his fine qualities and potential. He was made great because he had demonstrated the potential for greatness, not because of the coincidental circumstances of his birth. The case of Octavian being exalted to emperor of Rome serves to demonstrate the truth of how an adopted son oft had greater respect from his family than the natural-born son, and also how the adopted son within

---

and the Immanently Creative Spirit," 337–50.

54. There is some patristic support for such a contention; indeed, in *Against Heresies*, Irenaeus of Lyons writes, "For it was for this end that the word of God was made man and he who was the son of God became the son of man, that man, having been taken into the word, and by receiving adoption, might become the son of God" (3.19.1, as translated in *Ante-Nicene Fathers*, 1:448.). Further, in Origen of Alexandria, we see that "with Jesus human and divine nature began to be woven together, so that by fellowship with divinity human nature might become divine, not only in Jesus, but also in all those who believe and go on to undertake the life which Jesus taught" (Origen, *Against Celsus* 3.29, as translated by Chadwick in *Origen: Contra Celsus*, 146).

55. Cf. Peppard, *Son of God in the Roman World*.

a family often inherited the position of his adopted father over and above the natural-born one.

Julius's truly eldest son, Caesarion, is merely a footnote to history, only relevant in the reconstruction of bloodlines within the ancient world. However, the duly adopted son, Octavian, in contrast, became arguably the greatest Caesar in history, with his name forever etched in history as Caesar Augustus, the envy of the ancient world. He—not Julius's biological son—inherited the property, wealth, status, power, and influence that Julius Caesar had while alive. As Roman historian Christiane Kunst has put it: "The adopted son . . . exchanged his own [status] and took over the status of the adoptive Father."[56] I propose that just as Caesarion was adopted by Julius and thereafter became exalted higher than his brethren to the earthly throne as the heir of the first Caesar, so too was Jesus of Nazareth adopted by God, and that actually led to a *heightened* sense of significance and honor for him in relation to Father God than were he truly an offspring via the overshadowing of Mary by the Spirit of God, as recounted in the Christian Scriptures. By no means is Jesus "merely" the *adopted* Son of God; he is *the* Son of God. Moreover, Jesus' *adoptive* Father is not merely "a Father," he is *the* Father of all—God blessed forever. This is clearly an *exaltation* Christology, not a devaluing one. If we were all but so lucky to be the adopted child of God! According to the apostle Paul, however, we *are* the adopted children of God (cf. Rom 9:8; Gal 3:26). We are made such, I claim, through the primary adopted Son of God—Jesus of Nazareth—and the descent of his Spirit upon us, which will "deitize"[57] us in the same manner in which it had formerly deitized him.

I do not wish to merely deconstruct the doctrine of the Trinity, but rather proffer something in its stead. In light of the exaltation Christology I have offered in this chapter, I would like to offer several suggestions as to how we may approach the doctrine of the Trinity in the twenty-first century, so let me spell it out in a seven points: first, and in danger of begging grace from everyone, I declare we must do so with the utmost perspicuity. That is, we need to be lucid about what we affirm and what we disagree with, offering clarity and not merely obfuscating matters more so. Clearly, based on how I have argued thus far, the direction I would like to go forward concerning the doctrine of God is something akin to the following: second, the Spirit's descent upon the man Jesus of Nazareth constitutes his deity; third, that Jesus is the "Son of God" need not connote that he participated in the

---

56. Kunst, *Römische Adoption*, 294.

57. I coin this term so as to connote the process by which Jesus of Nazareth became the Son of God through the descent of the Spirit upon him.

divine essence, but instead was only taken up into it at a later period of time. Thus, fourth, God's presence through his Spirit was bestowed upon Jesus at his baptism, and that presence remained upon Jesus of Nazareth for a long time, if not the remainder of his life.[58]

Sixth: although the Gospels refer to Jesus as the Son of God, Jesus himself refers to himself as the Son of Man, the underlying Aramaic of which means a son of a human.[59] So then, finally, perhaps we need to go back in order to go forward. If they got it right or approximately so some two thousand years ago, why cannot we now? Christ's elevation to sonship was a reward for his performance, and this performance is within the capacity of those who believe in him.[60] This type of statement is congruent with the advocation of the adoption of Jesus by God the Father as asserted throughout this chapter. Interestingly, as aforementioned, the early Christian writing named *Shepherd of Hermas* taught the very same thing in the mid-second century that I seek here to establish: that Jesus of Nazareth was an utmost virtuous man filled with the Spirit of God, and thereafter adopted by the Father.[61]

I contend—though this revisioning of the deity of the Son may be a hard pill to swallow for a number of Christians—"[D]espite their orthodox confession of the Trinity, [most] Christians are, in their practical life, almost mere 'monotheists' . . . [and,] should the doctrine of the Trinity have to be dropped as false, the major part of religious literature could well remain virtually unchanged."[62] As such, it is my contention that the adoption of an adoptionist perspective on the deity of Jesus of Nazareth will not amount to much change in the practical lives of Christians, day to day. It should, therefore, receive a fair hearing by all comers.

In this chapter, I have argued that there are problems with the inherited doctrine of the Trinity, which at least needs to be reconsidered, if not extremely "massaged" in the formulation that currently exists. Indeed, Jesus becomes the Son of God by adoption through the divine power that descends upon him at baptism, and he thereafter becomes an instrument of revelation and salvation for all of his fellow humanity. The details of my adoptionism proposal will have to be worked out later, in another article (or two, or three . . .), to be sure. A Process-panentheistic doctrine of the Trinity may be the way forward. Perhaps adoptionism itself is the way to go;

---

58. For this point, see Pannenberg, *Jesus: God and Man*, 117.
59. Ward, *Christ and Cosmos*, Kindle ed., pos. 767.
60. Cf. Peters, *God as Trinity*, 204n87.
61. Cf. Ehrman, *How Jesus Became God*, 62.
62. Rahner, *Trinity*, 10–11.

perhaps it is not. Nevertheless, as the Anglican Keith Ward stipulates—with whom I agree wholeheartedly on this point—there is need to restate the doctrine of the Trinity in a twenty-first-century context.[63] May we proceed forward, then, in attempting to reformulate the doctrine of God for our contemporary context. I know I will . . .

---

63. Ward, *Christ and Cosmos*, Kindle ed., pos. 345.

Part 4

Theological Perspectives on Evolution and Responsive Divine Love

9

The Connection between Kenosis and Emergence

INTRODUCTION

Modern advances in scientific study reveal a vastly more complicated world than the reductionist program of the late nineteenth and twentieth centuries ever envisioned. As Philip Clayton writes, "[i]t is unfortunate that in recent years the explosion of knowledge in molecular biology has caused all of biology to be painted with a reductionist stroke."[1] In the book entitled *Mind & Emergence*, Clayton seeks to offer a third way of understanding the world and human relationship: *emergentism*. Clayton contends that emergence is a viable option in contrast to the waning explanatory power of *physicalism* and *dualism*, its competitors. No longer can one seek to explain all things as being merely reducible to their physical entities or microphysical causes (i.e. physicalism), as physicalism is inconsistent with standard research theories and practices within biology.[2] Physicalism is also incompatible with emergence because it "rules out forms of natural causality that are more than merely a sum of physical forces."[3]

Although substance dualism was probably the dominant metaphysical view in Western history from Aristotle to Kant, one cannot continue to seek full explanation of all things as being composed of a bipartite construction

---

1. Clayton, *Mind & Emergence*, 94.
2. Clayton, *Mind & Emergence*, 66.
3. Clayton, *Mind & Emergence*, 174.

of physical components and spiritual components. Emergence is, in brief, the view that novel and unpredictable occurrences are naturally produced in nature, and that said novel structures, organs, and organisms are not reducible to their component parts.[4] One can find at least five distinct levels in which the term "emergence" is used in varying fields of study.[5] Clayton proffers that emergence is a fruitful paradigm in explaining evolutionary progress in the physical world, which represents explanatory power beyond that of physics alone. Whereas Clayton has offered an explanative survey of emergence theory, I posit that he has not given a sufficient account of the metaphysical realities that may give rise to emergence. It is these metaphysical realties that I seek to unpack in this chapter, using Clayton's text as the source of my extrapolations, for a richer metaphysical account *ironically* may result in greater autonomy for the biological sciences.

In *Creation and Reality*, Michael Welker "offers initial steps toward correcting both the classic theistic caricature of God the Creator and a corresponding religious understanding of reality."[6] New approaches to creation are a "burning theological interest," for modern religious depictions are "boring, vapid, and banal."[7] In this chapter, I seek to offer a new approach to creation, building upon the notions of emergence and kenosis. Pointedly, I offer the notion that the existence and viability of emergence theory depends upon the primal kenotic act of God the Spirit *pouring* himself *into* creation. In the following paper one will find three distinct parts. In the first part, I shall review and interact with Clayton's seminal work, *Mind & Emergence*. In the second part, I will present the biblical basis of kenosis of the Spirit *into* creation, and discuss former conceptions of the kenosis and science connection. In the third and final part of this paper, I will make my own contribution of the connections between kenosis of the Spirit into creation and emergence theory.

---

4. Clayton, *Mind & Emergence*, vi.
5. The term "emergence" is used, first, within *specific fields* within science; second, to describe *levels* within the natural world; third, to describe *patterns across* scientific disciplines; fourth, to describe patterns of *transitions between* scientific disciplines; fifth, to describe a metaphysical theory (Clayton, *Mind & Emergence*, 40–42).
6. Welker, *Creation and Reality*, 2.
7. Welker, *Creation and Reality*, 4.

REVIEW OF CLAYTON'S *MIND & EMERGENCE*

Clayton's book explicitly covers the revolution brought about by the study of evolution that undercuts both *physicalism* and *dualism*.[8] Clayton argues that *emergence* is the philosophical position that best accounts for the data derived from the study of evolution. Emergentists argue that the reductionary tendencies within the natural sciences are not tenable. In fact, "actualizing the dream of a final reduction 'downwards', it now appears, has proven fundamentally impossible."[9] The pompous nature of the physics of former years has been *humbled*— epistemically and practically—by a series of revelations within nature that place inherent limitations upon what physics can explain, predict, or know.[10]

Clayton rejects the *exclusive* explanatory power of three of Aristotle's forms of causality (i.e. efficient, material, and final), and posits instead that *formal* causality might have more application in emergent systems than any of the other three Aristotelian forms of causality.[11] While not advocating the notion that formal causality is the exclusive form of causation found within nature, Clayton wants to remind us not to forget the importance of it. However, I take issue here, especially in light of a pneumatic understanding of the lure/woo of God toward eschatological fulfillment, and posit instead that it may indeed be likely that *final* causality has more import in this discussion of emergence than Clayton seemingly allows for it, especially when viewed from the kenotic position argued by this current paper.[12] Clayton claims

---

8. Clayton, *Mind & Emergence*, 1.

9. Clayton, *Mind & Emergence*, 70.

10. For example, Heisenberg's uncertainty principle delimits our ability to predict with accuracy the exact location and momentum of subatomic particles, and makes one realize that there exists an inherent indeterminacy within the physical world itself. Moreover, chaos theory has shown that the future states of complex systems are unpredictable, due to finite knowledge of initial conditions.

11. Clayton, *Mind & Emergence*, 7.

12. In personal communication on June 6, 2007, Clayton said that he holds the assumption that final causation conflicts with the explanatory paradigm of the biological sciences. So then, if he argues that God does something biologically impossible, then Clayton opens up a chasm between himself and other biological scientists. Clayton said that he follows Thomas Aquinas, with God being the primary cause and creation being the secondary cause(s). Moreover, Clayton stated that God as the primary cause never conflicts with secondary causes. However, "one can accept an epistemic presumption in favor of naturalistic interpretations and still hold that it is metaphysically possible that . . . the regularities of the natural world are occasionally, or perhaps frequently, broken by direct interventions of God" (Clayton, *Mind & Emergence*, 163). Moreover, Clayton states that emergentists must "give up" the principle of causal closure, which is common to physics (Clayton, *Mind & Emergence*, 56).

that Aristotle's principle of *entelechy* foreshadows the rise of the emergentist position.[13] Aristotle defined entelechy as the internal principle of growth and perfection that guides an organism toward the attainment of qualities that it already contains, though merely in a *potential* state. Disputing the scientists who relate emergence as a "magic pill" of "mystical power," Clayton intimates that scientists could have found in emergence the *vital power* or the divine "lure/woo" (as I advocate) that lifts (or *pulls*) the universe toward new levels of reality.[14] However, Clayton gives three reasons why we must resist the strict equation of emergence with entelechy, especially considering that entelechy (internal) and wooing (external) are incompatible: 1) in the long run, we need a robust theory of divine providence; 2) the place to reconcile providence and the evolution of agency is *theology*, not science; and 3) the theologians must show how this robust theological account is consistent with biological explanation, not the scientists. Clayton does not want to tell the biologists that they are wrong in their own domain.[15]

Before offering his own definition of emergence, Clayton first depicts the two main classifications of emergence theories within the twentieth century: *strong* and *weak*. The *strong* emergentist position can be labeled *ontological* emergence, whereas the *weak* emergentist position could be aptly labeled as *epistemological* emergence. Strong emergentists postulate that evolution produces *ontologically* distinct levels of organs/isms that are characterized by their own distinct regularities and causal forces. In opposition, weak emergentists maintain that as new patterns emerge the causal processes remain those that are *fundamental* to known physics. A property of an organ/ism is weakly emergent if it is reducible to its intrinsic qualities, insomuch as weakly emergent properties are "novel" only at the level of description (*epistemologically*). This contrasts with strongly emergent organs/isms in which the cause is reducible *neither* to any intrinsic causal capacity of the parts *nor* to any relation between the component parts.[16] Clayton asserts that weak emergence in effect leaves us with the same old dichotomy of physicalism and dualism.[17]

---

13. In personal communication on June 6, 2007, Clayton also noted to me the connection between *e'lan vital*, entelechy, and vitalism, as they all refer to inward working out of a prearranged outcome. Clayton thinks that we need a more robust theological and metaphysical account regarding how the agency of God is more effective than that of nature.

14. Clayton, *Mind & Emergence*, 47.

15. Clayton, personal communication, June 6, 2007.

16. Clayton, *Mind & Emergence*, 10.

17. In further recounting the emergence theories within the twentieth century, Clayton notes that Conway Lloyd Morgan anticipated, by some sixty-five years, Niles

Clayton notes that in the 1990s strong emergence theories resurfaced with great vigor through the rediscovered writings of Michael Polanyi.[18] Whereas I agree with Clayton's critique of Polanyi in that he *went too far* in reference to finalistic causes in biology, I would like to suggest that instead of the organs/isms being *guided* by the potentialities that are open to it, that they are instead *lured* by the potentialities that are open to it. The concept of *lure*, instead of guide, would entail the Spirit to be ever before the evolutionary advancement of organs/isms, *wooing* them toward their eschatological fulfillment in complexity and in Christ, while nevertheless allowing them their own autonomy in "deciding" their trajectory.[19]

After reviewing and critiquing twentieth-century views of emergence (i.e., *strong* and *weak*), Clayton offers his *own* view regarding emergence theory in chapter 2. In so doing, Clayton radicalizes the *immanence* of God.[20] I posit that this radicalization of immanence comports well with my advocacy of kenosis of the Spirit *into* creation, for in said notion, the Spirit is *intimately interior* to nature, as its *source, sustenance,* and *end*.[21]

Eldredge's postulation of "punctuated equilibrium." Morgan perceived that emergence entails an evolution that is punctuated. Morgan resisted his contemporary's view that an *e'lan vital* (vital energy) was introduced from a force outside of nature. In contrast, Morgan advocated a position in which the underlying forces driving evolution toward greater emergence are *thoroughly immanent* in the natural world. In personal communication on June 6, 2007, Clayton relayed to me that perhaps "punctuated equilibrium" could be thought of in terms of final causation. If so, the big transitions in "punctuated equilibrium" are signs of divine intervention (Clayton, *Mind & Emergence*, 13–14).

18. Clayton, *Mind & Emergence*, 18.

19. These statements are reminiscent of A. N. Whitehead, who posits that the divine lure is at work since the moment of creation. In personal communication on June 6, 2007, however, Clayton noted that he breaks away from Whitehead because Whitehead's theory entails the notion that every unit of reality is a *fully* experiencing agent, whereas Clayton follows biologists in thinking that the degree of agency evolves over time, conditioned on the level of complexity of the specie in question. Samuel Alexander stated that there is a principle of development *within* evolution, i.e., something that drives the whole process, which Alexander terms the "nisus" (Cf. Alexander, *Space, Time, and Deity*). Alexander noted this was a creative metaphysical principle that bore resemblance to Whitehead's principle of creativity. Clayton contends that if we could wed Whitehead and Alexander, it could be very effective because Whitehead has a theory of agency and lure whereas Alexander has the eight evolving levels of agency.

20. Clayton also acknowledges this throughout *Mind & Emergence* (e.g., p. 187). Note, however, that Clayton is a *theological* dualist, but not a metaphysical dualist. As a theological dualist, Clayton contends that God will work supernaturally to establish the eschaton, and that what we now know of *Homo sapiens* will not be reflected at the eschaton, as it will be a "new order," as per revelation. Clayton notes that the new creation is an act of pure and free grace on God's part.

21. Recognize that if theism is to be more than mere deism, it must allow for some sort of divine involvement in the natural world, which leads to the plausibility of some

Clayton writes that emergence is "that which is produced by a combination of causes, but cannot be regarded as the sum of their individual effects."[22] Moreover, "emergence is the theory that cosmic evolution repeatedly includes unpredictable, irreducible, and novel appearances."[23] Clayton here approvingly cites Archinov and Fuchs in saying that any adequate theory of emergence must contain reference to: 1) synergy, 2) novelty, 3) irreducibility, 4) unpredictability, 5) coherence, and 6) historicity.[24] Further, Clayton argues that emergence cannot be adequately explained by reference to only one scientific discipline, for "emergence is a pattern that runs on a variety of different platforms."[25]

In chapter 3, Clayton seeks to develop the *role* of emergence—as he understands it— in the natural sciences and in evolution, which is Clayton's most important contribution to theology and science within *Mind & Emergence*, and as a result is an important contribution to this current paper. He notes that, particularly within biology, one can see multiple instances of where that which emerges becomes a causal agent in its own right. He states that the biggest question facing scientists today is "how nature obtains order 'out of nothing', that is, how order is produced in the course of a system's evolution when it is not present in the initial conditions."[26] Clayton argues that whereas "biological processes in general are the result of systems that create and maintain order (stasis) through massive energy input from their environment," there comes a point of sufficient complexity after which a phase transition suddenly becomes almost inevitable.[27] Emergence in evolution therefore "consists of a collection of highly convoluted processes that produce a remarkably complex kind of combinatorial novelty."[28]

Clayton implies that the resurgence of emergence in the twentieth century has done much to deflate the *bottom-up* "new synthesis" that

---

degree of *immanence*.

22. Clayton, *Mind & Emergence*, 38.
23. Clayton, *Mind & Emergence*, 39.
24. Archinov and Fuchs, *Causality, Emergence, Self-Organization*, 5–6.
25. Clayton, *Mind & Emergence*, 47.
26. Clayton, *Mind & Emergence*, 73. Clayton then considers three examples of mechanisms that make such emergence possible: 1) autocatalysis in biochemical reactions, wherein the presence of the product is required for its own synthesis; 2) reactions that suggest emergence is ontological in nature and not merely epistemological (i.e., Belousov-Zhabotinsky reactions); and 3) self-organization (seen, e.g., in some slime molds).
27. Clayton, *Mind & Emergence*, 78. Note Clayton's general agreement with Kauffman, *Investigations*, 35.
28. Clayton, *Mind & Emergence*, 85. Cf. Deacon, "Hierarchic Logic of Emergence," 273–308.

resulted from Watson and Crick's discovery of the DNA molecule in 1956 being linked to Neo-Darwinian evolutionary thought.[29] Said "new synthesis" posits that the behavior of organisms—and even *ecosystems*—can be explained solely by referencing the gene reproduction and mutation that underlies them. As Leon Kass notes in his discussion of evolutionary biology, it never would have occurred to Darwin that "certain differences of degree—produced naturally, accumulated gradually (even incrementally) and inherited in an unbroken line of descent—might lead to a difference in kind."[30] However, due in part to the resurgence of emergence in the late twentieth century, the "new synthesis" is *in process* of being replaced by an "interactionist consensus" (also referred to as Meta-Darwinism) in which neither genes nor environments, neither nature nor nurture, suffice wholly for the production of phenotypes.[31] Within this interactionist paradigm, "fully adequate explanations of biological phenomena require the constant interplay of both bottom-up and top-down accounts."[32] Genotypes produce phenotypes that interact with specific environments, which then reproduce genotypes (*ad infinitum*).

In a logical move from the "interactionist consensus" just mentioned, the *new* "systems biology" approach has established four levels of complexity along the proverbial pyramid of life: 1) the base functional organization,[33] 2) the metabolic pathway, 3) the larger functional modules,[34] and 4) the large-scale organization arising from functional modules.[35] Understanding that complex cellular and intercellular processes are products of both upward and downward forces, according to systems biology, offers crucial insight

---

29. Note this implication is inferred by his placement of the section describing the "new synthesis" in biology into this chapter.

30. Kass, *Hungry Soul*, 62. I am not sure that Darwin would not consider *difference in degree* able to produce *difference in kind*, despite his reaction against the Lamarckian genetics of his day.

31. Cf. Jason S. Robert, *Embryology, Epigenesis and Evolution*, 2. See also Fowler and Kuebler, who analyze the Meta-Darwinian interpretation, which posits that different natural mechanisms are required to explain evolution other than natural selection and random mutation. These other mechanism include endosymbiosis, which is the engulfing of other structures and systems by existent cells; morphogenetic fields, which describes the general developmental area within which the system grows; and exaptation, which describes the co-opting of seemingly useless structures and systems from the environment within which the evolution of complexity occurs (Fowler and Kuebler, *Evolution Controversy*, 277–328).

32. Clayton, *Mind & Emergence*, 95.

33. Composed of the gene, genome, etc.

34. Responsible for cell function, note.

35. Clayton, *Mind & Emergence*, 91.

into the role of downward causation in nature. Indeed, "the development of large networks is governed by robust self-organizing phenomena that go beyond the particulars of the individual systems."[36] Clayton agrees, and states that there "is increasing evidence that emergence represents a fruitful . . . meta-scientific . . . framework for comparing the relations between the diverse realms of the natural world."[37] As Neil Campbell, in his highly used introductory biology college textbook, writes, "with each upward step in the hierarchy of biological order, novel properties emerge that were not present at the simpler levels of organization. These emergent properties arise from interactions between the components . . . Unique properties of organized matter arise from how the parts are arranged and interact . . . [insomuch as] we cannot fully explain a higher level of organization by breaking it down to its parts."[38] In the next section, I seek to fill in the gap, so to speak, left from Clayton's view of emergence with relevant biblical data that supports the notion of the Spirit's kenosis into creation.

BIBLICAL BASIS OF KENOSIS OF THE SPIRIT INTO CREATION AND FORMER CONCEPTIONS OF THE KENOSIS AND SCIENCE CONNECTION

The Bible gives good grounds for illustrating the Holy Spirit as being the *active* agent of God in the world, particularly regarding the Spirit as *life-giver* and *animator* of all creation.[39] It is the position of this paper that just as the Spirit kenotically entered into the chaotic seas through which the Jews passed in their exodus and parted them (Exod 14:21), so too did the Spirit of God part the chaotic primordial waters, thereby *preparing* and *causing* creation to leap forth (Gen 1:2).[40] The Spirit of life hovered over the primordial waters and transformed the *chaos* into the *cosmos*. As the Spirit blows, God speaks forth his creative Word, imparts information, and something that is separate from God comes into existence. Creation begins not with the Word, but rather with the Spirit, as the Spirit's presence precedes and is presupposed by the speaking of the Word.[41] One could perceive this creative activity of the Spirit as being either *inside* the chaos (picturing God as *immanent*) or as the Spirit *reaching down* to create order according

36. Barabási and Albert, "Emergence of Scaling in Random Networks," 509.
37. Clayton, *Mind & Emergence*, 93.
38. Campbell, *Biology*, 2–3.
39. Cf. Paul's assertion that the Spirit of God "gives life" in 2 Cor 3:6.
40. Lodhal, *Shekhinah/Spirit*, 43.
41. Dabney, "Nature of the Spirit," 73.

to the laws of nature (picturing God as *transcendent*).[42] It should be noted that the term *ruach* denotes God's active and creative presence throughout creation. Moreover, according to Dunn, *ruach* connotes the meanings of wind, breath, and power, usually with attending connotations of strength or violence.[43]

In Genensis 1:2, the Spirit moves upon the face of the waters, which constitutes an obvious creative act. The Hebrew word used in Genesis 1:2 for "moved" is *rahap*, which literally means "to vibrate" (recognize that vibration is energy). So then, it was the Spirit that introduced *energy* (or pure information) into the formless void. This verb used in Genesis 1:2 depicts the presence of the Spirit hovering mysteriously over the waters, preparing for the acts of creation to follow. It is interesting to note that the Hebrew verb עָרָה has been translated as "hovering" (as a bird over her young; see Deut 32:11), whereas the Syriac cognate term means "to brood over; to incubate." That the Spirit was hovering like a mother stork might hover over her nest is a portent of life to come from the dark, murky depths of the chaotic primordial waters.[44] Additionally, the original terms תהו (*tohu*) and בהו (*bohu*) of Genesis 1:2, which are often translated as "without form and void," are of uncertain etymology; but wherever they are used, they convey the idea of *confusion* and *disorder*. So then, the Spirit, one may postulate, is ultimately responsible for both the conditions for life as well as life itself. The Spirit is the "executive arm" (i.e., the *enacting* or *effectual* arm) of the Trinity in that he was active as the Son spoke each word in the primal creating moments recorded in Gen 1.

After the introduction of energy (or pure information) by the Spirit into the formless, chaotic matter, there was light (Gen 1:3). So then, the light that first illuminated the Earth was caused by the *impartation* of information and order by the *inspiriting* of the Spirit of God. When God *inspirits* formless and chaotic matter, nothing becomes *something*, and the disorderly becomes *orderly*. Since the level of order required for the origination of complex life was extremely high,[45] it is especially important to acknowledge that the Old Testament begins by presenting the function of the Spirit as being the giver and communicator of orderly information, and consequently, of complex biological life.

A rereading of Genesis 1 and 2 shows the currently predominant conceptions of creation to be false abstractions. The summarizing conceptions

---

42. Crain, "God Embodied In, God Bodying Forth the World," 666.
43. Dunn, "Towards the Spirit of Christ," 5.
44. Note that the Spirit is described as a *dove* in Matt 3:16.
45. As per Stuart Kaufman, cited in Popa, *Between Necessity and Probability*, 73.

of creation, according to Welker, are "very vague, mostly even obscure."[46] I declare that creation in Genesis 1 and 2 is not a creation out of nothing, as a one-time event, but is instead a *continuous* creation, a transformative process of producing higher aggregate conditions out of an absence of structure and order. *Creatio continua* operates as an enabling condition for all that occurs thereafter. According to Welker, neither Genesis 1 nor 2 "describes God as a highest being who in pure self-sufficiency does nothing other than produce and cause creaturely being."[47] Welker stipulates that God's action in Genesis 1 and 2 corresponds to only a few ways in which we normally construe causation and production.[48] Seven times God is listed as *evaluating*.[49] Three times God is listed as *naming*.[50] Twice God is listed as *acting* upon what is already created in order to separate it and give it order.[51] The latter two instances of God's action give credence to the notion of God acting upon formless matter, and thereby giving it order, structure, and complexity. Thus, the creating God is not merely an *actor* within creation, but also a *reactor* within creation. Indeed, God's action is an action that reacts, and is an action that lets itself be determined. Genesis 1 and 2 depict a creation that has its own activity, is itself productive, and is itself causative. In the Genesis narrative, we are not able to derive a clear demarcation between God's creativity and creation's/creature's activity.[52] On the one hand, God's activity is clearly active in production and causation. On the other hand, God is equally reactive to that which is created. An abstract, minimal definition of creation as related within the Genesis narrative is as follows: "creation is the construction and maintenance of associations of different, interdependent creaturely realms."[53] The study of creation must, therefore, focus upon the interdependencies of natural and providential processes. Creation as a whole, both the *reality* and *nature* of it, continually flow into each other.

Not only did God the Spirit create the world at one point in the past, but he now continually upholds it.[54] Paul the apostle expresses God the Son's creative work as that by which "all things were created" (Col 1:16),

---

46. Welker, *Creation and Reality*, 6–7.
47. Welker, *Creation and Reality*, 9.
48. Welker, *Creation and Reality*, 9.
49. Gen 1:4, 10, 12, 18, 21, 25, and 31.
50. Gen 1:5, 8, and 10
51. Gen 1:4 and 7.
52. Welker, *Creation and Reality*, 12.
53. Welker, *Creation and Reality*, 13.
54. This statement is adapted from Newton, as cited in Southgate, *God, Humanity, and the Cosmos*, 281.

which is an act of *definitive* causation (a "coming to be"). The speaking forth of the Word of God, which Paul here has in mind, necessarily presupposes the *breath* of God (i.e., *pneuma/ruach*, God the Spirit). The very next verse explains that "in him all things hold together" (Col 1:17), which connotes the *continual* creative act of the Spirit.[55] It is important, therefore, to view the Spirit not only as *originator* of creation, but also as *sustainer* of creation, upholding its order, and *giving it life*.[56] As Polkinghorne writes, "[p]art of a notion of *creatio continua* must surely be that an evolving universe is one which is theologically understood as being allowed, within divine providence, 'to make itself.'"[57] Rather than bringing into being a ready-made world of unalterable character, God the Father allows the creation, kenotically empowered by the Spirit, to develop according to its own pace. As Vanstone notes, the activity of the Spirit within creation proceeds by no assured program, but is precarious instead.[58] This *evolving fertility* is not a linear progression, but is staggered, as the Spirit is not the *manipulator* of creation, but its *director* instead. So then, the Spirit makes things able to make themselves, which affirms a *panentheistic* perspective.[59] Theologians today are correct, then, to perceive this long process of evolutionary emergence as God's continued creation, mediated by the interplay of laws and chance.[60] No picture of creation is complete that neglects either the *definitive* or the *continual* creative work of the Spirit. The reality of creation, then, deals with both *origins* and *continual* operation.

The Spirit is seen at various junctures within the Bible to operate via *proximate* causation. For example, Psalm 104:30 (NKJV) states, "[w]hen you send your Spirit, they are created, and you renew the face of the earth." Here the term "create" (*bara*) is used, not of the initial *generation* of life, but of its continual *regeneration*, as the context speaks of the Spirit causing "the grass [to] grow for the cattle, and plants for man to cultivate" (v. 14). It is "He [the Spirit, i.e., who] makes springs pour water into the ravines; [and flow] between the mountains" (v. 10) and who "bring[s] darkness, [and] it becomes night" (v. 20). It is the Spirit that continually provides food for all

---

55. For support of this notion, see Ward, *God, Chance, and Necessity*, 78.
56. Bonting, "Spirit and Creation," 724.
57. Polkinghorne, *Serious Talk*, 84.
58. Vanstone, *Love's Endeavor, Love's Expense*, 62.
59. In short, what is herein meant by "panentheism" is that God is in the world and permeates it, but simultaneously is greater than the world.
60. Doncel, "Kenosis of the Creator and of the Created Co-Creator," 798. Note that as a consequence of positing *creatio continua*, one must insist that the Spirit of God's providential power is manifest in the unfolding of creation in evolutionary history (Polkinghorne, "Kenotic Creation and Divine Action," 96).

living things (v. 28). The repeated emphasis within Psalm 104 is the notion that God *preserves* of the world, which *presupposes* that God creates through the power of the Spirit, as well as that the presence of the Spirit is the condition for both *potentialities* and *realities* of creation.[61] So then, the psalmist knows nothing of outright *spontaneous* generation, for God sends forth his Spirit, and they (i.e., all things) are created. Instead, the Spirit is repeatedly depicted in this psalm as the *presence* of God, as well as the means by which God acts *within* his creation.[62]

The Greek verb *kenown* can mean either "to empty" or "to pour out." In the literal sense, its Hebrew equivalent is used, for example, in Isaiah 32:15: "Until the spirit be *poured upon* us from on high . . ." The various cognates of the verb translated by *kenosis* in the Septuagint (LXX) appear fourteen times in biblical Hebrew. In its original sense, the verb עָרָה refers to a cause of movement leading to a mass being poured out of a container. Thus, the word means "to pour out" in reference to Rebekah's *pouring out* water from her pitcher *into* the trough (Gen 24:20; the verb in the LXX is *exekenōsen*). In the original Hebrew of Genesis 24:20, the term is עָרָה, a primitive root meaning "to be" (i.e., causatively "to make"). Hence, it is appropriate to translate said term as either "to empty" or "to pour out." Whereas the *pitcher* was *emptied*, the *trough* was made *full* (which is in effect an *addition*) by the emptying of the pitcher. I therefore conclude that a fruitful approach to understanding the verb *kenown* is to realize that it also means "to pour out." I posit that the *kenosis* of the Spirit *into* creation had a similar effect to Rebekah's pouring out water *into* the trough.

Christ poured himself *into* humanity so that it could be reconciled to the Father and that it might become acceptable to the Father (Phil 2:5–11). God the Son enters *into* the limited, finite situation of mankind, descending *into* it, thereby embracing the whole of human existence in his being.[63] It needs to be noted that the *kenosis* of the Son referred to in Philippians 2:5–11 *cannot* be understood as a *subtraction* of deity, but the *addition* of humanity instead. In the Philippians passage, the verb often translated as "emptied" is *explained*, *expanded*, and *extrapolated* by three participles that directly follow it: 1) "taking" the form of a servant, 2) "becoming" in the likeness of men, and 3) "being found" in fashion as a man. This reference to Christological *kenosis*, then, has the net effect of *addition*. Furthermore, the Philippians usage of the term *kenosis* eerily resembles that which is found in Isaiah 53:12, which reads, "[h]e *poured out* his soul to death." What God

---

61. Moltmann, *God in Creation*, 10.
62. Bonting, "Spirit and Creation," 715.
63. Moltmann, *Crucified God*, 176.

does *particularly* and *punctiliously* by the *kenosis* of the Son into human form, I posit, God does *generally* and *continually* by the *kenosis* of the Spirit into creation. The Spirit is the *breath of life*, the very giver of life, and is thus the creative power of the Father. The Spirit, then, is the *vital energy* that enlivens, as well as the *potent force* that enervates innovation. The kenosis of the Spirit *into* creation, the *pouring out* of life, makes possible not only *otherness* as properly conceived, but also its actualization. So then, a principle that one may draw from the usage of kenosis in reference to God the Son is illustrative of the kenosis in reference to God the Spirit.[64] There is an inherent others-centeredness in *kenosis*, as one can see in Rebekah's case, as well as in Christ's *kenosis*. It may be extrapolated, further, that the same others-centeredness is applicable to the Spirit's *kenosis into* creation.

The science and religion dialogue has long wrestled with the topic of God's action in the world, and models for conceiving divine action heretofore have been unsatisfactory.[65] Classical interventionism should be dismissed as illogical because God's action in the world would be inconsistently intermittent if actualized as pure intervention; God acting only as the creator of the world is deistic, and thereby delimits divine action in perpetuity; Thomistic understandings of God as the primary cause and creatures as secondary causes results in unnecessary bifurcations; and Process theology is unable to sustain the eschatological guarantees of God as revealed in scripture.[66] The resurgence of kenotic theology has been helpful in reformulating divine action in an evolutionary world.

Several years ago, a collection of essays by theologians and scientists explored creation as *The Work of Love*, pointing to divine action as *kenosis*.[67] In said book, Polkinghorne adopts the understanding of *kenosis* as an affirmation of God's voluntary self-limitation that allows creatures to enjoy power and freedom. Classical theology, according to Polkinghorne, envisions God in total control and invulnerable, such that there is no reciprocal effect of creatures upon the divine nature. According to Polkinghorne's view of *kenosis*, however, the kenotic creator interacts with creatures. The word "interact" is preferable to "intervene," in this volume, apparently because "intervene" carries interruption connotations. For Polkinghorne,

---

64. This *kenosis* of the Spirit can also be seen, for example, in his descent upon Jesus at his baptism. Indeed, the Spirit was *poured into* Jesus so as to *empower* Jesus for his crucial ministry of imparting life to the masses, which resulted in Jesus' own temporal and bodily death.

65. See Southgate, *God, Humanity, and the Cosmos*.

66. Yong, "From Quantum Mechanics to the Eucharistic Meal: John Polkinghorne's Vision of Science and Theology."

67. Cf. Polkinghorne, ed., *Work of Love*.

kenosis connotes the risk of the creating Spirit in submitting to the quasi-free process of evolutionary creation, which qualifies the operation of the Spirit. The Spirit was, as it were, "taking a risk" in creating a world kenotically, for it necessarily involves both chance and randomness through the processes of evolution.[68] Polkinghorne notes that the kenotic Spirit is the exemplar of humility, for he kenotically interacted with the created world, and as such, at least in some qualified sense, limited his eternality and omnipotence.[69] Polkinghorne conceives of *kenosis* as God's entirely voluntarily self-limitation.

Polkinghorne's view of *kenosis* is similar to Moltmann's view, who notes that kenotic self-surrender is "God's Trinitarian nature, and is therefore the mark of all his works 'outward.'"[70] The kenotic creating Spirit does not overrule his creation or its creatures, but continuously *interacts* with them instead. Polkinghorne summarizes his view by intimating that God allows the created other to be and to act, so that, while all that happens is permitted by God's general providence, not all that happens is in accordance with God's will or brought about by divine special providence. Such an understanding is basic to the interpretation of evolutionary history as creation making itself.

CONNECTION BETWEEN KENOSIS AND EMERGENCE THEORY

I find Polkinghorne's theory of *kenosis* as found within *The Work of Love* helpful, but incomplete (especially when one considers the problem of evil). The kenotic theology posited by this paper maintains that the Spirit *completely* shares and imparts himself *into* creation. The Spirit of God "poured herself out" into creation, thereby causing it to emerge from chaos and become a structured and orderly system of life-bearing entities. As a result of this *Breath* of God imparted, nature gives birth to life, and *life-bearing* creatures burst upon the environ.[71] So then, the Spirit is the life-giving force that enables creation to strive toward becoming its fullness via the process of evolution. The creation of ordered matter has its *ontological origin in* and *through* the agency of the Spirit of God. Creation is thus a kenotic act of *self-offering*. Therefore, one may accurately posit that creation, in a *qualified* sense, possesses the Spirit of God from its very *origin*, though one needs to

68. Peacocke, "Cost of New Life," 27.
69. Polkinghorne, "Kenotic Creation and Divine," 106.
70. Moltmann, "Kenosis in the Creation and the Consummation of the World," 141.
71. Ralston, "Kenosis and Nature," 58.

be weary of falling into pantheism. Instead of reducing the created world into a pantheistic entity, God is an "all-embracing unity" and the world exists "in" (panentheism) God in the sense that God is the ground of being for the created world. Being panentheistic in relation, there is both distinction and relatedness between the Spirit and creation.

According to Kathryn Tanner, the Spirit has historically been seen to either work immediately (i.e., proximately) or gradually.[72] So then, the Spirit could be seen just as much at work in the ordinary events of history as in its unusual happenings. Just as God usually works within, rather than overriding, the normal course of human affairs, so too does God work within the natural processes of nature, for "the same Spirit doth not breathe contrary notions."[73] The gradual model of the working of the Spirit requires methods of inquiry typical of modern science, and holds great promise for the science and religion dialogue.[74] The Spirit works modestly, in a continuous fashion, *in* and *through* natural processes.[75] The notion of emergence is compatible with the impersonal kenotic working of the Spirit in empowering creation from within in an almost hidden manner.[76] This hiddenness of the Spirit comports well with the Orthodox theologian Vladimir Lossky's statements to the effect that the Spirit remains "unmanifested, concealing himself even in his appearing."[77] By the Spirit's *kenosis* into creation, creation itself is then enabled to participate in the processes of production and reproduction. In the following two sections, I will explore further the notion of the Spirit's kenosis into unordered matter in discussing primordial chaos, as well as the potentialities that are inherent within matter.

Kenosis and Primordial Chaos

In an interesting contribution to the compilation edited by Michael Welker, *The Work of the Spirit*, Amos Yong discusses the contributions of

---

72. Tanner, "Workings of the Spirit: Simplicity or Complexity?," 87.

73. Sibbes, *Works*, 5:427.

74. Tanner, Workings of the Spirit: Simplicity or Complexity?," 105.

75. Welker, "Spirit in Philosophical, Theological, and Interdisciplinary Perspectives," 227.

76. Hiddenness is at the heart of *kenosis*, notes Ernest Simmons (Simmons, "Towards Kenotic Pneumatology," 11–16). The creation is, in a sense, *larva dei*, the *mask of God*. We encounter God through said masks because that is the only way in which finite beings can associate with the infinite *ground of being* (Tillichian overtones). Simmons notes that the Hebrew *ruach* as well as the Greek *pneuma* both carry with them a sense of hidden and unseen forces (Simmons, "Towards kenotic Pneumatology," 14).

77. Lossky, *Mystical Theology of the Eastern Church*, 169.

pneumatology to the broad notion of divine action.[78] In so doing, Yong invokes the Spirit of God as acting upon primordial chaos. Primordial chaos is the great confusion of matter out of which the Spirit, by *kenosis*, generated order, structure, and ultimately all of life. Primordial chaos, in and of itself, it must be reckoned, is utterly incapable to produce the formation of an ordered, structured, and functional collocation of atoms, because it is by definition random processes. Indeed, primordial chaos lacks the favorable environment that is requisite for enduring and functional patterns of matter to emerge. In fact, in primordial chaos matter did not exist as such, but indeterminate and unconditioned disorder instead.

According to Yong, the Spirit causes the emergence of order and presides over it from within through the processes of division, distinction, differentiation, and particularization.[79] This creating the Spirit did by infusing the primordial chaos with pure and directed information, which resulted in an evolutionary process that was imbibed with fertility. Yong's assertion gains support by Morowitz, who argues that the Spirit powers—even empowers—emergence by *being* the selection rules between God's immanence and the development of the Earth. Morowitz writes, "emergence selects the restricted world of the real from the super-immense world of the possible."[80] So then, the Spirit is the intermediate between physical laws and chaotic matter. In this sense, then, the Spirit acted as a liaison between the primordial chaos, which was the source of variation and novelty, and the resultant ordered and structured creation of the Genesis account.

This primordial chaos did not contain its own information (only *non-directed* energy instead), and therefore had to be infused with such by the Spirit. Thus, one may accurately note that the Spirit is the *agent of causation* by the interjection of both concretion and specification through information.[81] So then, the movement from chaos to cosmos was directed by the Spirit. Primordial chaos without an input of active information by the Spirit of God would remain forever indeterminate and unstructured.[82] For Bulgakov, ordered matter is the direct result of the kenotic action of the Spirit of God into creation.[83] Matter's receptivity to spirit, which has form as a requisite, also has as its precondition the creaturely descent of the Spirit, his

---

78. Yong, "Ruach, the Primordial Chaos, and the Breath of Life," 183–204.
79. Yong, "Ruach, the Primordial Chaos, and the Breath of Life," 194–95, 202.
80. Morowitz, *Emergence of Everything*, 197.
81. Polkinghorne, "Hidden Spirit and the Cosmos," 169.
82. Cf. Huchingson, "Chaos, Communications Theory, and God's Abundance," 395–414.
83. Bulgakov, *Comforter*, 345.

kenosis into creation.[84] Thus, the Spirit of God seems at first to have created the elementary principles of all things, creating formless masses of matter, which was *without* arrangement or distinction of parts.

Kenosis and Creation Understood as Potentiality

Primordial chaos, due to its intrinsic unpredictabilities, allows the *Possibility of God* (i.e., the Spirit[85]) much leeway in action. This primordial chaos was essential to God's subsequent creation because it was the source of innumerable potentialities[86] and novelties, without which the immense variety of nature would not be possible.[87] So then, the Spirit's *kenosis* into creation leads to the realization of manifold potentialities. This divine *Possibility* swept over the primordial chaotic abyss, and by *kenosis* into the primal creation, the complex activity of ordering within the chaotic primordial waters was onset. Because of the Spirit hovering over the waters, "the chaos becomes promise."[88]

In creation, the Spirit kenotically bestows both *potentiality* and *being* ("Let there be . . ."). In this view, "instead of being daunted by the role of chance in genetic mutations as being the manifestation of irrationality in the Universe, it would be more consistent with the observations to assert that the full gamut of potentialities of living matter could be explored only through the agency of the rapid and frequent randomization which is possible at the molecular level of DNA."[89] The way in which "chance" operates within the world to produce new structures, new entities, and even new species can only be understood as an actualization of the potentialities that the creating Spirit imbibed *within* creation. Thus, the creating Spirit's intention and purpose is actualized through the operation of "chance" and "random" events. One can perceive God within evolution, then, as the processes themselves, unveiled by the biological sciences, are God-acting-as-creator.

---

84. Bulgakov, *Comforter*, 221.

85. For justification of this terminology, see Dabney, "Naming the Spirit," 58. Also, creation from a pneumatological standpoint begins with the Spirit, and thus one should interpret the world as not defined by necessity, but by possibility instead, for the Spirit is the *possibility of God* (Dabney, "Naming the Spirit," 78). Michael Lodahl also notes that the "Spirit of God is identified as the possibility of God" (Lodahl, "From God to Creation," 4).

86. Note that within this section, the terms "potentialities" and "possibilities" are used virtually synonymously.

87. Huchingson, "Chaos, Communications Theory, and God's Abundance," 398.

88. Montague, *Holy Spirit*, 67.

89. Peacocke, *Creation and the World of Science*, 94.

Perhaps these potentials are delimited through what Polkinghorne refers to as "informational causality,"[90] which bears some similarity to the *formal cause* of Aristotle. Polkinghorne advocates a divine causation by God inputting pure and active information at the level of chaotic systems, and therefore it operates from *within* the causal nexus of nature.[91] Polkinghorne similarly asserts that this pure information is finely tuned and extremely sensitive to initial conditions, while also being open to the future at the same time.[92] His conception of God's input of information does not violate the law of conservation of energy, and also avoids the criticism of the God of the gaps.[93]

Chaotic systems, perhaps wrongfully labeled, interlace both order and disorder. If the system is too far on the orderly side, the possibility for novelty is greatly reduced, as the system itself is too rigid for anything except a rearrangement of what already exists. Conversely, if the system strays too far on the side of disorder, a random world of proverbial anarchy results. The potential for novelty and relative stability lies between the two poles of order and disorder within chaotic systems. I posit that the endowment of potentiality and regularity was instituted by, and relies upon, the kenosis of the Spirit *into* creation. The Spirit, in this kenotic model, is seen as working *within* the seeming openness of nature, in conjunction with the unfolding of potentiality, and hence is not what some could call a "Spirit of the gaps" (akin to the God of the gaps). Moreover, the Spirit enables emergence by endowing creation and creatures with the ability to unfold by apparent natural processes according to their own inherent potentialities and possibilities.

George Gaylord Simpson writes that "within the framework of the evolutionary history of life, there have been not one but many different kinds of progress," which is a correlate to the notion of the actualization of possibilities. (Of which these are examples: the increasing specialization with its corollary of improvement and adaptability, increase in the general energy or maintained level of processes, increasing complexity, and so forth.[94]) Moreover, Popper points out that the realization of possibilities, which may be random, depends upon the total situation within which the possibilities are being actualized so that there "exist weighted possibilities which are more than mere possibilities, but [at the same time are] . . . tendencies or

---

90. Polkinghorne, *Work of Love: Creation as Kenosis*, 99.
91. Polkinghorne, "Hidden Spirit and the Cosmos," 180.
92. Polkinghorne, *Belief in God in an Age of Science*, 66–67.
93. Polkinghorne, *Belief in God in an Age of Science*, 52–53.
94. Simpson, *Meaning of Evolution*, 236.

propensities to become real."⁹⁵ Peacocke suggests that there are propensities in evolution—of the Popperian sense noted above—towards the possession of certain features and characteristics, propensities that are built into the evolutionary process. Among these propensities of evolution are complexity and information-processing and -storage ability.

Regarding these propensities in evolution, Conway Morris notes that "within certain limits the outcome of evolutionary processes might be rather predictable . . . [as] nearly all biologists agree that convergence is a ubiquitous feature of life . . . [for] again and again we have evidence of biological form stumbling on the same solution to a problem."⁹⁶ Gould contends that there can be overall direction and implantation of divine purpose through what may popularly be called "chance" that operates within a rule-obeying context.⁹⁷ However, neither Gould nor Peacocke see these "propensities" as a special providential action by God, but rather a consequence of how God continuously creates through the processes that he has made (and hence merely a general providential action).

Contra Gould, however, I posit that there is a definitive *lure* of the Spirit within the *propensities* of nature, which seamlessly coalesces with the notion of the Spirit's *kenosis* into creation; for this potential, as it were, is directed by the ordering activity of the Spirit. The *kenosis* of the Spirit *into* creation is certainly not a picture of the traditional monological act of creation by direct production. Instead, by creating in a kenotic manner, the Spirit both *allows* and *invites* the input of creatures in the activity of creation, and *reacts* according to that input. Thus, God has chosen to allow the *other* to act, and has chosen to invite creation into a *cooperative* relationship. Indeed, the Spirit did not need to create in a manipulative, single act, but was able instead to create a process in which creation was allowed to develop. This can be seen, for example, by coalescing pneumatology with the modern Big Bang theory, whereby the Spirit can be viewed as the *Originator*, creating unformed matter, setting the Big Bang in motion, and then working with it over time to produce complexity. Instead of creating a *finished* product by divine fiat, the Spirit allows the world to *develop* within the framework he set up. This notion of creation through *development* also leads to an understanding of *biological evolution* in which the Spirit is seen as using the development of creatures via a type of *continuing creation*. There exists overwhelming evidence of a universe marked by development, which points to creation by *kenosis*. And it should be noted that the Spirit is present "in,

---

95. Popper, *World of Propensities*, 12.
96. Conway Morris, *Crucible of Creation*, 205.
97. Gould, *Wonderful Life*, 51.

with, and under" the processes of biological evolution within the created world. The kenotic creating Spirit is present within the *historical contingency of evolution*, as well as its *lawful regularity*. Seen in this manner, the Spirit acts within the *causal nexus* of creation (i.e., natural law, providence, and later human action) to input pure informational content by means of the impartation of active energy. Thus, the Spirit did not bring about creation in a *single*, definitive action, but instead used a process of evolution guided by natural laws.

CONCLUSION

The Earth is an active, empowering environment— even an empowering agent—that brings forth life by various independent processes of self-reproduction. Evolution is the overall process, but emergence punctuates the steps of the evolutionary epic. At the same time, the Earth must be seen as an environment of various heterogeneous life processes. So then, the Earth brings forth, but it does not bring forth *itself*. By releasing the power of the self-directed Earth, the Spirit enables—potentially—the continual production, variation, and sustenance of vegetable and animal life.[98] Moreover, in order to be consistent within the causal nexus, the Spirit of God kenotically bestows causal power unto the created order, and in effect thereafter becomes the chief Cause *amongst* causes. However, the created world is ever docile before the Spirit, and therefore ever open to his causal influence.

The entire mission of the Spirit could be succinctly envisioned as one of *kenosis*.[99] By extrapolation, one may infer that the Spirit was *poured into* creation so that it might develop fully in complexity into what the Father had intentioned from the beginning. By focusing on the Spirit, via *kenosis* into creation, as both *originator* and *operator* of creation, one can see that the Spirit is both *directly* and *indirectly* involved in the world from *beginning* to *end*. So then, whereas the Spirit is the *primary* cause of all things, he also works through *secondary* causes. This implies, therefore, that what may commonly be referred to as "*natural* processes," or even what may be termed "*random* processes," are in reality the *indirect* acts of the Spirit through *secondary* causes. It is the postulate of this paper that distinctive, seemingly nondependent actions are in fact Spirit-caused, though they may appear to be *secondarily* caused.[100] The apparent *secondary* causation is due

---

98. Welker, *Creation and Reality*, 42.

99. Lucien, *Kenosis and Creation*, 116.

100. Compare this postulation with a Neo-Thomist conception of divine "double agency," as mentioned by Southgate, *God, Creation, and the Cosmos*, 281.

in large part to the fact that the Spirit is the agent of discovery within the various *possibilities* of God.[101] In this *secondary* capacity, the Spirit is the *remote* cause, while natural forces are *proximate* causes of events. Because the Godhead created all of the natural processes and laws, via *kenosis* into creation, the Spirit is God's *agent of creation* within all of the forces of nature.

The Spirit, it is herein affirmed, ennobles and enables creation to possess emergent capabilities.[102] The Spirit imparted *propensities* into creation that eventuate the rise of information-processing systems, as well as information-storage systems, which were both necessary for the realization of higher forms of life. The Spirit is the very *power of being* this paper posits. The *Breath of Life* enables and empowers the emergence of creation and creatures. Moreover, this Spirit of emergence endows creation with the ability to unfold by "natural" processes according to their inherent potentialities.

In this chapter, I have reviewed and interacted with Clayton's seminal work *Mind & Emergence*. In that book, Clayton contends that emergence is a viable option in contrast to the waning explanatory power of both *physicalism* and *dualism*. Moreover, I have presented the biblical basis of *kenosis* of the Spirit *into* creation, arguing that the Bible presents the Spirit as being the *active* agent of God in the world, particularly regarding the Spirit as *life-giver* and *animator* of all creation. I also have made my own contribution of the connections between *kenosis* of the Spirit into creation and emergence theory, which complements Clayton's explanative survey of emergence theory. In so doing, I have posited that Clayton has not given a sufficient account of the metaphysical realities that give rise to emergence, and therefore have sought to unpack these metaphysical realties in this chapter. In using Clayton's text as the source of my extrapolations, I have contended that a richer metaphysical account may *ironically* result in greater autonomy for the biological sciences.

---

101. Dabney, "Naming the Spirit," 58.
102. Cf. Welker, *Work of the Spirit*, xii.

10

Nygren and Oord on Love: A Critique[1]

In a not-so-funny way, we are all prisoners of love.

—ROBERT E. WAGONER[2]

INTRODUCTION

Both Anders Nygren and Thomas Jay Oord are modern-day theological giants when it comes to the exposition of Christian love. Oord's thoroughly relational concept of love is an apt portrayal that I will appropriate in my depiction of love within this chapter as fully kenotic—that is, kenotically donated and self-giving.[3] By the newly minted terminology of "kenotically donated," I am referring to the methodology by which the Spirit of God's

---

1. This article originally appeared as McCall, "Nygren & Oord on Love: A Critique." Reprinted with permission.

2. Wagoner, *Meanings of Love*, 135.

3. Robert Wagoner also pictures preeminent love to be of the self-giving variety. In fact, he calls it "the epitome of love . . . [for] there is enormous power in selflessness" (Wagoner, *Meanings of Love*, 137). Further, according to Wagoner, however love is defined, it must be understood as a relation of some kind (14). In fact, "from the Christian point of view love is something held in trust, something given, something I can enjoy only if I do not attempt to possess it" (Wagoner, *Meanings of Love*, 47). Wagoner's view is that love is something I can enjoy only if it is self-giving in its orientation, which backs up one of the main thrusts of this current essay. This condition, I would submit, applies both to God as well as humans.

self-giving, uncontrolling love imbibes creation. After all, in many ways, the utmost expression of love is the utmost gift of the self.[4]

Charles Hartshorne is right when he opines, "Theologians have never taken really seriously the proposition that God is love."[5] Historically speaking, people have always had a hard time with love. Dealing with it, that is. All the more so when speaking of divine love, which we often cannot either empirically detect or directly discern mentally. In recent years, Oord has written several books regarding God's love, its affects, as well as what it effects in the world. In fact, one could legitimately say that Oord is the leading theologian of love in today's academic context. This is but one reason why I have chosen to use his extensive writing to help me flesh out kenotically donated, self-giving, and uncontrolling love. Some of these terms are Oord's own words, while some are not; the distinction will become apparent in what follows.

The *fully* kenotic concept of God's love developed herein is consistent with Oord's portrayal of an essentially kenotic God who has an eternal nature marked by others-centered and others-empowering, uncontrolling love. This uncontrolling love, as the contingentist (a word that refers to someone who emphasizes contingency in his or her philosophy of life) Oord likes to say, necessarily provides freedom and agency to members of each species within the natural world—especially human animals—with God working to empower and inspire creation toward well-being and wholeness.[6] Regardless of our attitude about religion, there is something very compelling about this radical image of self-giving as the epitome of love. In what follows, I will seek to build on the insights regarding love by both Nygren and Oord, with an assist by Karol Wojtyla. I seek to illustrate the notion that God's kenotically donated love is a synergistic symbiosis enacted through the Spirit of creativity that achieves greater evolutionary results combined than either aspect of the symbiosis alone.[7]

This means, then, that God's kenotically donated love is both productive of emergent entities and effectual for the derivation of greater complexity within those entities in the natural environ. This kenotically donated love onsets an evolving fertility, which most proximately is a result of the panentheistic relationship of God and world. This panentheistic relationship was initially wrought by the kenotic donation of God's very self *into* chaotic matter eons ago, and is now continually sustained and upheld by

---

4. Wagoner, *Meanings of Love*, 5.
5. Charles Hartshorne, "Ethics and the New Theology," 97.
6. Oord, *Uncontrolling Love of God*, 94.
7. see McCall, "Whitehead, Creativity, and the Immanently Creative Spirit," 337.

the repetitive impartation of God's very self—through imbibification of the Spirit—into the natural world. Thereafter, marked by the embeddedness of Spirit, which is the agent of contingency within evolution, the natural world progressed in a serpentine manner in the advancement toward greater complexity, of which *Homo sapiens sapiens* is the pinnacle (at present, anyway). In fact, God's world is teeming with randomness. It is, I like to say, smothered in contingency. Indeed, it is both smothered and stuffed with it. As such, it is marked by contingentist entities. Things do not happen according to a divine plan, but God intends for entities to cooperate with kenotically donated love.

KENOTIC LOVE AS SELF-DONATION AND SELF-GIVING

The terminology of love as "self-donation," which originated with Karol Wojtyla, is a principle on which my "kenotically donated love" is based. Neither did I originate the terminology of "self-giving, uncontrolling love" (Oord did). If one looks at Wojtyla's *Love and Responsibility*,[8] one can find several different ways that he applies Thomistic principles to the modern study of love as self-donation, which is, according to his reasoned judgment, a defining characteristic of love with relation to the other. This conception of self-donating love by Wojtyla entails the Spirit going outside herself (*ad extra*) to both find and produce a fuller existence in another entity, whereby the epic of evolution is empowered. It should be noted, also, that Wojtyla's self-donating love is a strong correlate to Oord's characterization of uncontrolling love. Accordingly, I will employ both terms—or at least their application—in what can be called "kenotically donated love." This depiction is based fundamentally upon the notion that *kenosis* of the Spirit amounts to self-giving (literally a "pouring out" of the Spirit or an "infilling") with reckless abandonment, and *not* a mere self-emptying (or self-abnegation). Oord and I have both been picturing *kenosis* as essentially self-giving (or, to use my terminology, a "pouring out" into the other, an "infilling," or even as a "self-donation" to the other) since or about the year 2008.

The Greek word for "empty," *keneos*, from which the term *kenosis* is derived, can mean either "to empty" or "to pour out." I contend that the Spirit's "pouring herself out" into creation (i.e., her *kenosis*) enables the derivation of life and love itself.[9] The view I am defending is similar to Wojtyla's description of love as "self-donation." The biblical tradition and the theological tradition give good grounds for illustrating the Spirit as the

---

8. See, e.g., Wojtyla, *Love and Responsibility*, 82.
9. McCall, "Kenosis of the Spirit into Creation."

active agent of God in the world, particularly as *life-giver* and *animator* of all creation through kenotic, self-donating, and self-giving love.[10] These latter two—self-donating and self-giving love—I now note, are manifestations of God's love *to* his creatures, *for* his creatures, and *through* his creatures. In what follows, I shall use the terms "self-donating love" and "self-giving love" *to* and *for* creation as illustrative metaphors with which to picture God's dynamic presence within the world in our postmodern context through kenotic donation.

In noting that the love of God is kenotically donated, I intend to highlight that God not only gives us love itself, but also *her-self* in the very act of love. Further, in characterizing love as self-giving, I intend to once again draw attention to the fact that God gives of himself (liberally) to his creation and creatures of the creation. He imparts part of himself to it and them, both, in a *kenotic* (i.e., a self-giving, a self-donated, or an "infilling") manner. Hence, I say God's love is kenotically donated. Picking up Oord's view of love as being "uncontrolling," I gather that he means God gives out of his fullness, but does not insist on controlling the response(s) of his creation to his impartation of love; hence, the designation of his love as "uncontrolling." So then, God does not insist on having control. In point of fact, due to her nature primarily being kenotically donated, self-giving love, God *cannot* (totally) control other entities, be they animate or not, although she could—and does!—lure, woo, and beckon entities toward herself. Not simply "will not," but "cannot." That is the *radical* assertion everywhere made by Oord, and especially in his newest title, *God Can't*.[11] And I join him in it.

I will argue in what follows for a notion of love that is kenotically donated, self-giving, creative, and uncontrolling. In so doing, I will use several of Oord's texts as my launching points, and will aim at substantiating that kenotically donated, self-giving, creative, and uncontrolling love is empowering of the other and allows for the interactivity of matter and the Godhead, since it is principally pneumatologically derived (i.e., Spirit-based) and based upon an imbibification of matter with the Spirit of God, which onsets a panentheistic orientation between God and the world. I have coined the term "imbibification" to refer to the process by which some entity, some thing, or someone is imbibed by the Spirit of God. There is a danger that such a position could be labeled pantheism, but if one were to consciously stipulate at all times that God is in the world thoroughly, but at the same is also more than the world, one could avoid such a distorting moniker.

---

10. McCall, "Thomistic Personalism in Dialogue with Kenosis," 21–32.
11. Oord, *God Can't*, 22.

I will be reinforcing the statement of Stephen G. Post to the effect that the energy of love should be studied intently by religion.[12] This type of study is illustrated by Oord's oft-employed terminology of a "love, science, and theology symbiosis," wherein issues of love are given paramount importance in all areas of our lives, not just in what has been historically been seen to lie within its domain (i.e., in interpersonal relationships).[13] This idea of a synergistic symbiosis of kenotically donated love is itself highly instructive, because it invokes the terminology of close, long-term biological associations wherein both entities benefit from the relationship, which is known as *mutualism*. Or, alternatively, it could refer to close, long-term biological associations wherein one of the entities benefits solely, but not to the detriment of the other entity, which is a relation known as *commensalism*. Although *parasitism* is theoretically possible in such biological relationships that I am herein envisioning, I choose not to either include it or elaborate upon it because I view love, following Oord, to be inherently self-giving, others-centered, and others-empowering, versus being self-centered to the exclusion of the other entity, which would be the meaning of parasitism in this context. In many ways, I posit that the commensalistic association just spoken of is an apt metaphor for our relationship with God, in part because I cannot conceive how an entity such as God would "benefit" from our reciprocated love (contra *mutualism*). This rejection of mutualism concerns God's *existence*, which is necessary, and not God's *actuality* (or how God exists), which is compatible with mutualism.

LOVE, THEOLOGY, AND *KENOSIS* SYMBIOSIS: IN DIALOGUE WITH OORD

In what follows, I largely preserve Oord's insights into love, and I mention such here so as to later build upon Oord's definition of love, wherein he asserts that it is "to act intentionally, in sympathetic/empathetic[14] response to others (including God), to promote overall well-being."[15] Oord breaks this definition down into the following components: "to act intentionally" means, for him, that love refers to "deliberations, motive, and self-determination,"

---

12. Post, *Unlimited Love*, viii.

13. see Oord, *Science of Love: Wisdom of Wellbeing*.

14. Note that Oord published two texts dealing with love in calendar year 2010: *Defining Love* and *The Nature of Love*, the latter of which added "empathetic" to the definition of love.

15. Oord, *Defining Love*, 15.

to which he later adds "freedom."[16] The decisionality of love, as presented in the above definition by Oord, seemingly refers to the claim that a degree of mentality must needs accompany action that is regarded as loving, though this mentality need not be marked by depth and complexity. This has explicit process philosophical overtones. This is itself intentional in that I view Process philosophy to offer the most cogent view of the subject matter in question.

Oord's next phrase, "in sympathetic/empathetic response to others," indicates that actual relationality, not just theoretical relationality, is required for there to be an instance of love shown.[17] Oord here uses the terms "sympathy and empathy" in reference to love because they are "technical word[s]," which refer to the "internal, constituting influence of one or more objects or individuals on the loving actor."[18] In so doing, he highlights the "feeling-with/suffering-with" of sympathy and empathy. Bluntly, love is inherently relational. Love takes at least two entities, if not more. Entirely isolated individuals/entities could not love, according to Oord. Further, creatures could not love if a relational God were not the lover who empowers, inspires, and beckons them to do so.

Charles Hartshorne notes that sympathy entails "the doctrine . . . that all feeling feels other feeling, all reaction has an object which itself is reactive, [and] that we have objects at all is due entirely to the . . . immanent sociality of experience."[19] Further, Alfred North Whitehead contended that sympathy is equivalent to "prehension," a point that also stands out in this context. Herbert Spencer, the great nineteenth-century Darwinian, notes that sympathy is "fellow-feeling." Oord avers that his usage of the terminology of "sympathetic/empathetic" with reference to love is meant to conjure up the internally influencing nature of love itself.[20] In addition, love is a decision that is made: it is both tendential and judgmental, which is captured rather well by process theologians John Cobb and David Ray Griffin's phraseology of "creative-responsive love."[21] Oord joins these scholars in noting that love has both passive and active dimensions to it.[22]

The last phrase of Oord's definition of love, "to promote overall well-being," highlights the positive character of love's aim: well-being. To

16. Oord, *Nature of Love*, 8.
17. Oord, *Nature of Love*, 42.
18. Oord, *Defining Love*, 19.
19. Hartshorne, *Beyond Humanism*, 185.
20. Oord, *Defining Love*, 20.
21. Cobb and Griffin, *Process Theology*, Cf. ch. 3.
22. Oord, *Defining Love*, 22.

promote well-being is to increase flourishing in at least one of the following dimensions: a person's dispositions, habits, or character. According to the mutuality tradition of love, to love is to engage in personal interaction or relationship. Love *is* relation, meaning that the reciprocity inherent in any relationship is itself love. Indeed, contemporary theologian Vincent Brümmer calls love "a reciprocal relation," and he claims that love "must by its very nature be a relationship of free mutual give and take."[23] Charles Hartshorne offers a similar view of love as mutuality when he says that "love means realization in oneself of the desires and experiences of others, so that one who loves can in so far inflict suffering only by undergoing this suffering himself."[24] Invoking the symbiotic associations in biology once more, I posit that to love is to be "mutually related."

ANDERS NYGREN AND THE THREEFOLD DELINEATION OF LOVE

The fifteenth-century French philosopher Francois de la Rochefoucauld once said, "There is only one kind of love, but there are a thousand different versions of it."[25] Today we might say that love has trillions of versions. Indeed, love is highly pluralistic in that love is multiform and multiexpressive.[26] Authored by the Swedish theologian Anders Nygren (1890–1978), *Agape and Eros: The Christian Idea of Love*[27] was the most successful and influential theological book on love in the twentieth century. Nygren therein, somewhat helpfully (I have a split opinion of his view of love, as will become evident later), divides love into three different conceptions: *agape*, *eros*, and *philia*. Throughout the world, countless students of theology and related disciplines have learned from Nygren's book that Christian love (*agape*) stands in radical opposition to both the Greek concept of *eros* and the Jewish treatment of love in law (*nomos*).[28] Nygren distinguishes sharply between two irreconcilable concepts of love, namely the Platonic and the Christian. He identifies the Platonic understanding of love in terms of *eros*

---

23. Brümmer, *Model of Love*, 162.
24. Hartshorne, *Man's Vision of God*, 31. Hartshorne is inconsistent in his use of "love." Sometimes he uses the word to speak of simple mutuality; other times he uses the word to speak of acting for the good. And he does not believe that mutuality always promotes the good.
25. La Rochefoucauld, *Moral Maxims and Reflections*, 31.
26. Oord, *Defining Love*, 32.
27. Cf. Nygren, *Agape and Eros*.
28. Jeanrond, *Theology of Love*, 113.

and the Christian in terms of *agape*. *Agape*, the word most frequently used in both the New Testament and the Greek translation of the Old Testament, is charged here with a different, particularly Christian meaning, namely, the belief that Christian love comes from God.

According to Nygren, "*eros* and *agape* are the characteristic expressions of two different attitudes to life, two fundamentally opposed types of religion and ethics. They represent two streams that run through the whole history of religion, alternately clashing against one another and mingling with one another. They stand for what may be described as the egocentric and the theocentric attitude in religion."[29] They are essentially opposite of one another because "*Eros* is an upward movement . . . [whereas] *agape* comes down."[30] In fact, Nygren pursues a twofold aim: he wishes to expose *eros* as that human form of egocentric and desiring love that strives to reach the divine sphere by its own strength, and he recommends *agape* as that form of love that originates in God and therefore requires a human attitude of receptivity and passivity. An erotic attitude focuses on something that is of great attraction and value to us human beings and thus causes desires in us, whereas *agape* is addressed to every human being and as such creates a value in that being.[31] *Agape* is God's way to humankind.[32] For Nygren, there "cannot actually be any doubt that *eros* and *agape* belong originally to two entirely separate spiritual worlds, between which no direct communication is possible."[33]

Nygren distinguishes sharply between two irreconcilable concepts of love, namely the Platonic and the Christian. He identifies the Platonic understanding of love in terms of *eros* and the Christian in terms of *agape*. As such, *eros* is the aspiration of a lower drive toward a higher drive. *Eros* is the attitude of *eudaemonism*.[34] *Agape*, on the other hand, is the attitude of the higher entity stooping down in service to the lower entity. Indeed, for Nygren, *agape* is essentially the love of God who, in divine grace, stoops down *toward* human persons in order to save them. "There is thus no way for man to come to God, but only a way for God to come to man: the way of divine forgiveness, divine love. *Agape* is God's way to man."[35]

29. Nygren, *Agape and Eros*, 205.
30. Nygren, *Agape and Eros*, 205.
31. Nygren, *Agape and Eros*, 78.
32. Nygren, *Agape and Eros*, 81.
33. Nygren, *Agape and Eros*, 31
34. This cumbersome term means simply that we are to pursue the highest ethical goal, which is happiness.
35. Nygren, *Agape and Eros*, 80–81.

Eros is born from want, whereas *agape* from abundance; in fact, "*Eros* is the will to get and possess which depends on want and need . . . *agape* is freedom in giving, which depends on wealth and plenty."[36] *Eros*, then, is need-love, which is motivated by the desire for what it lacks, whereas *agape* is gift-love, which flows spontaneously from its own abundance. Thus, God's love for us is not *eros*, but pure *agape* instead. In fact, "*Eros* is yearning desire; but with God there is no want or need and therefore no desire nor striving. God cannot ascend higher. . . . Since *agape* is a love that descends, freely and generously giving of its superabundance, the main emphasis falls with inescapable necessity on the side of God."[37] Therefore, God's love for us has its origin in God, that is, in the abundance of the Divine's own *agape*, and not in us.[38]

Eros is inherently conditional, whereas *agape* is completely unconditional. *Eros* is the love I have for the other because the other has potential to either realize the good within me or enabling me to achieve the good. As such, it is conditional on the other having this potentiality—I can only desire goodness from you on condition that you have this possibility. *Agape*, on the other hand, is unconditional since it is not motivated by the qualities of the other, but by the abundance of the giver instead. Indeed, *eros* is determined by the quality, or beauty and worth, of its object, and is not spontaneous, but "evoked," whereas *agape* is directed to both "the evil and the good"—and it is spontaneous, "overflowing," "unmotivated."[39] This situation applies especially to God's love for us: God's love is "groundless"—not in the sense that there is no ground for it, or that it is arbitrary, but that it is shown to us based upon no extrinsic grounds for it. At this point, a further difficulty surfaces in Nygren's view of love: it is incoherent to claim both that *agape* bestows value on its object and that it is indifferent to the value in the object. After all, the fact that I am loved by another indeed bestows a value on me that I would not have had lest I be loved by him or her. It is not clear whether the *agape* that Nygren conceives is the kind of love that can do this.

Another problem concerns the nature of God's love for us. For the same reason as Plato and Augustine before him, Nygren denies that God's love for us can be of the *eros* form: "With God there is no *want* or *need*, and therefore no desire or striving."[40] On the contrary, God's love is pure *agape*, and that for two reasons: first, God's love is *agape* by definition—"All love

---

36. Nygren, *Agape and Eros*, 210.
37. Nygren, *Agape and Eros*, 212.
38. see Brümmer, *Model of Love*, 129.
39. Nygren, *Agape and Eros*, 210.
40. Nygren, *Agape and Eros*, 210. Italics added.

that has any right to be called *agape* is nothing else but an outflow from the divine love. It has its source in God. 'God is *agape*'. This, too, is a simple consequence of the meaning of the word *agape*."[41] Further, this is a "real definition": it is not a mere contingent fact about God that God is *agape*, but a necessary consequence of God's essential nature as the superabundant love behind, before, and for all things—"Since *agape* is a love that descends, freely and generously giving of its superabundance, the main emphasis falls with inescapable necessity on the side of God."[42] This view of God's love raises a number of difficulties. First, if Nygren holds that there is in God "no need or want or desire," then God cannot *need* nor *want* nor *desire* that we return God's love—God would be unable to receive our love in any meaningful sense, as well, which is an incoherent and an abominable assertion, for God would then care *for* us but not *about* us.[43]

Another "dimension of love" discussed by Nygren is our love *toward* God. Nygren stipulates that this can very well be *eros*: "Human want and need seeks for satisfaction in the divine fullness. *Eros*-love is acquisitive desire, appetite, which as such strives to obtain advantages. Since God is the Highest Good, the sum of all conceivable good or desirable objects, it is natural that he should attract to himself all desire and love."[44] Strictly speaking, our love for God cannot be *agape*, since "*agape* is spontaneous, unmotivated love. But in relation to God, man's love can never be spontaneous and unmotivated. God's love always comes first and awakens man's love in response."[45] This is because our love for God is always motivated by an extrinsic cause in God. Nygren thus doubts whether *agape* can appropriately be used to denote a human's attitude toward God. In relation to God, people are never spontaneous; we are not an independent center of activity. Hence it *lacks* all the essential marks of *agape*.

All forms of *eros*, however, aim at self-realization and are therefore expressions of self-love. Unlike *eros*, *agape* "excludes all self-love. Christianity does not recognize self-love as a legitimate form of love . . . It is self-love that alienates man from God, preventing him from sincerely giving himself up to God, and it is self-love that shuts up man's heart against his neighbor."[46] In brief, according to Nygren, in all cases *eros* equals self-love, and *agape* in all cases is God's love toward human beings. The most we can hope to be are

41. Nygren, *Agape and Eros*, 212.
42. Nygren, *Agape and Eros*, 212.
43. see Brümmer, *Model of Love*, 132.
44. Nygren, *Agape and Eros*, 212.
45. Nygren, *Agape and Eros*, 213.
46. Nygren, *Agape and Eros*, 217.

impersonal "reservoirs" or "canals" by which God can let *agape* flow to the world. But then, it seems to me, we are *not* the ones who love, but rather, God does all the loving—*God* loves through us, and we do nothing. Nygren's claims make the Christian faith explicitly deny that human beings are "independent centers of activity," and as such, it denies that they are persons.[47]

Because the problem of love is whether and how there can be a self-denying and sacrificial love for others that is at the same time fulfilling and perfective of oneself, Nygren only admits two extreme forms of love, which he claims are mutually exclusive. On the one hand, we can love other humans and God with a love of *eros*, in which we love them out of self-interest in order to acquire from or possess them; or we can love others and God with a love of *agape*, in which we reject all self-gain and interest and surrender ourselves to others and love them purely for themselves. Thus, Nygren presents us with an unbridgeable dichotomy: either we love others and God purely for ourselves, in which case we do not really love them at all; or we love them for themselves with a true love, in which case we act against our own self-interest and happiness.[48]

Rather than the definition and elaboration of *agape* that Nygren gives us, I would like to propose the following litany of terms as descriptive of God's *agape* love (if we are forced to even use that term; more on this later): *agape* love is, according to Reinhold Niebuhr, a "self-sacrifice."[49] Moreover—and I truly appreciate this definition due to my reimagining of the oft-used, but rarely understood, term *kenosis*—it is a "letting-be," according to John Macquarrie.[50] Further, it is a representation of "the divine extravagance of giving that does not take self into account."[51] It is also, in another definition that I particularly appreciate, "God giving himself," or even a "divine bestowal," according to Irving Singer.[52] Finally, there is yet another definition that I greatly appreciate from Paul Fiddes, who claims that it is "self-giving," insomuch as a person "spends himself freely and carelessly for the other person."[53] I would now like to appropriate many of these senses of the word *agape* for my own purposes in joining Oord, building from the previous section, in picturing God's love

---

47. See Brümmer, *Model of Love*, 137.
48. see Rousselot, *Problem of Love in the Middle Ages*, 13.
49. Niebuhr, *Nature and Destiny of Man*, 2:82.
50. Macquarrie, *Principles of Christian Theology*, 349.
51. Grant, *Altruism and Christian Ethics*, 188.
52. Singer, *Plato to Luther*, 1:269.
53. Fiddes, *Creative Suffering of God*, 170.

as always "self-giving." Thus, ideally I would not divvy love up into various "types"—be it *agape,* or *eros,* or *philia.*

"FULL-OORDED" LOVE

I follow Oord in noting that *agape* is simply one form of love, according to the biblical witness, and as such it is not the be-all, end-all substance of love. *Agape* is just one out of a multitude of ways that we humans may self-givingly and intentionally respond to others to promote well-being, which we can refer to as "full-Oorded" love. In my conception, "full-Oorded" love would encompass what is ordinarily contained within the definition of *agape* love, but it would also include *eros* love, for the latter is the love of colaborment. Indeed, Martha Nussbaum says that *eros* "involves an opening of the self toward an object, a conception of the self that pictures the self as incomplete and reaching out for something valued."[54] Thus, when *eros* is expressed, the responsive, affective, or emotional element in love exerts considerable influence—but intentionality is never completely absent.[55]

In my appropriation of this terminology of "*eros* love," it would be the type of love that has the desire to, for example, expand one's territory or one's domain, which makes it applicable to the modern theory of evolution by natural selection. Evolution—i.e., "descent with modification," to invoke a Darwinian phrase—then, recognizes self-giving love, and the goodness thereof, in that species regularly undergo commensalist relationships in nature, whereby one is aided by the other, while the other is neither aided nor harmed. This is self-giving love and a proper demonstration of it. We are *not* just "reservoirs," to invoke Nygren; we are also generators of self-donating, self-giving, kenotic love. Oord and Wojtyla would entirely agree with this contention, for kenotic, self-donating, and self-giving love is inherently relational. But it must not be seen to be only a "desire," for it is also an intentional response to promote overall well-being when affirming that which is valuable. Self-giving, it should be noted, is the central aspect of reflections upon God as love. God makes the object of divine love first of all worthy of this love. The love flowing from the cross makes the ugly person beautiful in the eyes of God. For Jüngel, Christ's self-giving (*kenosis*) is the ultimate qualification of love.[56] I agree with Jeanrond, for he indicates that God's "self-giving love" "defines love."[57]

54. Nussbaum, *Upheavals of Thought,* 460.
55. see Oord, *Defining Love,* 46.
56. Eberhard Jüngel, *God as the Mystery of the World,* 358.
57. Jeanrond, *Theology of Love,* 132.

My understanding of "full-Oorded" love would also include dimensions of *philia* love. *Philia*, if we must retain the differentiation, could be akin to mutualism or commensalism in biology, especially since *philia* love has historically been associated with friendship or the interrelatedness of the natural world. Notably, Aristotle indicates that even nonhuman animals can express *philia* love.[58] The relationships marked by *philia*, then, could be identified by mutuality, reciprocity, and cooperation, which fits the above biological connotation well. While *agape* or *eros* might benefit from cooperation, reciprocity, and mutuality, those two forms of love do not require any of those three abstract nouns. *Philia* does, flatly. I contend, in fact, that the *kenosis* of the Spirit *into* creation amounts to self-giving, betrothed love through self-donation. Several years ago, a collection of essays by scientists and theologians pondered creation as *The Work of Love*, pointing therein to divine action as *kenosis* in which it is asserted that the Spirit has chosen to invite creation into a *cooperative* relationship, which also coalesces with Wojtyla's conception of love as self-donation. Further, because the love of God is uncontrolling, it always donates freedom, agency, and self-organization to the other, and thereby God sustains the regularities of nature.[59]

Notably, even *after* Darwin, Petr Kropotkin indicated that cooperation was everywhere present within the natural world, an argument that belies the oft-rehearsed "selfish" nature of Darwinian evolution. Kropotkin spent years studying organisms within and on frozen ice in Siberia. He notes:

> Wherever I saw animal life in abundance, as, for instance, on the lakes where scores of species and millions of individuals came together to rear their progeny; in the colonies of rodents; in the migrations of birds which took place at that time on a truly American scale along the Usuri; and especially in a migration of fallow-deer which I witnessed on the Amur, and during which scores of thousands of these intelligent animals came together from an immense territory, flying before the coming deep snow, in order to cross the Amur where it is narrowest—In all the scenes of animal lives which passed before my eyes, I saw mutual aid and mutual support carried on to an extent which made me suspect in it a feature of the greatest importance for the maintenance of life, the preservation of each species, and of its further evolution.[60]

Kropotkin goes on:

58. Aristotle, *Nichomachean Ethics*, 1155a.
59. see Oord, *Uncontrolling Love of God*, 95.
60. Kropotkin, *Mutual Aid*, 5.

> Besides the law of Mutual Struggle there is in Nature the law of Mutual Aid, which, for the success of the struggle for life, and especially for the progressive evolution of the species, is far more important than the law of mutual contest. This suggestion—which was, in reality, nothing but a further development of the ideas expressed by Darwin himself in *The Descent of Man*—seemed to me so correct and of so great an importance, that since I became acquainted with it (in 1883) I began to collect materials for further developing the idea.[61]

The union, then, of *agape, eros,* and *philia* love could be expressed as mutual aid, or full-orbed love, or even, as I like to say, "full-Oorded" love. But again, that is only if we are absolutely resigned to continue to employ those three terms, for, as Edward Collins Vacek notes, "life typically includes all three loves in rhythmically occurring ways."[62] I would prefer not to retain them at all, however, and merely employ the terminology of "self-giving" or "full-Oorded" love instead. Flourishing lives, I aver, consistently express "full-Oorded" love.

Indeed, various problems arise when we regard *agape* love as the authentically Christian love, to the exclusion of either *eros* or (and?) *philia*. One problem is rather straightforward: there is just no consistent biblical basis for it. Sometimes authors of the New Testament seemingly may place *agape* on a different plane, whereas at other times they simply do not. The New Testament witness is erratic, and at most unreliable, if one tries to use it as a basis of extrapolating the meanings of the various "love words." To be sure, sometimes New Testament writers use *agape* in the "higher" sense, but almost as many times they simply do not. To attempt to base one's distinctions among these three regularly used words within the Judeo-Christian corpus on the variety of usage itself is questionable scholarship. Sometimes the biblical authors use *agape* as the highest form of love; sometimes they use *philia* as such.

There is, simply, no rhyme or reason with regard to their employment of either *agape, eros,* or *philia* love. Not simply with respect to the New Testament, but ancient literature generally uses these three terms for "love" indiscriminately, insomuch as it is hard to know what they mean by "love" simply by looking at the word employed. Similar problems arise when we look at texts predating Nygren's *Agape and Eros*. In fact, Robert Adams notes that "'Agape' is a blank canvas on which one can paint whatever ideal of . . .

---

61. Kropotkin, *Mutual Aid*, 6.
62. Vacek, *Love, Human and Divine*, 310.

love one favors."[63] *The Journal of Religious Ethics*, in a somewhat recent instance (1996), devoted an entire issue (24/1) to a delineation and discussion of these three love types: *agape*, *eros*, and *philia*. One author would argue for the distinction, and then one would argue against it, almost in whiplike fashion. For example, Colin Grant defends Nygren's thesis that there is a *bona fide* distinction between these three forms of love: *agape*, *eros*, and *philia*; he notes that *agape* is the highest form of love.[64] Carter Heyward argues that feminists like herself hold that *eros* should/could displace *agape* as the preeminent form of love.[65] And Edward Vacek defends the idea that *philia* love deserves the highest honor.[66] This small sample size demonstrates that a scholar working on love research has to have his or her discernment on tap, so to speak, when working with this topic. Oord suggests that Process philosophy can aid one to see that all three forms of love play important parts in the work to increase the common good of society as a whole. He posits such under the rubric of "full-orbed" love—that which I have designated "full-Oorded" love. "Full-Oorded" love would repay evil with good as *agape* would; such "full-Oorded" love would appreciate the intrinsic value and beauty in others, just like *eros* love does; and "full-Oorded" love would acknowledge the import of friendship and mutuality as does *philia* love.[67]

Following Oord and Wojtyla again, since God commands that we show "self-giving," "self-donating" love, we therefore indeed have the ability to love others as kenotically donating entities, much as God does. When we act as genuine conduits and amplifiers (note, not simply as "channels" or "reservoirs," as Nygren would say) of God's self-donating and self-giving love, we can truly love others, much as God does. Therefore, self-love is transformed by God's impartation of self-donating and self-giving love; and through that impartation, we are empowered—*kenotically*—to love others in a manner akin to how God loves us. In this manner, we may say that "since the beginning, the myriad creatures have been giving up their lives as a ransom for many." "The cruciform creation is, in the end, deiform" because of the struggle *and* mutual aid inherent within evolution by natural selection, not in spite of them. If humans cannot truly and authentically love, we are most to be pitied. Invoking the distinction that C. S. Lewis originally gave us—i.e., between "need love" and "gift love"[68]—I would like to close by

63. Adams, *Finite and Infinite Goods*, 136.
64. Grant, "For the Love of God: Agape," 3–21.
65. Heyward, "Lamenting the Loss of Love," 23–28.
66. Vacek, "Love, Christian and Diverse," 29–34.
67. see Oord, "Process Answers to Love Questions," 20–30.
68. Lewis, *Four Loves*, 3.

saying that Lewis is at least half right: there is a "gift" love, and it is a mark of all of our lives in that we can—*kenotically* empowered by God—self-donate and self-give our very beingness to others via kenotic donation, analogous to how God always does so. Of course, we cannot expect that we humans will always love as God does because we do not have an everlasting and unchanging nature that is necessarily inclined toward love, but we are at least *able* to love, however feebly and intermittently.

11

Necessary, Kenotically Donated, and Self-Giving Love[1]

In a not-so-funny way, we are all prisoners of love."[2]

—ROBERT E. WAGONER[3]

INTRODUCTION

The prompt to which I am responding in this chapter is related to whether or not God is necessarily loving, or whether he is freely loving. In attempting to answer this question, I will dialogue with Thomas Jay Oord, who is a giant when it comes to the exposition of Christian love. Further, I shall reiterate a minority view on the meaning and extrapolation of the Greek term *kenosis*—that is, that the term refers to, variously, a "kenotic donation,"[4]

---

1. This article originally appeared as McCall, "Necessary, Kenotically-Donated, & Self-Giving Love." Reprinted with permission.
2. Wagoner, *Meanings of Love*, 135.
3. Wagoner, *Meanings of Love*, 135.
4. By coining the phrase "*kenotically* donated," I am referring to the methodology by which the Spirit of God's self-giving, uncontrolling love imbibes creation.

a "self-offering,"[5] a "self-donation,"[6] or a "self-giving."[7] Indeed, the love to which God calls us is multidimensional and multiexpressive.[8] As such, it takes many forms. God calls his creatures to express "full-Oorded" love, because God's love is full-orbed.

This kenotically donated, "full-Oorded" love onsets an evolving fertility within the natural world, which is a result of the panentheistic relationship of God and world. This panentheistic relationship was initially wrought by the kenotic donation of God's very self *into* chaotic matter eons ago, and is now continually sustained and upheld by the repetitive imbibification[9] of the creating Spirit—i.e., the impartation of her very self—into the natural world.[10] Thereafter, marked by the Spirit of contingency within evolution, the natural world has progressed in a serpentine manner into the advancement of greater complexity, of which *Homo sapiens sapiens* is the pinnacle (at present, anyway).

Indeed, I will argue in the text that follows for a notion of love that is necessarily kenotically donated, self-giving, creative, and uncontrolling. In so doing, I will use several of Oord's texts as my launching point, and will aim at substantiating that this necessary, kenotically donated, self-giving, creative, and uncontrolling love is empowering of the other and allows for the interactivity of matter and the Godhead, since it is principally pneumatologically derived (i.e. Spirit-based) and established by an imbibification[11]

---

5. For support of *kenosis* as "self-offering," please Cf. McCall, "Kenosis of the Spirit into Creation."

6. For an elaboration of *kenosis* as "self-donation," I point you to McCall, "Thomistic Personalism in Dialogue with Kenosis," 21–32.

7. Cf. Brümmer, *Model of Love*, 3. Robert Wagoner also pictures preeminent love to be of the self-giving variety. In fact, he calls it "the epitome of love . . . [for] there is enormous power in selflessness" (Wagoner, *Meanings of Love*, 137). Further, according to Wagoner, however love is defined, it must be understood as a relation of some kind (Wagoner, *Meanings of Love*, 14). In fact, "from the Christian point of view love is something held in trust, something given, something I can enjoy only if I do not attempt to possess it" (Wagoner, *Meanings of Love*, 47). So then, I deduce from Wagoner's statement that love is something I can enjoy only if it is necessarily self-giving in its orientation, which backs up one of the main thrusts of this current chapter. This condition, I would submit, both applies to God as well as humans.

8. Oord, *Defining Love*, 32.

9. The term "imbibification" is similarly a word coined by me to refer to the descent of the Spirit into matter, which causes the Spirit to be *embedded* within nature, and thereby be *embodied* within it as well.

10. For a fuller treatment of this concept, see McCall, "Whitehead, Creativity, and the Immanently Creative Spirit," 337–50.

11. I have coined the term "imbibification" to refer to the process by which some entity, something, or someone is imbibed by the Spirit of God.

of matter with the Spirit of God. Some of these terms are Tom's, while some are my terms; the distinction will become apparent in what follows.

KENOTIC LOVE AS SELF-DONATION AND SELF-GIVING

I did not originate the terminology of love as self-donation, which is a principle upon which my "full-Oorded," "kenotically donated" love is based (Karol Wojtyla did).[12] Neither did I originate the terminology of "uncontrolling love" (Tom Oord did).[13] But it should be noted that Wojtyla's self-donating love is a strong correlate to Oord's characterization of uncontrolling love. Accordingly, I will employ both terms—or at least their application—in what I have come to refer to as "kenotically donated love." This depiction of my own is based fundamentally upon the notion that *kenosis* amounts to self-giving with reckless abandonment. Whereas I originated neither of the two aforementioned terms, I did, however, originate the usage of the term *kenosis* as self-offering.[14] As a result, Tom Oord and I have both been picturing *kenosis* as essentially self-giving (i.e., an "infilling," a "self-offering," or even a "self-donation" to the other) since or about the year 2008. Self-donating love and self-giving love are both manifestations of God's love *to* his creatures, *for* his creatures, and *through* his creatures. In what follows, I shall use the terms "self-donating love" and "self-giving love" *to* and *for* creation as highly illustrative, essentially equivalent metaphors with which to picture the creating Spirit's dynamic presence within the world in our postmodern context through kenotic donation.

In noting that the love of the creating Spirit is kenotically donated, I mean to draw attention to the idea that she not only gives us love itself, but also *her-self* in the very act of love, and that necessarily so. Further, in characterizing love as self-giving, I intend to once again draw attention to the fact that the creating Spirit gives of herself (liberally) to her creation and the creatures of creation. She, in fact, imparts part of herself to it and them, both, in a kenotic manner. Hence, I say the creating Spirit's love is kenotically donated. Picking up Oord's illustration of "uncontrolling love,"[15] I gather that he means God gives out of God's fullness, but does not insist on controlling the response(s) of creation in response to that impartation of love; hence, the designation of God's love as "uncontrolling." As such, God does *not* insist on having control. I would like to transfer Oord's comments

12. Cf. McCall, "Thomistic Personalism in Dialogue with Kenosis," 21–32.
13. Reference the book by the same name: Oord, *Uncontrolling Love of God*.
14. McCall, "*Kenosis* of the Spirit into Creation."
15. Cf. Oord, *Uncontrolling Love of God*.

regarding God's love just mentioned to the creating Spirit's love. In so doing, I note that due to her nature primarily being kenotically donated, self-giving love, the creating Spirit *cannot* control other entities, be they animate or not, although she could—and does!—lure, woo, bid, and beckon entities toward herself. Not simply "will not," but "cannot!," and that necessarily so. That is the *radical* assertion everywhere made by Oord, and especially in his newest title, *God Can't*.[16] And I join him in it.

A DEEPER EXPLICATION OF "FULL-OORDED" DIVINE LOVE

I contend that Tom has proposed a doctrine of God's love in several texts over the last decade that is adequate both to science and theology.[17] We will meet two of his texts in what directly follows: that is, *Defining Love* and *The Nature of Love*, both of which were published in the calendar year 2010. His proposal of an adequate doctrine of the love of God begins with the claim that love is an *essential*, necessarily exhibited divine attribute.[18] It is, then, *necessarily* the case that God always acts intentionally, in sympathetic response to others (including past divine actions), to promote overall well-being.[19] Loving other entities, be they animate or not, is not an arbitrary divine decision but a central and necessary aspect of God's eternal, unchanging nature.[20] Simply spoken, God cannot *not* love.[21] It is a necessarily expressed attribute of his person. With the writer of John's gospel, Oord affirms that "God is love." Oord is quick to point, however, that in suggesting that love is an essential aspect of the divine nature, he is not suggesting that God has no choice whatsoever with regard to love. *That* God will love others is necessarily the case. However, *how* God loves others is a free choice on God's part.[22] So we see here both necessity and freedom with regard to God's love.

16. Oord, *God Can't*, 22.

17. Oord, *Nature of Love*; *Defining Love*; *Uncontrolling Love of God*; and *God Can't*.

18. Instead of "essential," some philosophers prefer "superessential" to refer to divine attributes. The latter term implies that a particular attribute applies to God in all possible worlds. Oord means by "essential" essentially the same.

19. Oord, *Defining Love*, 15.

20. Cf. Oord, *Defining Love*, 15.

21. Here Oord affirms both the theology of Jürgen Moltmann and some of the philosophical conclusions of William L. Rowe. Moltmann argues that divine freedom does not include the freedom *not* to love (Moltmann, *Trinity and the Kingdom*, 52–56). Rowe argues that God is not free to do some things—God is not free to make something less than the best of all possible worlds, for example (Rowe, *Can God Be Free?*).

22. On this, see Oord, "Divine Love."

"In ongoing love relations," Tom writes, "we can rest assured that God will always act intentionally, in sympathetic response to others (including God's own past actions), to promote overall well-being."[23] In fact, this "relentless, steadfast love is a necessary aspect of what it means to be divine."[24] The fact *that* God loves others, therefore, is an aspect of God's eternal essence,[25] and is essential to his person. However, the manner in which God chooses to promote overall well-being in particular instances arises from *how* God sympathetically responds to others in that particular instance itself. There is neither a formula nor circumstances exterior to God that entirely determine what the manifestation of love by God will be. How God loves others, therefore, is a matter of the divine will, and that alone—somewhat ad hoc even—that is, there is no exterior compulsion. *How* God loves is a free choice on God's part, and in this sense and in this alone, God *freely* chooses to love. But the compulsion itself is inalterable.

God expresses *philia* by working cooperatively with creatures—and also by aiding creatures to work cooperatively with other creatures—to increase the common good. Notably, Oord defines *philia* as acting intentionally, in response to God and others, to promote overall well-being by seeking to establish deeper levels of cooperative friendship. *Philia*, then, is the love of colaborment. Oord points out that *philia*—both the word and the concept—plays a significant role in the New Testament.[26] He notes that we have a strong biblical basis for affirming the notion that God expresses *philia* often in his relations with the other. While God's *agape* refers to repaying evil with good and *eros* refers to creating and enhancing value, *philia* refers to God's work to promote friendship with those capable of such. *Philia* is *alongside of* love.[27] Like *agape* and *eros*, creaturely expressions of *philia* require God's prevenient and empowering action. God is both the exemplar of *philia* as well as the source of *philia*. *Philia* is a form of love that works *alongside of* God and others to promote overall well-being. We are, in a very real sense, God's fellow *agents of creativity* and God's fellow *workers*. God's love is "full-Oorded"—i.e., composed of *agape*, *eros*, and *philia* dimensions.

The notion that God's love is "full-Oorded" presupposes that God is a thoroughly relational being;[28] and as relational, God both *affects* and is

---

23. Oord, *Defining Love*, 190.

24. Oord, *Defining Love*, 190.

25. For a scholarly analysis of the notion that love is an essential divine attribute, see Taylor, *God Is Love*.

26. For more on the implications of *philia*, see Oord, *Science of Love*, ch. 5.

27. Oord, *Nature of Love*, 114.

28. Cf.. Oord, *Defining Love*, 190.

affected by those with whom God relates. In a greatly positive development of the last generation or so, almost invariably, contemporary relational theologians have rejected the idea that God is an aloof monarch uninfluenced by others. Instead, relational theologians affirm that God suffers and is passible, which means that God is influenced by the ups and downs, joys and sorrows, sins and loves of others. God truly cares, and is, in fact, the "most moved mover."[29] Although his creatures truly affect this truly relational God, God's eternal nature of kenotically donated, self-giving, and uncontrolling love remains unchanging. God's eternal nature is fixed. God's nature is love, and that nature never alters. The responses of creaturely entities influence the particular way—*agape, eros, philia*—that God chooses to love others. The theology that Oord proposes suggests that God's own characteristics and God's own relations with others influence the extent of divine love, as well as the manifestations of divine love. God is always everywhere present to all creatures (theologians refer to this as "omnipresence"), and God's loving omnipresence plays a distinctively crucial role for understanding divine action in relation to the natural world. Divine omnipresence pertains directly to love's breadth and width and height and depth. Indeed, because God is present to all creatures and because God loves perfectly in a kenotically donated, self-giving, and uncontrolling manner, all creatures are necessarily loved; they are in fact, smothered with love. Pelted by it, one might say.

GOD'S LOVE FOR THE OTHER

Building off of Oord's position, I claim that the creating Spirit necessarily loves "the other," to invoke Bultmannian language. Indeed, what he suggests agrees with adherents to the idea of *kenosis* who say that the three-word sentence "God is love" is the highest revelation of God. The best of the Christian tradition also confirms the supreme importance of divine love.[30] In fact, God's loving actions are expressions of a loving divine nature. Throughout Oord's *Defining Love*, we encounter the proposition that love requires relations with others.[31] Simply put, love is inherently relational. As Oord is fond of saying, loving actions require intentional sympathetic responses to others with whom the lover possesses relations, and love involves promoting the well-being of those with whom the lover relates.[32] Thus, if love is an essential

---

29. Notably, Clark Pinnock titles one of his most highly regarded books *Most Moved Mover*.
30. Oord, *Science of Love*, ch. 1.
31. Oord, *Defining Love*, 19.
32. Oord, *Defining Love*, 206.

divine property and love always requires relations, we should conclude that God at all times requires relations with an other. To say it succinctly, divine relatedness is an aspect of the divine trifold being at rudiment. In the same manner that God did not voluntarily decide the necessarily loving feature of God's own nature, God does not voluntarily decide to be relational. God has to be so. It is a necessary expression of who and what God is. Whereas God does not depend upon relations to creatures to exist—as God exists necessarily—the *ways* in which creatures respond to God affect the moment-by-moment constitution of the divine trifold being. It is indeed true that some Christian theologians agree that relational love is a necessary aspect of the divine being. However, many of them argue that God only necessarily loves others in the immanent Trinity. Love for creatures, then, is contingent upon God's wholly voluntary decision.[33] Love for those in the Trinity is necessary; love for those in the universe is arbitrary.

The hypothesis that Oord offers in *Defining Love*,[34] by contrast, claims that God necessarily relates to and loves all creatures, be they worthy or not. God necessarily relates to and loves whatever God creates,[35] and God everlastingly creates, relates, and loves. One may or may not argue that God relates necessarily within the Trinity, but either way it is Oord's contention that that sort of necessary relation is not sufficient to account for the sum of God's relationality; God needs an other to relate to as well. For Oord, God necessarily relates within the Trinity and God necessarily relates to creatures, at one in the same time. For Oord, these two ideas are not mutually exclusive. A being that both exists necessarily and loves necessarily requires nothing outside itself to exist. Oord is keen to argue that God exists necessarily. Indeed, Oord strongly suggests that a scheme supposing that God necessarily and everlastingly relates to some creaturely world or another is preferable to a scheme that claims God's relations to the world are accidental or arbitrary.[36] Only a God who necessarily relates to and loves the world should be said to love the world essentially and eternally. In contrast, the God whose relations with the world are arbitrary can/should be said to love the world arbitrarily. This God would not be worthy of worship.

33. Oord, *Defining Love*, 207.

34. Oord, *Defining Love*, 207.

35. Oord stipulates that the world was not created out of absolutely nothing, and *creatio ex nihilo* should therefore be abandoned. In fact, it should be abandoned because of its shaky theological, scriptural, historical, scientific, and philosophical warrants, or, rather, the lack thereof. For work related to the inadequacy of *creatio ex nihilo*, and the possibilities of a positive case for Chaos theory, see Bonting, *Chaos Theology*; Hutchingson, *Pandemoneum Tremendum*; and Keller, *Face of the Deep*.

36. Oord, *Defining Love*, 207.

This vision of Oord's proffers a God who is love at rudiment, and to use my own language, who necessarily "kenotically donates," "pours out herself," or "self-offers" as a moment-by-moment cause among causes, and who relates with entities that possess God-given freedom. God's self-offering is a necessary part of what it means for God to empower creatures. This kenotic donation, to again use my own wording, is an essential and necessary property of God's very being, and does not entail voluntary self-limitation whatsoever.

THE CREATING SPIRIT'S NECESSARY LOVE FOR THE NATURAL WORLD

The creating Spirit's self-giving—*kenotic*—love for the natural world is an essential and necessary component to her nature.[37] Indeed, to say that love is an essential feature of the creating Spirit's eternal nature means God loves necessarily. All of the creating Spirit's actions in the past, present, and future are acts of love.[38] To use the double negative: the God whose nature is love cannot *not* love.[39] According to Oord, God necessarily acts intentionally, in sympathetic/empathetic response to Godself and others, to promote overall well-being.[40] He names this "Essential *Kenosis*" theology.

Essential *Kenosis* theology—with its dual claims that God's love is necessary in Trinity and necessarily expressed for other entities as well—also offers a strong psychological advantage over other theologies of love. For example, it makes a difference psychologically whether we believe God necessarily loves us. Our personal experience is affected insomuch as to believe God cannot stop loving us because God's rudimentary nature is love for the world provides assurance and trust. Some theologies say that God chooses whether to love the world, because love for creatures is wholly voluntary. In such a view, God's love is conditional, in the sense that God may or may not choose to love creatures. Oord's Essential *Kenosis* theology, however, affirms the characteristically Christian testimony regarding God's unconditional love. God's necessary and essential unconditional love refers to God's unchanging nature—his essence, if you will. God essentially loves creation, because God's essential nature includes kenotically donated, uncontrolling love for the natural world.

37. Oord, *Nature of Love*, 124.
38. This is the position of Dunning, *Grace, Faith, and Holiness*.
39. Jürgen Moltmann argues this point well in *Trinity and the Kingdom*, 52–56. See also Taylor, *God Is Love*.
40. Oord, *Nature of Love*, 17.

CONCLUSION

For the God of self-giving, kenotically donated love, the decision to express love at all times comes first. In my conception, "full-Oorded" love would encompass what is ordinarily contained within the definition of *agape* love, but it would also include *eros* love, for the latter is the love of colaborment. In my appropriation of this terminology of *eros* love, it would be the type of love that the desires to, e.g., expand one's territory or one's domain, which makes it applicable to the modern theory of evolution by natural selection. Evolution—i.e., "descent with modification," to invoke a Darwinian phrase—then, recognizes self-giving love, and the goodness thereof, in that species regularly undergo commensalist symbiotic relationships in nature, whereby one is aided by the other, while the other is neither aided nor harmed. This is self-giving love in its entirety, and a proper demonstration of it.

My understanding of necessarily expressed, "full-Oorded" love also includes dimensions of *philia* love. *Philia* could be akin to the symbiotic relationship known as mutualism in biology, especially since *philia* love has historically been associated with friendship or the interrelatedness of the natural world. Notably, Aristotle indicates that even nonhuman animals can express *philia* love.[41] The relationships marked by *philia*, then, could be identified by mutuality, reciprocity, and cooperation,[42] which fits the above biological connotation well. While *agape* or *eros* might benefit from cooperation, reciprocity, and mutuality, those two forms of love do not require any of those three nouns. *Philia* does. I contend, in fact, that the *kenosis* of the Spirit *into* creation amounts to self-giving, betrothed love through self-donation.

The union, then of *agape*, *eros*, and *philia* love could be expressed as mutual aid, or full-orbed, or even, as I like to say, "full-Oorded" love. Flourishing lives—be they human or some other mammal—I aver, consistently and necessarily express "full-Oorded" love. Oord suggests that Process philosophy can aid one to see that full-orbed love—that which I have designated "full-Oorded" love—plays an important part in the work to increase the common good of society as a whole. Indeed, "full-Oorded" love would repay evil with good as *agape* would; such a "full-Oorded" love would additionally welcome the intrinsic value and beauty in others, just like *eros* love does; and "full-Oorded" love would also recognize the import of friendship and mutuality as does *philia* love.

---

41. Aristotle, *Nichomachean Ethics*, 1155a.
42. Oord, *Defining Love*, 49.

Following Oord and Wojtyla again, since God commands that we show necessarily "self-giving," "self-donating" love, we therefore indeed have the ability to love others as kenotically donating entities, just as the creating Spirit does. When we act as a genuine conduit and amplifier of the creating Spirit's self-donating and self-giving love, we can truly and entirely and infinitely love others, just as God does. Of course, we cannot expect that we humans will always love alike unto how God does, because we do not have an eternal and unchanging nature that is necessarily inclined toward love,[43] but we are at least always *able* to do it. May we go forth, then, and do likewise . . .

---

43. Oord, *Uncontrolling Love of God*, 77.

Bibliography

Adams, Robert M. *Finite and Infinite Goods: A Framework for Ethics*. Oxford: Oxford University Press, 1999.
Agamben, Gorgio. *Infancy and History: Essays on the Destruction of Experience*. Translated by Liz Heron. London: Verso, 1993.
Alexander, Samuel. *Space, Time, and Deity*. 2 vols. The Gifford Lectures for 1916–18. London: Macmillan, 1920.
Allen, Paul. "Augustine and the Systematic Theology of Origins." In *Augustine and Science*, edited by John Doody, Adam Goldstein, and Kim Paffenroth, 9–26. Lanham, MD: Lexington, 2013.
Archinov, N. A., and M. Y. Fuchs, *Causality, Emergence, Self-Organization*. Moscow: NIA-Piroda, 2003.
Arendt, Hannah. *Love & Saint Augustine*. Chicago: University of Chicago Press, 1929.
Aristotle. *Nichomachean Ethics*. Edited and translated by Sarah Brodie and Christopher Rowe. Oxford: Oxford University Press, 2002.
Augustine. *The Confessions*. With an Introduction by R. S. Pine-Coffin. Harmondsworth: Penguin, 1961.
———. *On Genesis: A Refutation of the Manichees, Unfinished Literal Commentary on Genesis, The Literal Meaning of Genesis*. With introductions, translations, and notes by Edmund Hill. Edited by John E. Rotelle. New York: New City, 2002.
———. *On Genesis: Two Books on Genesis Against the Manicheans and On the Literal Interpretation of Genesis: An Unfinished Book*. Translated by Roland J. Teske. Fathers of the Church: A New Translation. Washington, DC: Catholic University of America Press, 1991.
———. *The Literal Meaning of Genesis*. Vol. 1. Translated by John Hammond Taylor. New York: Paulist, 1982.
———. "The Retractationes." In *The Fathers of the Church*, vol. 60, translated by Sister M. Inez Bogan, edited by Roy Jospeh Deferrari. Washington, DC: Catholic University of America Press, 1968.
———. *The Trinity*. In *The Works of Saint Augustine: A Translation for the 21st Century*, edited by John E. Rotelle, translated by Edmund Hill. 2nd ed. New York: New City, 2011.

Ayala, Francisco J. "Can 'Progress' Be Defined as a Biological Concept?" In *Evolutionary Progress*, edited by M. Nitecki, 75–96. Chicago: University of Chicago Press, 1988.
———. "The Concept of Biological Progress." In *Studies in the Philosophy of Biology*, edited by F. J. Ayala and T. Dobzhansky, 339–54. London: MacMillan, 1974.
———. "The Evolutionary Concept of Progress." In *Progress and Its Discontents*, edited by G. Almond, M. Chodorow and R. H. Pearce, 106–24. Berkeley: University of California Press, 1982.
Badmington, Neil. "Derridanimals." *Oxford Literary Review* 29/1–2 (2007) v–vii.
Barabási, Albert-László, and Reka Albert. "Emergence of Scaling in Random Networks." *Science* 286 (1999) 509–12.
Bartholomew, David J. *God of Chance*. London: SCM, 1984.
Bauckham, Richard. *Jesus and the God of Israel: God Crucified and Other Studies on the New Testament's Christology of Divine Identity*. Grand Rapids: Eerdmans, 2008.
Bauer, Walter, and Frederick William Danker. *A Greek-English Lexicon of the New Testament and Other Early Christian Literature*. 3rd ed. Chicago: University of Chicago Press, 2001.
Benton, Michael J. "Progress and Competition in Macroevolution." *Biology Review* 62 (1987) 305–38.
Berger, Anne E., and Marta Segarra. "Thoughtprints." In *Demenageries: Thinking (of) Animals after Derrida*, 3–22. Critical Studies 35. Amsterdam: Rodopi, 2011.
Bernard, Robert W. "*In figura*: Terminology Pertaining to Figurative Exegesis in the Works of Augustine of Hippo." Ph.D. diss, Princeton University, 1985.
Bethune-Baker, J. F. *Early History of Christian Doctrine to the Time of Chalcedon*. London: Methuen, 1903.
Blowers, Paul M. *Drama of the Divine Economy: Creator and Creation in Early Christian Theology and Piety*. Oxford: Oxford University Press, 2012.
Bogan, Sister M. Inez. Translated and edited by Roy Jospeh Deferrari. In *The Fathers of the Church*, vol. 60. Washington, DC: Catholic University of America Press, 1968.
Blumer, M. J., F. L. von Salvini-Plawen, R. Kikinger, and T. Buchinger. "Ocelli in a Cnidaria polyp: The Ultrastructure of the Pigment Spots in *Stylocoronella riedli* (Scyphozoa, Stauromedusae)." *Zoomorphology* 115 (1995) 221–27.
Bonner, John T. *The Evolution of Complexity*. Princeton, NJ: Princeton University Press, 1987.
Bonting, Sjoerd L. *Chaos Theology: A Revised Creation Theology*. Ottawa: Novalis, 2002.
———. "Spirit and Creation." *Zygon: Journal of Religion and Science* 41/3 (2006) 713–26.
Boorman, S. A., and P. R. Levitt. *The Genetics of Altruism*. New York: Academic Press, 1980.
Bottjer, D. J. "'The Ecology of Evolutionary Innovation: The Fossil Record." In *Evolutionary Innovations*, edited by M. Nitecki, 253–88. Chicago: University of Chicago Press, 1990.
Bowler, Peter J. *Evolution: The History of an Idea*. Berkeley: University of California Press, 1984.
———. *Fossils and Progress*. New York: Science History, 1976.
Boyd, R., and P. Richerson. *Culture and the Evolutionary Process*. Chicago: University of Chicago Press, 1985.
Bracken, Joseph A. *God: Three Who Are One*. Engaging Theology: Catholic Perspectives. Collegeville, MN: Liturgical, 2008.

———. "Infinity and the Logic of Non-Dualism." *Journal of Hindu-Christian Studies* 11 (1998) 39–44.

———. "Non-Duality and the Concept of Ultimate Reality." *Ultimate Reality and Meaning* 19/2 (1996) 140–47.

———. "Whitehead and the Critique of Logocentrism." In *Process and Difference: Between Cosmological and Poststructuralist Postmodernisms*, edited by Catherine Keller and Anne Daniell, 91–110. Albany: State University of New York Press, 2001.

Bradley, James. "Transcendentalism and Speculative Reason in Whitehead." *Process Studies* 23/3 (1994) 155–91.

Bradnick, David, and Bradford McCall. "Making Sense of Emergence: A Critical Engagement with Leidenhag, Leidenhag, and Yong." *Zygon: Journal of Religion and Science* 53/1 (2018) 240–57.

Brown, Andrew J. "Augustine's View of Creation and Its Modern Reception." In *Augustine and Science*, edited by John Doody, Adam Goldstein, and Kim Paffenroth, 27–42. Lanham, MD: Lexington, 2013.

———. *The Days of Creation: A History of Christian Interpretation of Genesis 1:1—2:3*. Dorset, UK: Deo, 2014.

Brown, Harold O. J. *Heresies: Heresy and Orthodoxy in the History of the Church*. Grand Rapids: Hendrickson, 1984.

Brümmer, Vincent. *The Model of Love: A Study in Philosophical Theology*. Cambridge, Cambridge University Press, 1993.

Buchanon, Brett. *Onto-Ethologies: The Animal Environments of Uexküll, Heidegger, Merleau-Ponty, and Deleuze*. New York: State University of New York Press, 2008.

Bülgakov, Sergius. *The Comforter*. Grand Rapids: Eerdmans, 2004.

Butler, Dom Cuthbert. *Western Mysticism: The Teaching of Augustine, Gregory and Bernard on Contemplation and the Contemplative Life*. 2nd ed. Eugene, OR: Wipf and Stock, 2001.

Caiazza, John. "Augustine on Evolution, Time, Memory." In *Augustine and Science*, edited by John Doody, Adam Goldstein, and Kim Paffenroth, 111–26. Lanham, MD: Lexington, 2013.

Cain, A. J. "The Perfection of Animals." *Biological Journal of the Linnaean Society* 36 (1989) 3–29.

Calarco, Matthew. *Thinking Through Animals: Identity, Difference, Indistinction*. Stanford: Stanford University Press, 2015.

———. *Zoographies: The Question of the Animal from Heidegger to Derrida*. New York: Columbia University Press, 2008.

Campbell, Neil A. *Biology*. 3rd ed. Menlo Park: Benjamin Cummings, 1991.

Caragounis, Chrys C. *The Son of Man: Vision and Interpretation*. Tubingen: Mohr, 1986.

Cassidy, J. "Philosophical Aspects of the Group Selection Controversy." *British Journal for the Philosophy of Science* 45 (1978) 575–94.

Cederholm, E. Andersson, A. Björck, K. Jennbert, and A-S Lönngren, eds. *Exploring the Animal Turn: Human-Animal Relations in Science*. Pufendorf Institute of Advanced Studies, Lund University Press, 2014.

Chadwick, Henry. "Augustine." In *A Dictionary of Biblical Interpretation*, edited by R. J. Coggins and J. L. Holden, 64–75. London: SCM, 1990.

———. *Augustine*. Edited by K. Thomas. Oxford: Oxford University Press, 1986.

Charlton, James. *Non-Dualism in Eckhart, Julian of Norwich and Traherne: A Theopoetic Reflection*. New York: Bloomsbury Academic, 2012.
Christian, William A. "The Creation of the World." In *A Companion to the Study of St. Augustine*, edited by Roy W. Battenhouse, 315–42. Grand Rapids: Baker, 1979.
Clatterbaugh, Kenneth B. *The Causation Debate in Modern Philosophy, 1671–1739*. London: Routledge, 1999.
Clayton, Philip. *Mind & Emergence: From Quantum to Consciousness*. Oxford: Oxford University, 2004.
Cobb, John B., and David Ray Griffin. *Process Theology: An Introductory Exposition*. Louisville: Westminster, 1976.
Corrington, Robert S. *An Introduction to C. S. Peirce: Philosopher, Semiotician and Ecstatic Naturalist*. Lanham, MD: Rowman and Littlefield, 1993.
Craig, David Alexander. "Rationality, Animality, and Human Nature: Reconsidering Kant's View of the Human/Animal Relation." *Konturen* 6 (2014). http://journals.oregondigital.org/konturen/article/view/3506/3272.
Crain, Steven D. "God Embodied In, God Bodying Forth the World: Emergence and Christian Theology." *Zygon: Journal of Religion and Science* 41/3 (2006) 665–74.
Crisp, Oliver D., and Fred Sanders, eds. *Advancing Trinitarian Theology: Explorations in Constructive Dogmatics*. Grand Rapids: Zondervan, 2014.
Crouse, Robert. "*Paucis Mutatis Verbis*: St. Augustine's Platonism." In *Augustine and His Critics: Essays in Honour of Gerald Bonner*, edited by Robert Dodaro and George Lawless, 37–50. London: Routledge, 2002.
Curtis, E. *European Literature and the Latin Middle Ages*. Translated by W. R. Trask. London: Routledge and Keegan Paul, 1953.
Dabney, D. Lyle. "Naming the Spirit: Towards a Pneumatology of the Cross." In *Starting with the Spirit*, edited by Gordon Preece and Stephen Pickard, 28–58. Adelaide: Openbook, 2001.
———. "The Nature of the Spirit." In *The Work of the Spirit*, edited by Michael Welker, 71–86. Grand Rapids: Eerdmans, 2006.
Darwin, Charles. *The Descent of Man*. London: John Murray, 1871.
———. *On the Origin of Species by Means of Natural Selection*. London: John Murray, 1859.
———. *On the Origin of Species: A Variorum Edition*. Edited by Morse Peckham. Philadelphia: University of Pennsylvania Press, 2006.
Darwin, Charles, and Alfred Russel Wallace. "On the Tendency of Species to Form Varieties; and on the Perpetuation of Varieties and Species by Natural Means of Selection." *Proceedings of the Linnean Society, Zoological Journal* 3 (1858) 46–62.
Darwin, Erasmus. *The Temple of Nature*. London: J. Johnson, 1803.
Davies, Brian. *Storm Over Biology: Essays on Science, Sentiment, and Public Policy*. Buffalo, NY: Prometheus, 1986.
Dawkins, Richard. *The Extended Phenotype*. Oxford: Oxford University Press, 1982.
———. *The Selfish Gene*. Oxford: Oxford University Press, 1976.
Deacon, Terrence. "The Hierarchic Logic of Emergence." In *Evolution and Learning*, edited by Bruce H. Weber and David J. Depew, 273–308. Cambridge, MA: MIT Press, 2003.
———. *The Symbolic Species: The Co-Evolution of Language and the Brain*. New York: Norton, 1997.

Deane-Drummond, Celia. *Animals as Religious Subjects: Transdisciplinary Perspectives.* Edited by Rebecca Artinian-Kaiser and David L. Clough. London: T. & T. Clark, 2013.
Del Colle, Ralph. *Christ and the Spirit: Spirit-Christology in Trinitarian Perspective.* Oxford: Oxford University Press, 1994.
Deleuze, Gilles. *Difference and Repetition.* New York: Columbia University Press, 1968.
———. *Fold: Leibniz and the Baroque.* Minneapolis: University of Minnesota Press, 1992.
Deleuze, Gilles, and Félix Guattari. *What Is Philosophy?* New York: Columbia University Press, 1994.
Derrida, Jacques. "The Animal That Therefore I Am (More to Follow)." Translated by David Wills. *Critical Inquiry* 28/2 (2002) 369–415.
———. *Aporias: Dying—Awaiting (One Another at) the Limits of Truth.* Translated by Thomas Dutoit. Stanford: Stanford University Press, 1993.
———. "'Eating Well', or the Calculation of the Subject: An Interview with Jacques Derrida." In *Who Comes After the Subject?*, edited by Eduardo Cadava, Peter Connor, and Jean-Luc Nancy, 96–119. London: Routledge, 1991.
———. "Geschlecht II: Heidegger's Hand." Translated by John P. Leavey Jr. In *Deconstruction and Philosophy*, edited by John Sallis, 161–96. Chicago: University of Chicago Press, 1987.
———. "Of Spirit: Heidegger and the Question." Translated by G. Bennington and R. Bowlby. Chicago: Chicago University Press, 1989.
Desmond, Adrian, and James Moore, *Darwin: The Life of a Tormented Evolutionist.* New York: Norton, 1991.
Doncel, Manuel G. "The Kenosis of the Creator and of the Created Co-Creator." *Zygon: Journal of Religion and Science* 39/4 (2004) 798–816.
Dunn, James D. G. *Christology in the Making: An Inquiry into the Origins of the Doctrine of the Incarnation.* London: SCM, 1989.
———. "Towards the Spirit of Christ." In *The Work of the Spirit: Pneumatology and Pentecostalism*, edited by Michael Welker, 3–26. Grand Rapids: Eerdmans, 2006.
Dunning, H. Ray *Grace, Faith, and Holiness: A Wesleyan Systematic Theology.* Kansas City: Beacon Hill, 1988.
Eaton, T. H. "The Aquatic Origin of Tetrapods," *Transactions of the Kansas Academy of Science* 63 (1960) 115–20.
Eckhart, Meister. *Passion for Creation: The Earth-Honoring Spirituality of Meister Eckhart.* Edited by Matthew Fox. Rochester, VT: Inner Traditions, 2000.
Edwards, J. L. "Two Perspectives on the Evolution of the Tetrapod Limb." *American Zoologist* 29 (1989) 235–54.
Effendi, Shoghi, trans. *Gleanings from the Writings of Baha'u'llah.* Wilmette, IL: Baha'i Publishing Trust, 1952.
Ehrman, Bart D. *How Jesus Became God: The Exaltation of a Jewish Preacher from Galilee.* San Francisco: HarperOne, 2014.
———. *Jesus Before the Gospels: How the Earliest Christians Remembered, Changed, and Invented Their Stories of the Savior.* New York: HarperOne, 2016.
———. *The Orthodox Corruption of Scripture.* New York: Oxford University Press, 1996.

Epiphanius of Salamis. *The Panarion of Epiphanius of Salamis, Book I: (Sects 1–46)*. Translated by Frank Williams. 2nd ed., rev. and exp. Nag Hammadi and Manichean Studies. Leiden: Brill, 2008.

Evans, Craig A. ed. *Encyclopedia of the Historical Jesus*. New York: Routledge, 2008.

Faber, Roland. *The Divine Manifold*. New York: Lexington, 2014.

———. *God as Poet of the World: Exploring Process Theologies*. Translated by Douglas W. Scott. New York: Westminster John Knox, 2008

———. "Whitehead and Postmodernity." Claremont School of Theology, August 27– December 12, 2018.

Fergusson, David. *Creation*. Grand Rapids: Eerdmans, 2014.

Fiddes, Paul. *The Creative Suffering of God*. Oxford: Clarendon, 1988.

Fletcher-Louis, Crispin. *Jesus Monotheism: Christological Origins*, vol. 1: *The Emerging Consensus and Beyond*. Eugene, OR: Cascade, 2015.

Fowler, Thomas B., and Daniel Kuebler. *The Evolution Controversy*. Grand Rapids: Baker Academic, 2006.

Freud, Sigmund *New Introductory Lectures in Psycho-Analysis*. Edited by James Strachey. New York: Norton, 1990.

Gardner, A., and A. Grafen. "Capturing the Superorganism—A Formal Theory of Group Adaptation." *Journal of Evolutionary Biology* 22 (2009) 659–71.

Gasper, P. "An Interview with Philip Kitcher." *Human Nature Review* 4 (2004) 82–89.

Ghiselin, Michael. *The Triumph of the Darwinian Method*. Berkeley: University of California Press, 1969.

Gilbert, Robert Andrew. *The Elements of Mysticism*. Shaftesbury, Dorset: Element, 1991.

Goergen, Donald J. *Fire of Love: Encountering the Holy Spirit*. New York: Paulist, 2006.

González, Justo L., and Catherine Gunsalus González. *Heretics for Armchair Theologians*. Louisville: Westminster John Knox, 2008.

Gould, Stephen Jay. "The Evolution of Life." In *Evolution!: Facts and Fallacies*, edited by J. William Schopf, 1–14. Amsterdam, UK: Academic Press, 1998.

———. *The Richness of Life: The Essential Stephen Jay Gould*. New York: Norton, 2007.

———. *The Structure of Evolutionary Theory*. Cambridge, MA: Belknap, 2002.

———. *Wonderful Life: The Burgess Shale and the Nature of History*. New York: Norton, 1989.

Gould, Stephen Jay, N. L. Gilinsky, and R. Z. German. "Asymmetry of Lineages and the Direction of Evolutionary Time." *Science* 236/4807 (1987) 1437–41.

Gould, Stephen Jay, and Richard Lewontin. "The Spandrels of San Marco and the Panglossian Paradigm: A Critique of the Adaptationist Programme." *Proceedings of the Royal Society of London B* 205 (1979) 581–98.

Gould, Stephen Jay, David M. Raup, John J. Seposki Jr., Thomas J. M. Schoff, and David S. Simberloff. "The Shape of Evolution: A Comparison of Real and Random Clades." *Paleobiology* 3 (1977) 23–40.

Grant, Colin. *Altruism and Christian Ethics*. Cambridge: Cambridge University Press, 2001.

———. "For the Love of God: Agape." *Journal of Religious Ethics* 24/ 1 (1996) 3–21.

Greene, J. "Darwin as a Social Evolutionist." *Journal of the History of Biology* 10 (1977) 1–27.

Greene-McCreight, Kathryn. *Ad litteram: How Augustine, Calvin, and Barth Read the "Plain Sense" of Genesis 1–3*. New York: Peter Lang, 1999.

Happold, Frank C. *Mysticism: A Study and an Anthology*. 3rd ed. Harmondsworth: Penguin, 1990.
Haraway, Donna. "A Manifesto for Cyborgs: Science, Technology, and Socialist Feminism in the 1980's." In *The Haraway Reader*, 7–46. London: Routledge, 2004.
Harnack, Adolf von. *Lehrbuch der Dogmengeschichte*, 4th ed. Tübingen: Mohr, 1909.
Hartl, D. L. *Principles of Population Genetics*. Sunderland, MA: Sinauer, 1980.
Hartshorne, Charles. *Beyond Humanism: Essays in the New Philosophy of Nature*. Gloucester, MA: Peter Smith, 1975.
———. "Ethics and the New Theology." *International Journal of Ethics* 45/1 (1934) 90–101.
———. *Man's Vision of God*. Chicago: Willit, Clark, 1941.
Harvey, A. E. *Jesus and the Constraints of History*. Philadelphia: Westminster, 1982.
Harvey, P., and M. Pagels. *The Comparative Method in Evolutionary* Biology. Oxford: Oxford University Press, 1991.
Hausman, Carl R. *Charles S. Peirce's Evolutionary Philosophy*. Cambridge: Cambridge University Press, 1993.
———. "Criteria of Creativity." In *The Idea of Creativity*, edited by Michael Krausz, Denis Dutton, and Karen Bardsley, 3–16. Leiden: Brill, 2009.
———. "Eros and Agape in Creative Evolution: A Peircean Insight." *Process Studies* 4/1 (1974) 11–25.
Heyward, Carter. "Lamenting the Loss of Love: A Response to Colin Grant." *Journal of Religious Ethics* 24/1 (1996) 23–28.
Hogan, Richard M. *Dissent from the Creed: Heresies Past and Present*. Huntington, IN: Our Sunday Visitor, 2001.
Hopkins, Jasper. *Nicholas of Cusa's Debate with John Wenk: A Translation and an Appraisal of De Ignota Litteratura and Apologia Doctae Ignorantiae*. 3rd ed. Minneapolis: Arthur J. Banning, 1988.
Huchingson, James E. "Chaos, Communications Theory, and God's Abundance." *Zygon: Journal of Religion and Science* 37 (2002) 395–414.
———. *Pandemoneum Tremendum: Chaos and Mystery in the Life of God*. Cleveland: Pilgrim, 2000.
Hulswit, Menno. *From Cause to Causation: A Peircean Perspective*. New York: Springer, 2002.
———. "Peirce's Teleological Approach to Natural Classes." *Transactions of the Charles S. Peirce Society* 33/ 3 (1997) 722–72.
———. "Teleology: A Peircean Critique of Ernst Mayr's Theory." *Transactions of the Charles S Peirce Society* 32/ 2 (1996) 184–99.
Hultgren, Arland J., and Steven A. Haggmark. *The Earliest Christian Heretics: Readings from Their Opponents*. Minneapolis: Augsburg Fortress, 1996.
Hurtado, Larry W. *One God, One Lord: Earliest Christian Devotion and Ancient Jewish Monotheism*. Philadelphia: Fortress, 1988.
Huxley, Julian. "At Random." Television ad aired on CBS, November 21, 1959.
Inge, William Ralph. *Christian Mysticism*. Whitefish, MT: Kessinger, 2012.
Jackson, F. and P. Pettit, "In Defense of Explanatory Ecumenism." *Economics and Philosophy* 8 (1992) 1–22.
Jaki, Stanley L. *Genesis 1 Through the Ages*. Edinburgh: Scottish Academic, 1998.Jarvie, I. C. "The Rationality of Creativity." In *The Idea of Creativity*, edited by Michael Krausz, Denis Dutton, and Karen Bardsley, 43–62. Leiden: Brill, 2009.

Jeanrond, Werner G. *A Theology of Love*. New York: T. & T. Clark, 2010.
Jüngel, Eberhard. *God as the Mystery of the World: On the Foundation of the Theology of the Crucified One in the Dispute between Theism and Atheism*. Translated by Darrell L. Guder. Edinburgh: T. & T. Clark, 1983.
Kärkkäinen, Veli-Matti. *The Trinity: Global Perspectives*. Louisville: Westminster John Knox, 2007.
Kass, Leon. *The Hungry Soul*. Chicago: University of Chicago, 1999.
Kaufman, Gordon D. *In the Beginning . . . Creativity*. Minneapolis: Augsburg Fortress, 2004.
———. "On Thinking of God as Serendipitous Creativity." *Journal of the American Academy of Religion* 69/2 (2001) 409–25.
———. *In Face of Mystery: A Constructive Theology*. Cambridge, MA: Harvard University Press, 1993.
Kauffman, Stuart. *Investigations*. Oxford: Oxford University, 2000.
Keller, Catherine. *The Face of the Deep: A Theology of Becoming*. New York: Routledge, 2003.
Kelly, J. N. D. *Early Christian Doctrines*. San Francisco: HarperOne, 1978.
Kim, Yoon Kyung. *Augustine's Changing Interpretations of Genesis 1–3: From De Genesi Contra Manichaeos to De Genesi ad Litteram*. Lewiston, NY: Edwin Mellon, 2006.
Kimura, M. *The Neutral Theory of Molecular Evolution*. Cambridge University Press, 1983.
Kirsch, John A. W. "The Six-Percent Solution: Second Thoughts on the Adaptedness of the Marsupialia." *American Scientist* 65 (1977) 276–88.
Kitcher, Philip, Kim Sterelny, and C. K. Waters. "The Illusory Riches of Sober's Monism." *Journal of Philosophy* 87 (1990) 158–61.
Koenigswald, Wigham V., and Francisco Goin. "Enamel Differentiation in South American Marsupials and a Comparison of Placental and Marsupial Enamel." *Palaeontographica, Abteilung* A 255 (2000) 129–68.
Krebs, J., and N. Davies. *An Introduction to Behavioral Ecology*. Sunderland, MA: Sinauer, 1981.
Kropotkin, Petr. *Mutual Aid: A Factor in Evolution*. 3rd ed. Montreal: Black Rose, 1989.
Kruger, Michael J. *Christianity at the Crossroads: How the Second Century Shaped the Future of the Church*. Downers Grove, IL: IVP Academic, 2018.
Kuhn, Thomas. *The Structure of Scientific Revolutions*. Chicago: University of Chicago Press, 1962.
Kunst, Christiane. *Römische Adoption: Zur Strategie einer Familienorganisation*. Hennef, Germany: Marthe Clauss, 2005.
Kurtz, Paul, ed. *The Humanist Alternative*. Buffalo, NY: Prometheus, 1973.
La Rochefoucauld, Francois, duc de. *The Moral Maxims and Reflections*. Translated by J. W. Willis Bund and J. Hain Friswell. New York: Scribner, Welford, 1871.
Lawlor, Leonard. "Animals Have No Hand: An Essay on Animality in Derrida." *New Centennial Review* 7/2 (2007) 43–69.
Lessa, Enrique P., and Richard A. Farina. "Reassessment of Extinction Patterns among the Late Pleistocene Mammals of South America." *Palaeontology* 39 (1996) 651–62.
Lewin, Roger. "Evolutionary Theory Under Fire." *Science* 210 (1980) 882–96.
Lewis, C. S. *The Four Loves*. San Francisco: HarperOne, 2017.
Lienhard, Joseph T. "Reading the Bible and Learning to Read: The Influence of Education on St. Augustine's Exegesis." *Augustinian Studies* 29/1 (1996) 7–25.

Lodahl, Michael. "From God to Creation: Pursuing the Trinitarian Reflections of Gregory of Nyssa as a Critique of Creation ex Nihilo." Paper presented to the American Academy of Religion, 2004 Annual Meeting.

———. *Shekhinah/Spirit: Divine Presence in Jewish and Christian Religion*. New York: Stimulus, 1992.

Loomer, Bernard M. "The Size of God." In *The Size of God: The Theology of Bernard Loomer in Context*, edited by William Dean and Larry E. Axel, 42–67. Macon, GA: Mercer University Press, 1987.

Losee, J. *A Historical Introduction to the Philosophy of Science*. London: Oxford University Press, 1972.

Lossky, Vladimir. *The Mystical Theology of the Eastern Church*. Cambridge: James Clarke, 1957.

Lovejoy, A. C. *The Great Chain of Being*. Cambridge, MA: Harvard University Press, 1936.

Loy, David R. *Nonduality: A Study in Comparative Philosophy*. New Haven, CT: Yale University Press, 1988.

———. *Nonduality: In Buddhism and Beyond*. Somerville, MA: Wisdom, 2019.

Lucas, George R. "Evolutionist Theories and Whitehead's Philosophy." *Process Studies* 14 (1985) 287–300.

Lucien, Richard. *Kenosis and Creation*. New York: Paulist, 1997.

Macquarrie, John. *Principles of Christian Theology*. 2nd ed. New York: Scribner, 1977.

Malle, Marie-Luis. "The Animal That Therefore Derrida Is: Derrida and the Posthuman Critical Animal Studies." *Bhatter College Journal of Multidisciplinary Studies* 3 (2013) 92–99.

Marjanen, Antti, and Petri Luomanen. *A Companion to Second-Century Christian Heretics*. Leiden, Netherlands: Brill Academic, 2008.

Matthews, Julie. "Compassion, Geography and the Question of the Animal." *Environmental Values* 21 (2012) 125–42.

May, R. M., ed. *Theoretical Ecology: Principles and Applications*. 2nd ed. Sunderland, MA: Sinauer, 1981.

Mayr, Ernst. "Biology in the Twenty-First Century." *Bioscience* 50 (October 2000) 895–97.

———. *Towards a New Philosophy of Biology*. Cambridge, MA: Harvard University Press, 1988.

McCall, Bradford. "Emergence and Kenosis: A Theological Synthesis." *Zygon* 45/1 (2010) 149–64.

———. "Emergence and Kenosis: A Wesleyan Perspective." In *The Future of Wesleyan Theology: Essays in Honor of Laurence Wood*, edited by Nathan Crawford, 155–70. Eugene, OR: Pickwick: 2011.

———. "Emergence Theory and Theology: A Wesleyan-Relational Perspective." *Wesleyan Theological Journal* 44/2 (2009) 189–207.

———. "Evolution, Emergence, and Final Causality: A Proposed Pneumatico-Theological Synthesis." *Wesleyan Theological Journal* 52/2 (2017) 148–64.

———. "The God of Chance." In *Uncontrolling Love: Essays Exploring the Love of God, with Introductions by Thomas Jay Oord*, edited by Chris Baker et al., 221–24. Nampa, ID: SacraSage, 2017.

———. "The God of Chance and Purpose." *Theology and Science* 16 2 (2018). DOI: 10.1080/14746700.2017.1413815.

———. "Kenosis of the Spirit into Creation." *Crucible: Theology & Ministry* 1/1 (2008).
———. "Necessary, Kenotically-Donated, & Self-Giving Love." *Studia Elckie* 21/2 (2019). DOI: 10.32090/SE.210210.
———. "Thomistic Personalism in Dialogue with Kenosis." *Studia Elckie* 19/1 (2017) 21–32.
———. "Whitehead, Creativity, and the Immanently Creative Spirit." *Zygon: Journal of Religion and Science* 54/2 (2019) 337–50.
McGinn, Bernard. *The Foundations of Mysticism: Origins to the Fifth Century*. New York: Crossroad, 1997.
McGrath, Alister. *A Fine-Tuned Universe: The Quest for God in Science and Theology*. Louisville: Westminster John Knox, 2009.
McKeough, M. J. The Meaning of the Rationes Seminales in St. Augustine." PhD dissertation, Catholic University of America, 1926.
McMullin, Ernan. "Cosmology and Religion." In *Cosmology: Historical, Literary, Philosophical, Religious and Scientific Perspectives*, 581–606. New York: Garland, 1993.
———. "Darwin and the Other Christian Tradition." *Zygon* 46/2 (2011) 291–316.
———, ed. *Evolution and Creation*. South Bend, IN: University of Notre Dame Press, 1985.
McShea, Daniel W. "Complexity and Evolution: What Everybody Knows." *Biology and Philosophy* 6 (1991) 303–24.
Meland, Bernard. *Fallible Forms and Symbols: Discourses on Method in a Theology of Culture*. Philadelphia: Fortress, 1976.
Mitchell, W., and T. Valone, "The Optimization Research Program: Studying Adaptations by their Function," *Quarterly Review of Biology* 65 (1990) 43–52.
Moltmann, Jürgen. *The Crucified God*. Minneapolis: Augsburg Fortress, 1993.
———. *God in Creation: An Ecological Doctrine of Creation*. The Gifford Lectures of 1984–1985. London: SCM, 1985.
———. "Kenosis in the Creation and the Consummation of the World." In *Work of Love: Creation as Kenosis*, edited by John Polkinghorne, 132–51. Grand Rapids: Eerdmans, 2001.
———. *The Trinity and the Kingdom: The Doctrine of God*. San Francisco: Harper and Row, 1981.
Montague, G. T. *The Holy Spirit: Growth of a Biblical Tradition*. New York: Paulist, 1976.
Moore, Stephen D. *Divinanimality: Animal Theory, Creaturely Theology*. New York: Fordham University Press, 2014.
Morowitz, Harold J. *The Emergence of Everything*. Oxford: Oxford University, 2002.
Morris, Simon Conway. *The Crucible of Creation: The Burgess Shale and The Rise of Animals*. Oxford: Oxford University Press, 1998.
———. *Life's Solution: Inevitable Humans in a Lonely Universe*. Cambridge: Cambridge University Press, 2003.
———. "The Predictability of Evolution: Glimpses into a Post-Darwinian World." *Naturwissenschaften* 96 (2009) 1313–37.
———. *The Runes of Evolution: How the Universe Became Self-Aware*. West Conshocken, PA: Templeton, 2015.
Naas, Michael. "Derrida's Flair (for the Animals to Follow)." *Research in Phenomenology* 40/2 (2010) n.p.

———. *The End of the World and Other Teachable Moments*. New York: Fordham University Press, 2014.
Nagel, Ernest. *The Structure of Science*. London: Routledge & Kegan Paul, 1961.
Nicholas of Cusa. "Apologia Doctae Ignorantiae." In *Nicolai de Cusa Opera Omnia*, edited by Raymond Klibanski, 2:163–69. Leipzig/Hamburg: F. Meiner, 1932.
Niebuhr, Reinhold. *The Nature and Destiny of Man: A Christian Interpretation*. 2 vols. New York: Scribner, 1964.
Nitecki, M. *Evolutionary Innovations*. Chicago: University of Chicago Press, 1990.
Nussbaum, Martha C. *Upheavals of Thought: The Intelligence of Emotions*. Cambridge, Cambridge University Press, 2001.
Nygren, Anders. *Agape and Eros*. Philadelphia: Westminster, 1953.
———. *Agape and Eros*. Translated by Philip Watson. Chicago: University of Chicago Press, 1982.
O'Connell, Robert J. *St. Augustine's Early Theory of Man*. Cambridge, MA: Belknap, 1968.
Oord, Thomas Jay. 2019. *Defining Love: A Philosophical, Scientific, and Theological Engagement* (Grand Rapids: Brazos, 2010.
———. *God Can't: How to Believe in God and Love after Tragedy, Abuse, and Other Evils*. Grasmere, ID: SacraSage.
———. *The Nature of Love: A Theology*. St. Louis: Chalice, 2010.
———. *Philosophy of Religion: Introductory Essays*. Edited by Thomas Jay Oord. Kansas City: MO: Beacon Hill, 2002.
———. "Process Answers to Love Questions." In *The Many Facets of Love: Philosophical Explorations*, edited by Thomas Jay Oord, 20–30. Newcastle, UK: Cambridge Scholars, 2007.
———. *Science of Love: The Wisdom of Well-Being*. Philadelphia: Templeton, 2004.
———. *The Uncontrolling Love of God: An Open and Relational Account of Providence*. Downers Grove, IL: IVP Academic, 2015.
Origen. *Against Celsus*. Translated by Henry Chadwick. Cambridge: Cambridge University Press, 1980.
Orzack, S., and Elliot Sober. *Adaptation and Optimality*. Cambridge: Cambridge University Press, 2000.
———. "Optimality Models and the Test of Adaptationism." *American Naturalist* 143 (1994) 361–80.
Ospovat, Dov. *The Development of Darwin's Theory: Natural History, Natural Theology, and Natural Selection 1838–1859*. Cambridge: Cambridge University Press, 1981.
Oster, G. F., and E. O. Wilson. *Caste and Ecology in the Social Insects*. Princeton, NJ: Princeton University Press, 1978.
O'Toole, Christopher J. *The Philosophy of Creation in the Writings of St. Augustine*. Washington, DC: Catholic University of America Press, 1944.
Otto, Rudolf. *The Idea of the Holy: An Inquiry into the Non-Rational Factor in the Idea of the Divine and its Relation to the Rational*. Translated by John W. Harvey. Oxford: Oxford University Press, 1959.
Pannenberg, Wolfhart. *Jesus: God and Man*. Philadelphia: Westminster, 1968.
———. *Systematic Theology*. Translated by G. W. Bromiley. Vol. 2. Grand Rapids: Eerdmans, 1994.
Papandrea, James. *The Earliest Christologies: Five Images of Christ in the Postapostolic Age*. Downers Grove, IL: IVP Academic, 2016.

Parker, G., and John Maynard Smith. "Optimality Theory in Evolutionary Biology." *Nature* 348 (1990) 27–33.

Peacocke, Arthur R. "The Cost of New Life." In *The Work of Love: Creation as Kenosis*, edited by John Polkinghorne, 21–42. Grand Rapids: Eerdmans, 2001.

———. *Creation and the World of Science*. Oxford: Oxford University Press, 1979.

———. *Theology for a Scientific Age: Being and Becoming—Natural, Divine, and Human*. Minneapolis: Augsburg Fortress, 1993.Pearse, John S., and Vicki B. Pearse. "Vision of Cubomedusan Jellyfishes." *Science* 199 (1978) 458.

Peckham, Morse, ed. *The Origin of Species: A Variorum Text*. Philadelphia: University of Pennsylvania Press, 1959.

Peirce, Charles Sanders. *Collected Papers of Charles Sanders Peirce*. Edited by Charles Hartshorne and Paul Weiss. 6 vols. 2nd ed. London: Thoemmes Continuum, 1992–97.

———. *The Essential Peirce: Selected Philosophical Writings*. Edited by Peirce Edition Project. 2 vols. Bloomington: Indiana University Press, 1998.

———. *Reasoning and the Logic of Things: The Cambridge Conferences Lectures of 1898*. Edited by Kenneth Lane Ketner. Cambridge, MA: Harvard University Press, 1993.

Peppard, Michael. *The Son of God in the Roman World: Divine Sonship in Its Social and Political Context*. Oxford: Oxford University Press, 2012.

Peters, Ted. *God as Trinity: Relationality and Temporality in Divine Life*. Louisville: Westminster John Knox, 1993.

Pinnock, Clark. *Most Moved Mover: A Theology of God's Openness*. Grand Rapids.: Baker, 2001.

Placher, William C. *The Domestication of Transcendence: How Modern Thinking About God Went Wrong*. Louisville: Westminster John Knox, 1996.

Polkinghorne, John C. *Belief in God in an Age of Science*. New Haven: Yale University, 1998.

———. "The Hidden Spirit and the Cosmos." In *The Work of the Spirit: Pneumatology and Pentecostalism*, edited by Michael Welker. Grand Rapids: Eerdmans, 2006.

———. "Kenotic Creation and Divine Action." In *The Work of Love: Creation as Kenosis*, edited by John C. Polkinghorne, 90–106. Grand Rapids: Eerdmans, 2001.

———. *Serious Talk*. Philadelphia: Trinity, 1995.

Popa, Radu. *Between Necessity and Probability: Searching for the Definition and Origin of Life*. New York: Springer, 2004.

Popper, Karl R. *Conjectures and Refutations*. London: Routledge & Kegan Paul, 1963.

———. *The Logic of Scientific Discovery*. London: Hutchinson, 1959.

———. *Objective Knowledge*. Oxford: Oxford University Press, 1972.

———. *A World of Propensities*. Bristol: Thoemmes, 1990.

Post, Stephen G. *Unlimited Love: Altruism, Compassion, and Service*. Philadelphia: Templeton Foundation, 2003.

Prestige, G. L. *God in Patristic Thought*. Eugene, OR: Wipf & Stock, 2008.

Price, Robert M. *Deconstructing Jesus*. Amherst, NY: Prometheus, 2000.

Rahner, Karl. *The Trinity*. Translated by Joseph Donceel. New York: Crossroad Herder, 1999.

Ralston, Holmes, III. "Kenosis and Nature." In *The Work of Love*, edited by John Polkinghorne, 43–65. Grand Rapids: Eerdmans, 2001.

Raup, David M., and Stephen Jay Gould. "Stochastic Simulation and Evolution of Morphology towards a Nomothetic Paleontology." *Systematic Zoology* 23/3 (1974) 305–22.
Raup, David M., Stephen Jay Gould, Thomas J. M. Schoff, and David S. Simberloff. "Stochastic Models of Phylogeny and the Evolution of Diversity." *Journal of Geology* 81 (1973) 525–42.
Richards, Robert J. *Darwin and the Emergence of Evolutionary Theories of Mind and Behavior.* Chicago: University of Chicago Press, 1987.
———. *The Meaning of Evolution: The Morphological Construction and Ideological Reconstruction of Darwin's Theory.* Chicago: University of Chicago Press, 1992.
Ridley, Matt. *The Explanation of Organic Diversity.* Oxford: Oxford University Press, 1983.
Robert, Jason S. *Embryology, Epigenesis and Evolution: Taking Development Seriously.* Cambridge: Cambridge University, 2004.
Robinson, James McConkey. *Jesus: According to the Earliest Witness.* Minneapolis: Fortress, 2007.
Rose M., and G. Lauder. *Adaptation.* Cambridge, MA: Cambridge Academic, 1996.
Roughgarden, Jan. *Theory of Population Genetics and Evolutionary Ecology: An Introduction.* New York: Macmillan, 1979.
Rousselot, Pierre. *The Problem of Love in the Middle Ages: A Historical Contribution.* Translated by Alan Vincelett. Milwaukee: Marquette University Press, 2002.
Rowe, William L. *Can God Be Free?* Oxford: Oxford University Press, 2004.
Rudwick, Martin J. S. *The Meaning of Fossils.* New York: Science History, 1972.
Ruse, Michael. "Darwin's Debt to Philosophy: An Examination of the Influence of the Philosophical Ideas of John F.W. Herschel and William Whewell, on the Development of Charles Darwin's Theory of Evolution." *Studies in History and Philosophy of Science* 6 (1975) 159–81.
———. "Evolution and Progress." *Tree* 8/2 (1993) 55–59.
———. *Evolutionary Naturalism: Selected Essays.* London: Routledge, 1995.
———. "How Evolution Became a Religion." *National Post*, May 13, 2000, B1.
———. *Monad to Man: The Concept of Progress in Evolutionary Biology.* Cambridge, MA: Harvard University Press, 2009.
Ruse, Michael, and Edward O. Wilson. "Moral Philosophy as Applied Science." In *Conceptual Issues in Evolutionary* Biology, edited by Elliot Sober, 173–92. Cambridge, MA: MIT Press, 1986.
Sagan, Carl *Cosmos.* New York: Random House, 1980.
Savi, Julio. "The Baha'i Faith and the Perennial Mystical Quest: A Western Perspective." *Baha'i Studies Review* 14 (2007) 5–11.
Scarborough, Milton. *Comparative Theories of Nonduality: The Search for a Middle Way.* New York: Continuum, 2011.
Sebright, J. *The Art of Improving the Breeds of Domestic Animals in a Letter Addressed to the Right Hon. Sir Joseph Banks, K.B.* London: privately printed, 1809.
Short, T. L. "Peirce's Concept of Final Causation." *Transactions of the Charles S Peirce Society* 17/3 (1981) 369–86.
Sibbes, Richard. *Works.* Edited by A. B. Grosart. 7 vols. Edinburgh: James Nichol, 1853–62.
Simmons, Ernest. "Towards Kenotic Pneumatology: Quantum Field Theory and the Theology of the Cross." *CTNS Bulletin* 19/2 (1999) 11–16.

Simpson, George Gaylord. *The Meaning of Evolution*. New Haven, CT: Yale University Press, 1971.
Singer, Irving. "On Racism, Animal Rights, and Human Rights." *The New York Times*, May 27, 2015. http://opinionator.blogs.nytimes.com/2015/5/27/peter-singer-on-speciesism-and-racism.
———. *Plato to Luther*. Vol. 1 of *The Nature of Love*. 2nd ed. Chicago: University of Chicago Press, 1987.
Sire, James W. *Discipleship of the Mind*. Downers Grove, IL: InterVarsity, 1990.
Smith, John Maynard. *Evolution and the Theory of Games*. Cambridge: Cambridge University Press, 1982.
———. "Group Selection and Kin Selection." *Nature* 201 (1964) 1145–46.
———. "How to Model Evolution." In *The Latest on the Best: Essays on Evolution and Optimality*, edited by J. Dupre, 117–31. Cambridge: MIT Press, 1987.
———. "J. B. S. Haldane." In *The Founders of Evolutionary Genetics*, edited by S. Sarkar, 37–51. Dordrecht: Kluwer Academic, 1992.
———. "Optimization Theory in Evolution." *Annual Review of Ecology and Systematics* 9 (1978) 31–56.
———. "Taking a Chance on Evolution." *New York Review of Books*, May 14, 1992, 36.
Sober, Elliot. "Did Darwin Write the Origin Backwards?" *Proceedings of the National Academy of Sciences* 106 (2009) 10051–57.
———. *Evidence & Evolution: The Logic Behind the Science*. Cambridge: Cambridge University Press, 2008.
———. "The Multiple Realizability Argument against Reductionism." *Philosophy of Science* 66 (1999) 542–64.
———. *The Nature of Selection*. Cambridge, MA: MIT Press, 1984.
———. *Philosophy of Biology*. Boulder, CO: Westview, 2000.
———. "Three Differences Between Evolution and Deliberation." In *Modeling Rationality, Morality, and Evolution*, edited by P. Danielson, 408–22. Oxford: Oxford University Press, 1998.
Sober, Elliot, and David Sloan Wilson. *Unto Others: The Evolution and Psychology of Unselfish Behavior*. Cambridge, MA: Harvard University Press, 1998.
Southgate, Christopher. *God, Humanity, and the Cosmos*. New York: T. & T. Clark, 2005.
Spiegel, James S. "Augustine, Evolution, and Scientific Methodology." In *Augustine and Science*, edited by John Doody, Adam Goldstein, and Kim Paffenroth, 196–213. Lanham, MD: Lexington, 2013.
Stace, Walter Terence. *Mysticism and Philosophy*. London: Macmillan, 1961.
Sterelny, Kim, and Paul Griffiths. *Sex and Death*. Chicago: University of Chicago Press, 1999.
Sterelny, Kim, and Philip Kitcher. "The Return of the Gene." *Journal of Philosophy* 85 (1988): 339–60.
Sweetman, Brendan. *Evolution, Chance, and God: Understanding the Relationship between Evolution and Religion*. New York: Bloomsbury, 2015.
Tanner, Kathryn. "Workings of the Spirit: Simplicity or Complexity?" In *The Work of the Spirit: Pneumatology and Pentecostalism*, edited by Michael Welker, 87–108. Grand Rapids: Eerdmans, 2006.
Taylor, John V., and David Wood. *The Go-Between God: The Holy Spirit and the Christian Mission*. Eugene, OR: Wipf & Stock, 2015.

Taylor, Mark Lloyd. *God Is Love: A Study in the Theology of Karl Rahner.* Atlanta: Scholars, 1986.
Thatamanil, John J. "Ecstasy and Nonduality: On Comparing Varieties of Immanence." *Journal of Hindu-Christian Studies* 22 (2009) 19–24.
———. *The Immanent Divine: God, Creation, and the Human Predicament.* Minneapolis: Fortress, 2006.
Tillich, Paul. *Love, Power, and Justice.* London: Oxford University Press, 1954.
———. *Systematic Theology.* 3 vols. Chicago: University of Chicago Press, 1951–63.
———. *Ultimate Concern.* London: SCM, 1965.
Turnbull, W. D. "Another Look at Dental Specialization in the Extinct Sabre-Toothed Marsupial Thlyacosmilus, Compared to Its Placental Counterparts." In *Development, Function and Evolution of Teeth*, edited by Percy M. Butler K. A. Josey, 319–414. London: Academic, 1978.
Turner, Alan, and Mauricio Antón. *The Big Cats and Their Fossil Relatives: An Illustrated Guide to their Evolution and Natural History.* New York: Columbia University Press, 1977.
Underhill, Evelyn *Mysticism: The Preeminent Study in the Nature and Development of Spiritual Consciousness.* New York: Image Classics, 1990.
Vacek, Edward Collins "Love, Christian and Diverse: A Response to Colin Grant." *Journal of Religious Ethics* 24/1 (1996) 29–34.
———. *Love, Human and Divine: The Heart of Christian Ethics.* Washington, DC: Georgetown University Press, 1994.
Vanstone, W. H. *Love's Endeavor, Love's Expense.* London: Darton, Longman and Todd, 1977.
Wagner, Walter F. *After the Apostles: Christianity in the Second Century.* Minneapolis: Fortress, 1994.
Wagoner, Robert E. *The Meanings of Love: An Introduction to Philosophy of Love.* Westport, CT: Greenwood, 1997.
Wald, G., and S. Raypart, "Vision in Annelid Worms." *Science* 196 (1977) 1434–39.
Wang, Henry. "Rethinking the Validity and Significance of Final Causation." *Transactions of the Charles S. Peirce Society* 41/3 (2005) 611–23.
Ward, Keith. *Christ and Cosmos: A Reformulation of Trinitarian Doctrine.* Cambridge: Cambridge University Press, 2015.
———. *God, Chance, and Necessity.* Oxford: Oneworld, 1996.
Waters, C. K. "Tempered Realism about Units of Selection." *Philosophy of Science* 58 (1991) 553–73.
———. "Why Genic and Multilevel Selection Theories Are Here to Stay." *Philosophy of Science* 72 (2005) 311–33.
Weber, Michael. *Whitehead's Pancreativism: The Basics.* Frankfurt: Ontos, 2006.
Welker, Michael. *Creation and Reality.* Minneapolis: Augsburg Fortress, 1999.
———. "Spirit in Philosophical, Theological, and Interdisciplinary Perspectives." In *The Work of the Spirit: Pneumatology and Pentecostalism*, edited by Michael Welker, 221–32. Grand Rapids: Eerdmans, 2006.
West, S., A. Griffin, and A. Gardner. "Social Semantics: Altruism, Cooperation, Mutualism, Strong Reciprocity, and Group Selection." *Journal of Evolutionary Biology* 20 (2006) 415–32.
Whitehead, Alfred North. *Adventures of Ideas.* New York: Free Press, 1967.

———. *The Concept of Nature: The Tarner Lecture Delivered in Trinity College, November, 1919*. Cambridge: Cambridge University Press, 1920.
———. *Process and Reality*. The Gifford Lectures, 1927–1928. New York: Free Press, 1979.
———. *Religion in the Making: Lowell Lectures, 1926*. New York: Fordham University Press, 1996.
———. *Science and the Modern World*. New York: Free Press, 1925.
Wild, G., A. Gardner, and S. West. "Adaptation and the Evolution of Parasite Virulence in a Connected World." *Nature* 459 (2009) 983–86.
Williams, Daniel D. "The Significance of St. Augustine Today." In *A Companion to the Study of St. Augustine*, edited by Roy W. Battenhouse, 3–14. Grand Rapids: Baker, 1979.
Williams, George C. *Adaptation and Natural Selection*. Princeton, NJ: Princeton University Press, 1966.
———. "A Defense of Reductionism in Evolutionary Biology." In *Oxford Surveys in Evolutionary Biology* 2, edited by Richard Dawkins and Matt Ridley, 1–27. Oxford: Oxford University Press, 1985.
———. "A Sociobiological Expansion of Evolution and Ethics." In *Evolution and Ethics*, edited by J. Paradis and G. C. Williams, 179–214. Princeton, NJ: Princeton University Press, 1989.
Williams, Rowan. "Creation." In *Augustine Through the Ages: An Encyclopedia*, edited by Alan D. Fitzgerald, 251–54. Grand Rapids: Eerdmans, 1999.
Wills, Garry. "Radical Creativity." *MLN* 89/6 (1974) 1019–28.
Wilson, David Sloan. *The Natural Selection of Populations and Communities*. Menlo Park, CA: Benjamin/Cummings, 1980.
Wilson, David Sloan. "Levels of Selection: An Alternative to Individualism in Biology and the Human Sciences." In *Conceptual Issues in Evolutionary Biology*, edited by Elliott Sober, 61–78. 2nd ed. Cambridge, MA: Bradford, 1994.
Wilson, Edward O. *The Origins of Creativity*. New York: Liveright, 2017.
———. *Sociobiology: The New Synthesis*. Cambridge, MA: Belknap of Harvard University Press, 1975.
Witherington, Ben, III. *What Have They Done with Jesus?* San Francisco: HarperCollins, 2006.
Wolfe, Cary. *Animal Rites: American Culture, the Discourse of Species, and Posthumanist Theory*. Chicago: University of Chicago Press, 2003.
———. "Flesh and Finitude: Thinking Animals in (Post)Humanist Philosophy." *SubStance* 37/3 (2008) 8–36.
Wojtyla, Karol. *Love & Responsibility*. San Francisco: Ignatius, 1993.
Yong, Amos. "From Quantum Mechanics to the Eucharistic Meal: John Polkinghorne's Vision of Science and Theology." *The Global Spiral: A Publication of Metanexus Institute* 5/5 (2005). http://www.metanexus.net/Magazine/ArticleDetail/tabid/68/id/9285/Default.aspx.
———. *Pneumatology and the Christian-Buddhist Dialogue: Does the Spirit Blow Through the Middle Way?* Studies in Systematic Theology. Leiden: Brill Academic, 2012.
———. "Ruach, the Primordial Chaos, and the Breath of Life: Emergence Theory and the Creation Narratives in Pneumatological Perspective." in *The Work of the Spirit: Pneumatology and Pentecostalism*, edited by Michael Welker, 183–204. Grand Rapids: Eerdmans, 2006.

———. *The Spirit of Creation: Modern Science and Divine Action in the Pentecostal-Charismatic Imagination*. Pentecostal Manifestos. Grand Rapids: Eerdmans, 2011.
Young, Davis A. "The Contemporary Relevance of Augustine's View of Creation." In *Augustine and Science*, edited by John Doody, Adam Goldstein, and Kim Paffenroth, 63–81. Lanham, MD: Lexington, 2013.
Young, Robert M. *Darwin's Metaphor: Nature's Place in Victorian Culture*. Cambridge: Cambridge University Press, 1985.

www.ingramcontent.com/pod-product-compliance
Lightning Source LLC
Chambersburg PA
CBHW070253230426
43664CB00014B/2522